THE QUOTABLE REBEL

Teishan Latner

Common Courage Press   Monroe, Maine

Library of Congress Cataloging-in-Publication Data is available from publisher on request.
ISBN 1-56751-356-5 paper
ISBN 1-56751-357-3 hardcover

ISBN 13 9781567513561 paper
ISBN 13 9781567513578 hardcover

Common Courage Press
121 Red Barn Road
Monroe, ME 04951

207-525-0900
fax: 207-525-3068

www.commoncouragepress.com
info@commoncouragepress.com

First printing
Printed in Canada

Cover images: starting with Martin Luther King at center top going clockwise, Arundhati Roy, Malcolm X, Cindy Sheehan, Bob Marley, Emma Goldman, Subcomandante Marcos, Winona Laduke, Noam Chomsky, Sojourner Truth, Geronimo, bell hooks.

CONTENTS

Work, Labor, Unions

Editor's Note

Another world is not only possible, she is on her way. On a quiet day, I can hear her breathing.

—Arundhati Roy

This anthology is a labor of love. I compiled this book with the desire to document the words of people who have changed the course of history through their everyday resistance and unshakable vision of a better future. I wanted to honor the voices of well-known and lesser known "radicals" in history and present them in one place in all of their wisdom and poignancy. It is a collection inspired by the power of ideas in the imaginations of those who believe that another world is indeed possible and is worth fighting for.

This book is also intended to fill a void. If the old saying—history is written by the winners—is true, it's not surprising then that the "winners" predominate in many political quotation volumes. In them we can easily find Andrew Jackson, for instance, who advocated mass theft of Native American land, but not Tecumseh, the Shawnee leader of the same era who urged his people to "brush from your eyelids the sleep of slavery" and unite against settler encroachment. Lyndon B. Johnson energized America's war to confront the "communist menace" in Vietnam and is ubiquitous in many political quotation volumes. We're hard pressed, however, to find many words from priest-activist Daniel Berrigan, who burned draft records in protest of the war and said caustically "Our apologies, good friends, for… the burning of paper instead of children."

I hope that with this book we will no longer have to struggle find quotations like these. As quotation books are updated to include George W. Bush and the architects of the "war on terror," we urgently need to hear poets like Suheir Hammad: "I will/ not kill for you. Especially/ I will not die/ for you. I will not mourn/ the dead with murder nor/ suicide." Or writers such as Bill Blum: "A terrorist is someone who has a bomb but doesn't have an air force." And we might consider journalists like Mumia Abu-Jamal, writing while incarcerated in a Pennsylvania prison: "The choice, as every choice, is yours: to fight for freedom or be fettered, to struggle for liberty or be satisfied with slavery, to side with life or death."

Wherever you stand in the spectrum of political worldview, I hope that you will find something in these pages that speaks to you. I have tried to present the quotations in a way that provokes thought and serves as a reference for the further study of the speakers. A great effort was made to ensure accuracy in every quotation and attribution. In the case that I was unable to find the original source or was unsure of the exactness of the transcription I listed the quotation as Attributed.

It must be noted that a book such as this cannot possibly include every "rebel voice" in history. I have deliberately emphasized perspectives that are marginalized elsewhere because of their controversial or militant nature. I welcome your help in making future editions of this collection even more inclusive and I invite you to contact me with suggestions for new material.

Teishan Latner
Philadelphia, October 2005
RebelVoices@Yahoo.com

All royalties from this book are donated to support the work of social justice initiatives.

Dedication

To all the U.S. political prisoners in the belly of America, "they are inside for us, we are outside for them."

Chapter 1

"Empire"

Colonialism, Imperialism, Occupation, Empire

Venality, brutality, and hypocrisy are imprinted on the leaden soul of every state. But when a country ceases to be merely a country and becomes an empire, then the scale of operations changes dramatically. So may I clarify that tonight I speak as a subject of the American Empire? I speak as a slave who presumes to criticize her king.

Arundhati Roy, Indian writer, activist. Speech, 5/13/2003

At its root, oppression is really quite simple. It's about looting. The rest is made up of the rules and institutions, rituals and agreements, mythologies, rationales and overt bullying by means of which small groups of people keep a firm grasp on way more than their share of the world's resources.

Aurora Levins Morales, historian, activist, writer. *Medicine Stories*, 1998

Why should you take by force from us that which you could obtain by love? Why should you destroy us who have provided you with food? What can you get by war?

Wahunsonacook, Powhatan leader. Statement to John Smith, Jamestown English settlement, 1609

The problem with our children is they are so full of self-hate but they don't know it, you see. We've been colonized for so long, so many hundreds of years really, and the young folk grow up brainwashed, like. They look to Europe to find out what's good, instead of looking at their own culture.

Patrick Connor, Irish man in town of Santry, describing Ireland, 1997. *Blu Magazine*, 2000

The American Empire? An oxymoron.
A compelling lust for political, economic and military hegemony over the rest of the world, divorced from moral considerations? Suggesting that to Americans is akin to telling them of one's UFO abduction, except that they're more likely to believe the abduction story.

William Blum, writer. *Rogue State*, 2000

[Black and Latino people] don't realize that America can't exist without separating them from their identities, because if we had some sense of who we really are, there's no way in hell we'd allow this country to push its genocidal consensus on our homelands.

> **Immortal Technique**, hip hop MC. From song "Poverty of Philosophy," Viper Records, 2001

Activists celebrate after being released from jail at a sit-in at a naval recruiting station in protest of the U.S. Navy's occupation of the island of Vieques, San Francisco, CA 2000. Photo by Bill Hackwell

When the white man landed on the moon, my father cried…I told him there weren't any Indians on the moon, so stop crying. He said nothing for a long time. Then he said our spirits were there, too—and he was sure Indians were crying up there, and trying to hide, and hoping that soon they'd go back to their Earth, the white men, where they make so many people unhappy, and where they don't know what to do next.

> **A young American Indian boy**, speaking to a psychiatrist. *New York Review of Books*, March 1975

When the European comes to the Gikuyu country and robs the people of their land, he is taking away not only their livelihood, but the material symbol that holds family and tribe together… When he explains, to his own satisfaction and after the most superficial glance at the issues involved, that he is doing this for the sake of the Africans, to "civilize" them, "teach them the disciplinary value of regular work," and "give them the benefit of European progressive ideas," he is adding insult to injury, and need expect to convince no one but himself.

Jomo Kenyatta, Kenyan political leader. *Facing Mt. Kenya*, 1965

There is a time coming…when many things will change. Strangers will appear among you. Their skins are light-colored, and their ways are powerful. They speak no Indian tongue. Follow nothing that these men do, but keep your own ways that I have taught you.

> **Sweet Medicine**, a figure from Cheyenne legend, based upon the life of a real person. From prophecy made before European arrival.

It is customary to contrast an immigrant and a colonialist by birth…I do not believe, however, that the distinction is a fundamental one. The material condition of a privileged person/usurper is identical for the one who inherits it at birth and the one who enjoys it from the time he lands… The immigrant who is prepared to accept anything, having come for the express purpose of enjoying colonial benefits, will become a colonialist by vocation.

> **Albert Memmi**, Tunisian writer, educator. *The Colonizer and the Colonized*, 1957

The greatest crime since World War II has been U.S. foreign policy.

> **Ramsey Clark**, human rights activist, former U.S. Attorney General. In *Another World is Possible*, 2001

The trouble with America is that when the dollar only earns 6 percent over here, then it gets restless and goes overseas to get 100 percent. Then the flag follows the dollar and the soldiers follow the flag.

> **Smedley Butler**, U.S. Marine Corps General, 1933

It is not so much that the U.S. tends "to back the wrong side in the Third World"—rather the U.S. *is* the wrong side.

> **David Gilbert**, writer, U.S. political prisoner. *No Surrender*, 2004

By definition, no country is free that has the army of a foreign government stationed on its territory.

> **Ramsey Clark**, human rights activist, former U.S. Attorney General, referring to the U.S. Military. Speech, 5/17/2003

"Under Occupation," collage by Theodore Harris

Will not all the new American nations, and the United States, who seem destined by Providence to plague America with torments in the name of freedom, be opposed to such a plan. I seem to foresee a universal conspiracy against our poor Colombia, which is already greatly envied by all the American republics.

> **Simón Bolívar**, Venezuelan revolutionary leader, military general.
> Letter to Colonel Patrick Campbell, 1829

Visit America, before America visits you.

> **Slogan used by an Indian travel agency**, Bombay, India 2003

There are times when one tragedy, one crime tells us how a whole system works behind its democratic facade and helps us to understand how much of the world is run for the benefit of the powerful and how governments lie.

> **John Pilger**, English filmmaker, writer, on the ethnic cleansing of
> Diego Garcia Island. *The Guardian*, UK, 10/2/2004

My name is Vieques.

I am a Puerto Rican girl.
My stepfather is the United States.
He comes into my room at night to do his
business.
My name is Vieques
And I will be free
> **Aya de León**, poet, activist. From poem "Grito de Vieques," 1999

The certainty that some are born to be free and others to be slaves has guided all empires since the world began.
> **Eduardo Galeano**, Uruguayan historian, educator. *Upside Down*, 1998

Conquerors always call themselves liberators.
> **Sami Abdul-Rahman**, Iraqi Kurdish administration leader. *The Independent*, 2/17/2003

To hide the ugliness of its regime of criminal exploitation, colonial capitalism always decorates its evil banner with the idealistic motto: Fraternity, Equality, etc.
> **Ho Chi Minh**, Vietnamese political leader, poet. Essay, "Equality!" 1922

Every empire, including America's, regularly tells itself and the world that it is unlike all other empires, and that it has a mission certainly not to plunder and control but to educate and liberate the peoples and places it rules directly or indirectly. Yet these ideas are not shared by the people who live there.
> **Edward Said**, writer, literary critic, educator. Essay, "Imperial Perspectives," 2003

We were colonized in the name of the West bringing civilization, democracy, bringing freedom to us. All of us recognize who is being talked about when that language is used. The terms crusade, infinite justice, cowboy imagery of dead or alive posters, we all know what they mean.
> **Sunera Thobani**, Canadian educator. Speech, Ottawa Women's Resistance Conference, 10/1/2001. Her speech made national news after she was accused under Canada's hate crime laws of "public incitement of hatred" against the U.S.

I say that between *colonization* and *civilization* there is an infinite distance.
> **Aimé Césaire**, Martiniquen poet, political leader. *Discourse on Colonialism*, 1955

I am an anti-imperialist. I am opposed to having the eagle put its talons on any other land.

Mark Twain, writer, circa 1900

Did you know that in Basra, some people drank their urine, and boiled their sewage water, so that they could have some liquid in their bodies because the U.S. invasion cut off their water. And we watched them do it, as we brought them democracy.

Elias Rashmawi, educator, activist. Speech, 5/17/2003

by John Jonik

As often as I consider the causes of war and our dire straights, I have great confidence that this day and your union will be the beginning of freedom for all Britain; for you have all joined together, you who have not experienced slavery, for whom there are no lands further on and even the sea is not safe, with the Roman fleet threatening us. Thus battle and weapons, which are honorable for the brave, are likewise the greatest source of safety even for cowards.

> **Calgacus**, of ancient Britain. Speech to the Caledonians, his tribal nation, occupied by the Roman empire. In "Agricola, Germany and Dialogue on Orators," 1967

Others of your accursed race have, in years past, poisoned our peaceful shores. They have taught me what you are. What is your employment? To wander about like vagabonds from land to land, to rob the poor, to betray the confiding, to murder in cold blood the defenseless. No! With such a people I want no peace—no friendship. War, never-ending war, exterminating war, is all the boon I ask.

> **Acuera**, Timucua leader, in message to Hernando de Soto, a Spanish "explorer" who came to what is now Florida with an army after the forces of another Spaniard, Ponce de Leon, had enslaved indigenous nations there. *The Indian Tribes of the United States*, 1884

The U.S. weaponry might be modern, but the model of occupying someone else's country is definitely an old one.

> **Medea Benjamin**, activist. *AlterNet*, July 2003

TO THE PEOPLE OF MEXICO:
MEXICAN BROTHERS AND SISTERS:
We are a product of 500 years of struggle: first against slavery, then during the War of Independence against Spain led by insurgents, then to avoid being absorbed by North American imperialism, then to promulgate our constitution and expel the French empire from our soil, and later the dictatorship of Porfirio Díaz...But today, we say ENOUGH IS ENOUGH. We are the inheritors of the true builders of our nation. The dispossessed, we are millions, and we thereby call upon our brothers and sisters to join this struggle as the only path, so that we will not die of hunger due to the insatiable ambition of a 70-year dictatorship.

> **Zapatista National Liberation Army**. From "Declaration of War" issued one day before their guerrilla military actions. Chiapas, Mexico, 12/31/1993

A Southern physician, Samuel Cartwright, argued that many of the slaves suffered from a form of mental illness, which he called "drapetomania," diagnosed as the uncontrollable urge to escape from slavery. In the second half of the 20th-century, this illness, in the Third World, has usually been called "communism."

William Blum, writer. *Killing Hope,* 1995

We wish to be fair and honorable in our dealings with the Caucasian inhabitants of this land, and hereby offer the following treaty: we will purchase said Alcatraz Island for twenty-four dollars ($24) in glass beads and red cloth, a precedent set by the white man's purchase of a similar island about 300 years ago. We know that $24 in trade goods for these 16 acres is more than was paid when Manhattan Island was sold, but we know that land values have risen over the years.

Indians of All Tribes, a coalition that took over Alcatraz Island and its abandoned prison in San Francisco Bay for 19 months beginning in 1969. From press statement.

European imperialism long ago made Tahiti a distant suburb of Paris, the missionaries made it a suburb of Christ's kingdom, and the radio made it a suburb of Los Angeles.

Cedric Belfrage, English writer, socialist, b. 1904. Attributed.

[The Third World] wasn't an impoverished world then, in fact the reason it was colonialized is because it had the wealth...None of these countries were impoverished. Today they are called the poorer part of the world because the wealth has been drained out.

Vandana Shiva, Indian scientist, activist. Interview, *In Motion Magazine*, 8/14/1998

Brother!...Your forefathers crossed the great waters, and landed on this island. Their numbers were small. They found friends and not enemies. They told us they had fled from their own country for fear of wicked men, and come here to enjoy their freedom. They asked for a small seat. We took pity on them, granted their request, and they sat down among us. We gave them corn and meat. They gave us poison in return.

Red Jacket, Seneca leader. Speaking to a missionary, 1805

Debating Imperialism is a bit like debating the pros and cons of rape. What can we say? That we really miss it?

Arundhati Roy, Indian writer, activist. Speech, World Social Forum, January 2004

We must study how colonization works to *decivilize* the *colonizer*, to *brutalize* him in the true sense of the word, to degrade him, to awaken him to buried instincts, to covetousness, violence, race hatred, and moral relativism.

> **Aimé Césaire**, Martiniquen poet, political leader. *Discourse on Colonialism*, 1955

Oppressors are their own first victims.

> **Nidal Sakr**, human rights activist.

When Africa becomes economically free and politically united, the monopolists will come face to face with their own working class in their own countries, and a new struggle will arise within which the liquidation and collapse of imperialism will be complete.

> **Kwame Nkrumah**, Ghanian political leader. *Neo-Colonialism*, 1965

Let us swear to the entire universe, to posterity, and to ourselves to renounce France forever and die, rather than live under her domination; wage war to the last gasp for independence of our country.

> **Jean Jacques Dessalines**, Haitian revolutionary leader. "Proclamation," 1804

And you motherfuckers that's for peace in Vietnam, the Black Panther Party is for victory in Vietnam... [The U.S. is] a bunch of Wall Street warmongers. And they need to be driven out of there.

> **Fred Hampton**, Black Panther leader, assassinated by Chicago police in December 1969. Speech, Northern Illinois University, November 1969

The blood and bones of those who were killed with spades and pickaxes, of those who were split with axes and hammered to death, pierced with bayonets, clubbed and stoned, of those who were burned alive with their little children in their homes, of those who perished of hunger and thirst in prison have been crying out for justice.

> **Haile Selassie**, Ethiopian political leader. Speech, May 1941

O Muscogees, brethren of my mother! Brush from your eyelids the sleep of slavery; once more strike for vengeance—once more for your country. The spirits of the mighty dead complain. The tears drop from the skies. Let the white race perish! They seize your land, they corrupt your women, they trample on your dead! Back! Whence they came, upon a trial of blood, they must be driven!

> **Tecumseh**, Shawnee leader, warrior. From speech to members of the Creek nation in appeal to join him in his fight against American settlers. *History of Fort Wayne*, 1868

Mural "Sun of Sons" painted by American artists Susan Greene and Eric Drooker, who were asked by members of Qadura Refugee Camp to paint a mural that would honor those from Qadura who were killed during the first and second infitadas. The mural also includes a portrait of an Italian journalist slain by Israeli tank fire. Ramallah, Palestine 2004. Photo by Susan Greene

We have a 9,000-year-old culture, you have a 200-year-old culture. I think we can figure out our own future.

> **Anonymous man**, Baghdad, Iraq. *Guerrilla News Network,* July 2003

I have undertaken to avenge you. I want liberty and equality to reign throughout Santo Domingo. I am working towards that end. Come join me, brothers, and fight by our side for the same cause.

Toussaint L'Ouverture, Haitian revolutionary leader. "Proclamation," August 1793

Your words are like a man knocking me in the head with a stick. What you have spoken has put great fear upon us. Whatever we do, wherever we go, we are expected to say, "Yes! Yes! Yes!"—and when we don't agree at once to what you ask of us in council you always say, "You won't get anything to eat! You won't get anything to eat!"

Standing Elk, Lakota leader, to U.S. officials threatening to cut off food rations if a land treaty was not signed, 1876

If it were necessary to give the briefest possible definition of imperialism, we should have to say that imperialism is the monopoly stage of capitalism.

Vladimir Lenin, Russian political leader. *Imperialism, the Highest Stage of Capitalism*, 1916

Imperialism was born when the ruling class in capitalist production came up against national limits to its economic expansion.

Hannah Arendt, German educator, political analyst. *Origins of Totalitarianism*, 1951

Working-class of Ireland... Join your voice with ours in protesting against the base assumption that we owe to this Empire any other debt than that of hatred of all its plundering institutions.

James Connolly, Irish socialist leader, referring to England. Essay, "Queen Victoria's Diamond Jubilee," 1897

The land is ours, it belongs to the peasants and the indigenous peoples, and we should take it back and make it produce for all, not just for a handful of the wealthy who wouldn't even recognize the color of the soil if you placed it before them.

Subcomandante David, Zapatista National Liberation Army, Mexico. From statement read at an anti-World Trade Organization protest in Cancun, Mexico, 9/11/2003

To survive, "Third World" must necessarily have negative *and* positive connotations: negative when viewed in a vertical ranking system—

"underdeveloped" compared to over-industrialized, "underprivileged" within the already Second sex—and positive when understood sociopolitically as a subversive, "non-aligned" force.

> **Trinh T. Minh-ha**, filmmaker, educator. *Woman, Native, Other,* 1989

They came here to drill oil. They ended up drilling blood.

> **Nigerian Delta resident**, anonymous, referring to U.S. oil companies. *Free Speech Radio News*, July 2003

I believe that if we had and would keep our dirty, bloody, dollar-soaked fingers out of the business of these [Third World] nations so full of depressed, exploited people, they will arrive at a solution of their own.... And if unfortunately their revolution must be of the violent type because the "haves" refuse to share with the "have-nots" by any peaceful method, at least what they get will be their own, and not the American style, which they don't want and above all don't want crammed down their throats by Americans.

> **General David Sharp**, former U.S. Marine commander, 1966. Attributed.

The colonists may kill in Indochina, torture in Madagascar, imprison in Black Africa, crack down in the West Indies. Henceforth the colonized know that they have an advantage over them. They know that their temporary "masters" are lying.

> **Aimé Césaire**, Martiniquen poet, political leader. *Discourse on Colonialism*, 1955

Divestment here means that all the oil companies who are responsible for the pollution of our lands; who are responsible for the desecration of our shrines; who are responsible for the destruction of our indigenous cultures; who are responsible for initiating violence on our land; who are responsible for destroying our future, our forests, our wildlife, those companies should be recalled back home. They are assassins in foreign lands.

> **Oronto Douglas**, Nigerian human rights activist, attorney. Interview, *CorpWatch Radio*, late 1990s

I may not be educated, but we understand what is happening, why they have come. I would rather drink sea water than accept a single bottle of water from the Americans or Kuwaitis. Do they think they can buy our loyalty with their hand-outs?

> **Elderly Iraqi man**, anonymous, as occupying U.S. troops passed out water. *Year Zero*, June 2003

Can't even be a citizen in my place that you livin' in
My religion and the color of my skin ain't fittin' in?

> **The Hammer Bros**, hip hop group. From song "Free Palestine," circa 2003

Laying claim to and denying the human condition at the same time: the contradiction is explosive. For that matter it does explode, you know as well as I do; and we are living at the moment when the match is put to the fuse.

> **Jean-Paul Sartre**, French writer. Introduction, *The Wretched of the Earth*, 1963

Colonial rule is like alcoholism or worse. As hard as it is to detoxify yourself from alcoholism, it's even harder to detoxify yourself from a colonial mindset, because you have to get rid of so many lies and complexes that they've drilled into your head.

> **Rafael Cancel Miranda**, Puerto Rican independence activist, former U.S. political prisoner. In *Puerto Rico,* 1998

At some time there shall come among you a stranger, speaking a language you do not understand. He will try to buy the land from you, but do not sell it; keep it for an inheritance to your children.

> **Aseenewub**, Red Lake Ojibwe leader, recalling a prophecy related by his father. The U.S. government later threatened Ojibwes with hanging if they did not sign over their land. In *The Wisdom of Native Americans,* 1999

In fourteen hundred and ninety-three,
Columbus stole all he could see

> **Traditional rhyme**, updated. In *Lies My Teacher Told Me*, 1995

Our fight is not over yet
Not all the blood was drained from
the limbs of the boriqua
It still flows inside my body

it lies in the gift of my name
that I was taught to despise
I am
Taína

> **Taína de Valle-Asili**, poet, activist, referring to Taino indigenous people colonized by Spanish invaders. From poem, 1998

Chapter 2

"It Takes a Nation"

Nations, National Self-Determination, Nationalism, Homeland

There are many people, even among those considered the most conscious circles, that were and are totally unaware of this fact, taking such statements of land and nationality as a joke. I, as a student, don't take it as a joke. What is your nationality and where is your land?

> **Marcus Ali Muhammad**, writer. *Black Star* newspaper, circa 2002

Let's not conflate nationalism with stateism. I am a member of a nation, I reject the state...I reject the notion of U.S. citizenship and if they don't like it they're free to deport me to—Oklahoma, I guess. I'd rather have my own land back in Georgia but that's another story.

> **Ward Churchill**, educator, activist, referring to his Cherokee ancestry. Speech, in *The Vinyl Project*, from the Freedom Archives, 2003

The State is not the nation, and the State can be modified and even abolished in its present form, without harming the nation.

> **Randolph Bourne**, writer. "The State," 1918

We have always lived here. We would rather die here. Our fathers did. We cannot leave them. Our children were born here—how can we go away? If you give us the best place in the world, it is not so good for us as this.

> **Celsa Apapas**, Cupa leader, arguing against leaving her ancestral land in California for a reservation, 1901

While you are under alien governments get the best out of them as the rights of citizenship; but always have in view doing something to make it possible for your race to have a nation and a government of its own.

> **Marcus Garvey**, Jamaican Black nationalist leader, circa 1937. *Message to the People*, 1986

It's hard to be a Nationalist without a nation. But if you're asking whether or not we advocate Puerto Rican independence, the answer couldn't be anything but yes.

> **Not4Prophet**, lyricist for band Ricanstuction. *Blu Magazine*, 2000

I have no country to fight for; my country is the earth, and I am a citizen of the world.

Eugene Debs, activist, labor organizer, socialist. Speech, 1914

The Vietnamese say Vietnam should be able to determine its own destiny. Power of the Vietnamese people. We also chant power of the Vietnamese people. The Latins are talking about Latin America for the Latin Americans. Cuba Si and Yanqui, No. It's not that they don't want the Yankees to have any power they just don't want them to have power over them. They can have power over themselves. We in the black colony in America want to be able to have power over our destiny and that's black power.

Huey Newton, co-founder, Black Panther Party. Interview, *The Movement*, August 1968

Whole nations have melted away like balls of snow before the sun.

Dragging Canoe, Cherokee chief, 1775

We prefer self-government with danger to servility with tranquility.

Kwame Nkrumah, Ghanaian political leader. *New York Times Magazine*, 7/2/1958

It is easy to sit back and intellectualize about our nationalism from the modernist, eurocentric framework of rational, scientific, materialist models. While one does that, it is our nationalism which constantly rallies our people to come together, remember our history, love ourselves, dream on and fight back.

Ashanti Alston, former Black Panther member, anarchist activist. Essay, "Beyond Nationalism, But Not Without It."

For all its differences, the Leninist, Social-democratic and "national liberation" traditions had one view in common: that we need to gain control over the state first, and then change society from above. But things do not seem to be so simple for us any more. For power is not located in the national states alone, but disseminated throughout society (including our minds).

Ezequiel Adamovsky, Argentinean educator, activist. *Z Magazine*, June 2003

I think that nationalism has undermined revolutionary Black struggle. It's no accident that people like Malcolm X and Martin Luther King were destroyed at those moments of their political careers when they had begun to critique nationalism as a platform of organization; and where, in fact, they replace nationalism with a critique of imperialism; which then, unites us with the liberation struggles of so many people on the planet.

> **bell hooks**, writer, educator, activist. Interview, *Z Magazine*, December 1995

Got land to stand on
then you can stand up, stand up for your rights

> **Arrested Development**, hip hop group. From song "Ache'n for Acres," 1994

Palestine belongs to the Arabs in the same sense that England belongs to the English or France to the French... If they must look to the Palestine of geography as their national home, it is wrong to enter it under the shadow of the British gun. A religious act cannot be performed with the aid of the bayonet or the bomb.

> **Mahatma Gandhi**, Indian activist, political leader, 1938. In *A Land of Two Peoples,* 1983

A desegregated lunch counter won't solve our problem. Better jobs won't even solve our problems. An integrated cup of coffee isn't sufficient pay for four hundred years of slave labor... The only lasting and permanent solution is complete separation on some land that we can call our own.

> **Malcolm X**, Black nationalist leader. Speech, June 1963

There can never be peace in Ireland until the foreign, oppressive British presence is removed, leaving all the Irish people as a unit to control their own affairs and determine their own destinies as a sovereign people, free in mind and body, separate and distinct physically, culturally and economically.

> **Bobby Sands**, Irish independence political prisoner. From prison diary before death from hunger strike, 1981

Do you know why they are taking me away? For trying to give you a country to honor and respect, for trying to shake off the shame of slavery, for getting rid of the whip that has slashed your backs and those of your children.

> **María Josefa Ortiz**, Mexican revolutionary in war of independence, during arrest by soldiers, 1810

The Negro needs a nation and a country of his own, where he can best show evidence of his ability in the art of human progress. Scattered as an unmixed and unrecognized part of alien nations and civilizations is but to demonstrate his imbecility, and point him out as an unworthy derelict, fit neither for the society of the Greek, Jew, nor Gentile.

> **Marcus Garvey**, Jamaican Black nationalist leader. *Black Nationalism*, 1962

Aztlán may be a myth or it may be a real place, but it always stands for the idea of a homeland, of freedom from that which we are not, of reclaiming what we are.

> **Rodolfo "Corky" Gonzales**, activist, writer, referring to the legendary place of origin of Aztec peoples, in Mexico and the American Southwest. *A War of Words*, 1985

If we are a part of America, then part of what she is worth belongs to us. We will take our share and depart, then this white country can have peace. What is her net worth? Give us our share in gold and silver and let us depart and go back to our homeland in peace. We want no integration with this wicked race that enslaved us.

> **Malcolm X**, Black nationalist leader. Speech, "God's Judgment of White America," December 1963

Chapter 3

"The Color of Justice"

Race, Ethnicity, Racism, Anti-Racism

I see unseen hands pitting you against me…
In boardroom they collectively divide the two
Telling you that my Black skull you should bash
Telling me you ain't nuttin' but white trash
We're both pawns in this new world order

> **Kirk Nugent**, poet. From poem "She Was Everything," circa 1999

When you removed the gag that was keeping these black mouths shut, what were you hoping for? That they would sing your praises? Did you think that when they raised themselves up again, you would read adoration in the eyes of these heads that our fathers had forced to bend to the very ground? Here are Black men standing, looking at us, and I hope that you—like me—will feel the shock of being seen.

> **Jean-Paul Sartre**, French writer. *Black Orpheus*, 1949

Racism seeps into our systems like poison, kills off pieces of ourselves as we build a tolerance for it. We have learned to survive with our insides, our essential selves, rotting away.

> **Virginia R. Harris**, writer, educator; and Trinity A. Ordoña, activist, photographer. In *Making Face, Making Soul*, 1990

We are not embattled with the color of man, but with the weakness of man, a mindset that lusts for power and wealth at the expense of life. Men of all colors, cultures and religions must stand together to oppose the genocidal policies that face us all as the corporate world seeks to enslave all, and pit one nation against another.

> **Leonard Peltier**, writer, U.S. political prisoner. "Anniversary Statement," 1/23/2004

Let's get this straight right now. Our entire system was constructed from day one on the subjugation, exploitation, or extermination of whole peoples. There has to be a cover story about that kind of practice, a justification. Racism provides that justification. Frontal racism, like slavery and Jim Crow, and implicit racism like 'white man's burden' and 'exporting democracy.'

> **Stan Goff**, writer, former U.S. Army sergeant. Interview, *Truthout*, 7/16/03

The white man has become the black man's burden.
> **Adam Clayton Powell, Jr.**, Congressman, writer. *Marching Blacks*, 1945

Race is, politically speaking, not the beginning of humanity but its end, not the origin of peoples but their decay, not the natural birth of man but his unnatural death.
> **Hannah Arendt**, German educator, political analyst. *The Origins of Totalitarianism*, 1951

The demon of racialism must be buried and forgotten; it has shed among us sufficient blood. We are one people.
> **Pixley Ka Isaka Seme**, South African lawyer. *Penguin Dictionary of South African Quotations*, 1994

What we never should lose sight of is that these may be socially constructed differences—but they are real… So we even find some middle-class white men claiming that they've "given up being white" (I can hear my grandmother saying, "More white foolishness!" with a dismissing headshake). Needless to say, they haven't given up anything. Race as a form of class is very tangible, solid, material, as real as a tank division running over you ... tank divisions, after all, are also socially constructed!
> **J. Sakai**, writer. Essay, "When Race Burns Class," 2000

Race may be a scientific fiction, but it is a social fact.
> **Tim Wise**, activist, educator. *White Like Me*, 2005

I would argue that unless we are going to in turn mimic the Nazis or the South Africans and try to define a constituency in purely racial terms, we would have to acknowledge that there is not a strict biological or racial definition of Indianness. It's generally assumed that there will be some lineal descent. We count in terms of lineage. We count in terms of kinship. Kinship is not biology.
> **Ward Churchill**, educator, activist. Interview, *Z Magazine*, December 1995

The price the white American paid for his ticket was to become white.
> **James Baldwin**, writer, educator. Essay, "The Price of the Ticket," 1985

'Racism' is a term that has been de-clawed by a purely psychological understanding as 'prejudice,' rather than as a category of oppression, and hence power and privilege.

> **Chris Wright**. Essay, "Marxism and White Skin Privilege."

If the white man doesn't want us to be anti-him, let him stop oppressing and exploiting and degrading us.

> **Malcolm X**, Black nationalist leader. Speech, "The Ballot or the Bullet," April 1964

We are oppressed people in the U.S. and don't even know it… Our problem is that we want to belong to a society that wants to oppress us. We want to be the plantation owner.

> **Assata Shakur**, former Black Panther, in exile in Cuba. Interview, "From Exile With Love," 2001

"Bound and Gagged" by Rodney Camarce

I have been everything in this country. I have nursed a nation of strangers—
strangers who I know—when they grew up, they would rape my daughters
and kill my son. I, black woman, I. I have fought for freedom. I have
enjoyed it. I have lost it. I have been on the very bottom of the strata. I have
somehow managed to keep myself intact enough to survive and to do better
then that—to thrive.

>   **Maya Angelou**, poet, educator. *Los Angles Times*, 1/17/1993

We gonna see to it that these few rich elites stop trickin' white folks... We
sayin' to America today, that when you white folks in America quit worrying
about where you live and what school you go to—Rockefeller and DuPont
wouldn't walk they dog through your neighborhood. The rich, rich elite
white folks in America wouldn't wash they feet in the pot you white folks
eat in. And the sooner white America stop getting put in a trick by a handful
of people who don't care nothing about you or me or your kids or my kids,
not until then will we be able to move this thing to where it have to go.

>   **Speaker unknown**. In *The Vinyl Project*, from the Freedom
>   Archives, 2003

White people with any sense of justice and with any hope for living in a
humane and cooperative society must fully ally with Black liberation.

>   **Kuwasi Balagoon, Judy Clark and David Gilbert**, black
>   liberation and white anti-imperialist activists captured during one
>   of their clandestine armed actions. From court statement during
>   pre-trial proceedings, September 1982

I'll have white kids come to me and say: 'I want to organize in the 'hood.'
Well, why would you want to do that? The 'hood isn't voting for high defense
budgets. The 'hood is not voting to go to foreign countries and blow folks
away, the 'hood has never really voted for putting more cops on the street
or, you know, supporting the death penalty—all those things, for the most
part, are coming from the communities that they left. If you want to help, go
back to where you came from and organize and educate there.

>   **Mario Hardy Ramirez**, activist. Interview, *Insubordination*,
>   September 2003

In a multicultural context, no one can speak to everyone. We need many
voices, and sometimes it needs to be white people who do that. Racism is
not our problem—it's an illness... I think white people have a lot of healing
to do, but maybe they're so scared to do it with us around. Some of it may

have to be a closed-door family kind of thing.
> **Rha Goddess**, activist, hip hop MC. In *No More Prisons,* 1999

We [Asian Americans and African Americans] are a kindred people, forged in the fire of white supremacy and struggle, but how can we recall that kinship when our memories have been massaged by white hands, and how can we remember the past when our storytellers have been whispering amid the din of Western civilization and Anglo-conformity?
> **Gary Okihiro**, educator, writer. *Margins and Mainstreams*, 1994

We have come over a way that with tears has been watered
We have come, treading our path through the blood of the slaughtered,
Out from the gloomy past till now we stand at last
Where the white gleam of our star is cast.
> **James Weldon Johnson**, poet. From poem "Lift Every Voice and Sing," 1900

Down in the Georgia and Carolina Sea Islands they still tell the story of the Ibos. They say that when the boat brought the Africans in from the big slaving ships, the Ibos stepped onto shore in their chains, took a look around, and, seeing what the Europeans further had in store for them, turned right around and walked all the way home to the Motherland.
> **Toni Cade Bambara**, writer, activist. Preface to *Daughters of the Dust,* 1992

African Americans have stories as varied as any other people in American society. As varied as any other people in the world. Our lives, our history, our present reality is no more limited to "ghetto" stories, than Italian Americans are to the Mafia, or Jewish Americans are to the Holocaust.
> **Julie Dash**, filmmaker. *Daughters of the Dust,* 1992

I have almost reached the regrettable conclusion that the Negro's great stumbling block in the stride toward freedom is not the White Citizen's Councilor or the Ku Klux Klanner, but the white moderate who is more devoted to "order" than to justice; who prefers a negative peace which is the absence of tension to a positive peace which is the presence of justice.
> **Martin Luther King, Jr.**, civil rights leader. "Letter from Birmingham City Jail," April 1963

The question really becomes whether you choose to be an oppressor or a revolutionary. And if you choose to be an oppressor, then you are my enemy—

not because you are white, but because you choose to oppress me. We are not an anti-white movement. We are anti-anybody who is anti-black.

> **H. "Rap" Brown**, Black power leader. Speech, 1967

I have these very deep feelings that white people who want to join black organizations are really just taking the escapist way to salve their consciences. By visibly hovering near us, they are "proving" that they are "with us." But the hard truth is this isn't helping to solve America's racist problem. The Negroes aren't the racists. Where the really sincere white people have got to do their "proving" of themselves is not among the black victims, but out on the battle lines of where America's racism really is—and that's in their own home communities; America's racism is among their own fellow whites. That's where the sincere whites who really mean to accomplish something have got to work.

> **Malcolm X.**, Black nationalist leader. *Autobiography of Malcolm X*, 1964

When I use the term European, I'm not referring to a skin color or a particular genetic structure. What I'm referring to is a mind-set, a worldview that is a product of the development of European culture. People are not genetically encoded to hold this outlook; they are acculturated to hold it. It is possible for an American Indian to share European values, a European worldview… What I'm putting out here is not a racial proposition but a cultural proposition. Those who ultimately advocate and defend the realities of European culture and its industrialism are my enemies. Those who resist it, who struggle against it, are my allies, the allies of American Indian people.

> **Russell Means**, activist, actor, former leader in the American Indian Movement. Speech, Black Hills International Survival Gathering, July 1980

Black man, white man, yellow man, put 'em in a can
Give 'em some guitars and make 'em have a jam
'Cause it might take a lesson in 'harmony'
To show these fools we're all from the same family

> **BLK Sonshine**, from song "Agitation," circa 2000

Colored Americans, in their fight for equality, must disabuse white people's minds of the opinion that the only equality the Negro desires is the association of white people.

> **William Pickens**, educator. *Atlanta World*, 1935

Do you know what white racists call black PhD's? . . . 'Nigger!'
  Malcolm X, Black nationalist leader. Attributed.

As long as white Americans take refuge in their whiteness—for so long as they are unable to walk out of this most monstrous of traps—they will allow millions of people to be slaughtered in their name, and will be manipulated into and surrender themselves to what they will think of—and justify—as a racial war. They will never, so long as their whiteness puts so sinister a distance between themselves and their own experience and the experience of others, feel themselves sufficiently human, *sufficiently worthwhile,* to become responsible for themselves, their leaders, their country, their children, or their fate.
  James Baldwin, writer, educator. "An Open Letter to My Sister,
  Angela Davis," November 1970

Our fathers had to fight Jim Crow. Now, we have to fight James Crow Jr., Esquire.
  Al Sharpton, civil rights activist, reverend. *CNN*, 1/12/2004

Treat us like men, and there is no danger but we will all live in peace and happiness together. For we are not like you, hard hearted, unmerciful, and unforgiving. What a happy country this will be, if the whites will listen.
  David Walker, slavery abolitionist, writer. "Appeal," 1829

The callousness and destructivness of this system damages everyone's humanity. No one can be blamed for where she or he was born, nor can one emerge magically free of the prevailing racism and sexism. The real issue is one of choices: whether or not to be an active ally against oppression and for a more humane society.
  David Gilbert, writer, U.S. political prisoner. *No Surrender*, 2004

There is the raw fear, the same fear the plantation owners felt when a slave revolution created the republic of Haiti, the same fear the Afrikaaners and British felt in South Africa: 'they will rise up and kill us in our sleep (and we will have deserved it).' We speak of the ancient instinctive fears that cause infants to startle and scream in the middle of the night, the shadow of the predator cat lurking in the back of the cave of a million years...waiting. I think that in the same way whites instinctively know that this favored status of ours cannot exist forever, because moral wrongs never can find a stable state in the universe.

> **Cynthia Gomez, a.k.a. Rootsie**, writer, educator. Essay, "The Burden of Privilege," 2004

"Stand Up," collage by Theodore Harris

Racism is the mental illness that will bring low the superpower.

> **Glen Ford and Peter Gamble**. *Blackcommentator.com*, August 2004

Justice is the most important word in race relations.

> **Rubén Salazar**, journalist, killed by a tear gas canister fired by police during a street protest against disproportionate Chicano deaths in the Vietnam war, 8/29/1970. Attributed.

I believe that there will ultimately be a clash between the oppressed and those that do the oppressing. I believe that there will be a clash between those who want freedom, justice and equality for everyone and those who want to continue the systems of exploitation. I believe that there will be that kind of clash, but I don't think that it will be based upon the color of the skin.

> **Malcolm X**, Black nationalist leader. Interview, *Pierre Berton Show*, 1/19/1965

My enemy is not the average white man, it's not the kid down the block, it's not the kids I see on the street. My enemy is the white man I don't see, the people in the White House, the corporate monopoly owners, fake liberal politicians, those are my enemies.

> **Immortal Technique**, hip hop MC. From song "Poverty of Philosophy," Viper Records, 2001

Now that we have enriched their soil and filled their coffers, they say that we are not capable of becoming like white men, and that we can never rise to respectability in this country. They would drive us to a strange land. But before I go, the bayonet shall pierce me through. African rights and liberty is a subject that ought to fire the breast of every free man of color in these United States.

> **Maria W. Stewart**, slavery abolitionist. Speech, Boston, MA, 1833

You've probably heard of "driving while black?" These days you've got to watch out if you're caught coughing while Asian. Ask any Asian American who's had hay fever in the past few weeks. A few hundred people get sick on the other side of the Pacific, and suddenly everyone who looks Asian is the new Typhoid Mary.

> **Gabrielle Banks**, describing the SARS virus outbreak of 2003. *ColorLines RaceWire*, 2003

The African-American has accepted something about America. The African in America said 'I'm just here against my will, and I'm still here against my will.'

> **Kwame Toure**, formerly Stokely Carmichael, civil rights and Black power activist. Speech, 1997

I have a dream that one day on the red hills of Georgia, sons of former slaves and sons of former slave owners will be able to sit down together at the table of brotherhood.

> **Martin Luther King, Jr.**, civil rights leader. Speech, August 1963

It's a peculiar mechanism of white supremacy where there is not a master-race mentality so much as a deficient-race ideology from which all others could self-exclude.

> **Stan Goff**, writer, former U.S. Army sergeant. Essay, May 2004

As soon as the organized white groups do not do the things that would benefit us in our struggle for liberation, that will be our departure point. So we don't suffer in the hang-up of a skin color. We don't hate white people; we hate the oppressor. And if the oppressor happens to be white then we hate him. When he stops oppressing us then we no longer hate him.

> **Huey Newton**, co-founder, Black Panther Party. Interview, *The Movement*, August 1968

Black body swinging in the Southern breeze,
Strange fruit hanging from the poplar trees.

> **Billie Holiday**, singer. From song written by Lewis Allen, "Strange Fruit," 1939

I think we have many common threads, but we've been programmed racially not to look at the common threads. You get right down to the reality of it, what are white people? White people are the descendants of tribes also. They come from tribes. It's just that the erasing of their tribal memory started 3,000 years ago. For us it started 500 years ago. When you look at what I call the Caucasian Americans, when they got here and the brutality that they carried out here was the only reality they knew, because that same brutality had been carried out on them.

> **John Trudell**, poet, activist, former chairman of the American Indian Movement. Interview, 1999

Going back centuries, there has been a displacement of anger by people who are at the lower rungs of the economic ladder, who opt for racism instead of fighting for progress.

> **Norman Solomon**, journalist. Interview, *Guerrilla News Network*, 9/9/2003

The problem arises then in what part [white radicals] can play. How can they aid the colony? How can they aid the Black Panther Party or any other black revolutionary group? They can aid the black revolutionaries first by simply turning away from the establishment, and secondly by choosing their friends. For instance, they have a choice between whether they will be a friend of Lyndon Baines Johnson or a friend of Fidel Castro. A friend of Robert Kennedy or a friend of Ho Chi Minh. And these are direct opposites.

> **Huey Newton**, co-founder, Black Panther Party. Interview, *The Movement*, August 1968

We wear the mask that grins and lies,
It hides our cheeks and shades our eyes, —
This debt we pay to human guile;
With torn and bleeding hearts we smile
>   **Paul L. Dunbar**, poet, writer. From poem, "We Wear the Mask,"
>   1895

Being a Negro in America means trying to smile when you want to cry.
It means trying to hold onto physical life amid psychological death. It
means the pain of watching your children grow up with clouds of inferiority
in their mental skies. It means having your legs cut off, and then being
condemned for being a cripple. It means seeing your mother and father
spiritually murdered by the slings and arrows of daily exploitation, and then
being hated for being an orphan.
>   **Martin Luther King, Jr.**, civil rights leader. *Where Do We Go
>   from Here: Chaos or Community?* 1967

We inherit a history that is not ours. We become stereotypes that are not
us. We allow self-hatred to consume us, and we fashion silence to suit us.
Asian Americans have pain and sorrow and anger that must be dealt with.
>   **Michelle Myers**, poet, educator. *Awol Magazine*, 2002

They fear
They fear the world.
They destroy what they fear.
They fear themselves.
>   **Leslie Marmon Silko**, writer, relating the story of a legend about
>   the coming of white settlers to American Indian land. *Ceremony,*
>   1988

Black people may find it hard to believe, but the main purpose of apartheid
was not racial separation, nor even racial domination; it was to enrich the
ruling class.
>   **Ken Owen**, South African editor. *Penguin Dictionary of South
>   African Quotations,* 1994

How can we exist together...with white people, if they are not ready to
hear the truth? The truth as it needs to be heard would have to consist of
the cries, the laughter, the hollers, the screams, the moans, all of which
constitute audible pain from racism that will phonically inscribe, upon the

white psyche.
> **Kelvin Monroe**, writer. Essay "My White Teeth: Counterpoint in F," 2003

No Vietcongs ever called me nigger.
> **Muhammad Ali**, champion boxer, activist, on his refusal to fight for the U.S. in Vietnam. Attributed.

Let us [white people] do it for our own dignity. Let us join this struggle so that we can lay honest claim to our own humanity. I say this because I believe that we give up our dignity when we evade the truth, and we surrender our humanity when we hold onto illegitimate power over others.
> **Robert Jensen**, writer. From essay "What the 'Fighting Sioux' Tells Us About Whites," 2003

Whiteness is ownership of the earth.
> **W.E.B. Du Bois**, scholar, educator. Attributed.

If White people are victims of, say, affirmative action's so-called reverse racism, the real claims of people of color and of women will make little sense. False claims of oppression dilute the force of real claims. White aggrieved victimhood is a smoke screen for White privilege.
> **Kendall Clark**, writer, educator. From essay "The Global Privileges of Whiteness," 2001

Treason to whiteness is loyalty to humanity.
> **Motto of the Race Traitor journal**

Being top of the pile means that whites are peculiarly and uniquely insensitive to race and racism, and the power relations this involves. We are invariably the beneficiaries, never the victims. Even when well-meaning, we remain strangely ignorant.
> **Martin Jacques**. *The Guardian*, UK, 9/20/2003

There is one thing that characterizes white privilege perhaps above all else, and that is the attempt to mitigate the pain of one's complicity in it.
> **Cynthia Gomez, a.k.a. Rootsie**, writer, educator. Essay, "The Falacies of the Hippie Movement," 2003

I would suggest that while a number of white anti-racists would join the struggle against white supremacy, when it really comes down to asking people to help destroy their own base of power, their dedication to their own privilege is likely to shine through.

Andi Shively, anti-racist activist. "Bullets, 'Burbs, and Backlash: Census 2000 and White Anxiety," 2001

The Black Family is still our No. 1 priority. As you prepare your delicious foods, cakes, pies and joyous entertainment, please remember that White people may be troublesome, but they are still a world minority. Always have been, always will be. Get away from them for awhile. If at all possible, get your family together or go see somebody that looks like you and communicates like you. Don't let these strange times keep us from coming together!

Nubian Network, "Black Consciousness Online," 2003

Protesting U.S. military intervention in Somalia, San Francisco, CA, 1993. Photo by Bill Hackwell

Is it wrong for me to love my own? Is it wicked in me because my skin is red; because I am a Sioux; because I was born where my father lived; because I would die for my people and my country?

Sitting Bull, Teton Lakota American Indian Leader. *Life of Sitting Bull and History of the Indian War of 1890-1891*, 1891

Up! You mighty race, you can accomplish what you will... No one knows when the hour of Africa's redemption cometh. It is in the wind. It is coming. One day, like a storm, it will be here.

    Marcus Garvey, Jamaican Black nationalist leader

Until the philosophy which holds one race superior and another inferior is finally and permanently discredited and abandoned; that until there are no longer any first and second class citizens of any nations; that until the color of a man's skin is of no more significance than the color of his eyes; that until the basic human rights are equally guaranteed to all—without regard to race—until that day, the dream of lasting peace and world citizenship and the role of international morality will remain but a fleeting illusion, to be pursued but never attained.

    Haile Selassie, Ethiopian political leader. Speech, United Nations, October 1963

It is hardly an exaggeration to say that white America is the biggest collective recipient of racial preference in the history of the cosmos. It has skewed our laws, shaped our public policy and helped create the glaring inequalities with which we still live.

    Tim Wise, activist, educator. Essay, "Whites Swim in Racial Preference," 2003

[There is] that sense of 'we are SO lucky' that often enters into the conversations of whites as they contemplate the world. 'Luck' is even equated by some to divine grace, to God's particular favor for his worthiest children. But of course neither luck nor grace has a thing to do with it. It's about ugly things like slavery and widespread thievery and the force of arms.

    Cynthia Gomez, a.k.a. Rootsie, writer, educator. Essay, "The Burden of Privilege," 2004

[White people] are like a biker with the wind so favorable at our backs that we don't even notice our advantage. It is difficult for us to imagine what it must be like—how it must change everything—to be born biking into a head wind. We have become so accustomed to having the wind at our backs, so spoiled by our good fortune, that it seems to us a great injustice that the wind should subside, or switch directions, and blow, even for a minute, in any other way.

    William Upski Wimsatt, writer, activist. *Bomb The Suburbs*, 1994

From the moment of your birth you are conscious of the fact that in apartheid South Africa you are not the same color as other persons who claim to be of higher quality than you are. You are made to feel from childhood that there is a race that is superior to you by virtue of its pigmentation and you sort of felt that all authority is white, and you grew up with that, becoming subservient to men of the other color.

> **Winnie Mandela**, South African human rights and political leader.
> In *The Roots of Resistance*, from the Freedom Archives, 2002

They saw themselves as others had seen them. They had been formed by the images made of them by those who had had the deepest necessity to despise them.

> **James Baldwin**, writer, educator. Attributed.

The ultimate sin
is to be ashamed of your skin

> **Immortal Technique**, hip hop MC. From song "Revolutionary,"
> Viper Records, 2001

You must remember, it's a human thing to want to be validated by the same system that misused you. You want them to say, "You OK" ...You know, any time I want to take on the same looks and characteristics of the oppressor, then they won.

> **Dick Gregory**, activist, nutritionist, comedian. Interview,
> *Nightlife*, July 1999

They have been made to feel inferior for so long that for them it is comforting to drink tea, wine or beer with whites who seem to treat them as equals.

> **Stephen Biko**, South African anti-apartheid leader, killed by
> police in 1977. Statement, circa 1975

Blond hair, pale sin, blue eyes: without them, one was considered ugly. Such attitudes prevailed in my mother's time, in her mother's time. They still exist today, but it stops here, with my generation, with me.

> **Jacqueline "Setra" Collins**, singer. *Dreads,* 1997

Whites must be made to realize that they are only human, not superior. Same with blacks. They must be made to realize that they are also human, not inferior.

> **Stephen Biko**, South African anti-apartheid leader, killed by
> police in 1977. *Boston Globe*, 10/26/1977

The most fundamental truth to be told in any art form, as far as Blacks are concerned, is that America is killing us.

> **Sonia Sanchez**, educator, poet, writer. In *Black Women Writers at Work,* 1983

We don't judge a man because of the color of his skin. We don't judge you because you're white; we don't judge you because you're black; we don't judge you because you're brown. We judge you because of what you do and what you practice. And as long as you practice evil, we're against you.

> **Malcolm X**, Black nationalist leader. Speech, 1965

An Indian who is as bad as the white men could not live in our nation... The white men do not scalp the head; but they do worse. They poison the heart.

> **Black Hawk**, Sac leader. Statement of Surrender, 1835

I, for one, can say that I am tired of burying innocent black and Latino people who die at the hands of this unjust system. I'm sorry, but I can't be calm if my baby is going to be shot or hurt by out-of-control police. I can't be calm when I drive through sections of Atlanta that look more like Kinshasa, Democratic Republic of Congo than America. I cannot be calm.

> **Cynthia McKinney**, former U.S. Congresswoman. Speech, Harlem, NY 8/6/2003

The destiny of colored Americans is the destiny of America. We shall never leave you.

> **Frederick Douglass**, slavery abolitionist, political theorist. Attributed.

Everyone says, "wow, she invents things! She is very powerfull!" But it is not I. It is Africa.

> **Zap Mama**, Belgian music group. Interview, *Blu Magazine,* 2001

I can't pay no doctor bills, but whitey's on the moon
ten years from now I'll be paying still, while whitey's on the moon

> **Gil Scott Heron**, poet, musician. From poem, "Whitey on the Moon," 1970

If Arabs can be automatically suspected of terrorism just because they are Arabs, then white people should be suspected of chicanery, thievery, and corruption, just because they are white... If Arabs should be suspect while in

flight, then white people should not be allowed near anyone's money.
> **Margaret Kimberley**, writer. Essay, "Arabs On Planes and White People in the Boardroom," 2004

Each man is good in the sight of the Great Spirit. It is not necessary for eagles to be crows.
> **Sitting Bull**, Teton Lakota American Indian leader. From speech.

Plenty of soapbox segregationists were bedroom integrationists.
> **Christy Oglesby**, writer, on the relationship between white former U.S. Congressman Strom Thurmond and Carrie Butler, a black house servant. *CNN*, 12/23/2003

I hear that melting pot stuff a lot, and all I can say is that we haven't melted.
> **Jesse Jackson**, civil rights activist, reverend. Interview, *Playboy*, November 1969

Much of the foundation and fabric of the African-American community itself has been quietly blowing away like sandy topsoil, scattered by the winds of integration. Yes, they have come to live with the white folks. But at what cost?
> **J. Douglas Allen-Taylor**, writer. *Colorlines* magazine, Summer 2004

Upwards to 20,000,000 Black people, knowing you for the rotten, racist, murdering nation of white thievish hypocrites that you are, are no longer interested in explaining anything to you, America.
> **Eldridge Cleaver**, writer, former black power activist. Essay, "Credo for Rioters and Looters," circa 1969

The color of the skin makes no difference. What is good and just for one is good and just for the other, and the Great Spirit made all men brothers.
> **White Shield**, Arikara leader, 1833-1883. Attributed.

Worn as exquisite fashion accessory, ever-present as exotic comic prop, liberally used as sex toy and servant, but invisible as empowered subject of history. That's you, bro. That's you, sister. Content to be the punchline in a dirty boy's club joke? Comfortable in your niche as silent partner to your own insignificance?
> **Announcement for Yellow Fist Campaign**, May, 2000, intended to combat misogynist, anti-Asian song lyrics.

The Negro's experience of the white world cannot possibly create in him any respect for the standards by which the white world claims to live.
> **James Baldwin**, writer, educator. *The Fire Next Time,* 1963

in how many back alleys, open fields, dark parks
did our bodies crumple, separate, flake
from the tar, feathers, knife, rifle, rope and flame
while they portrayed us as the beasts,
oblivious to pain
> **Michele Gibbs**, poet, activist. From poem, "Boot-black Blood-clot Blues," 1996

The leaders of this country can call out the Army and Navy to stop the railroad workers and stop the maritime workers; why can't they stop the lynchers?
> **Paul Robeson**, activist, scholar, athlete. Speech, 9/12/1946

What think you of a Christian land,
Where Christians on a Sabbath day
Upon their helpless brothers prey,
And oft their drowsy minds refresh
Thru sport of burning human flesh?
But none dare tell who led the band,
And this was in a Christian land
> **Walter Hawkins**, poet. From poem "The Mob Victim," depicting the lynching of a Black man and his pregnant wife, 1909

The white man must no longer project his fears and insecurities onto other groups, races and countries. Before the white man can relate to others he must forego the pleasure of defining them. The white man must learn to stop viewing history as a plot against himself.
> **Vine Deloria**, educator, writer. In *The Wages of Whiteness*, 1991

Your time of decay may be distant, but it will surely come, for even the white man, whose God walked and talked with him as friend with friend, cannot be exempt from the common destiny. We may be brothers, after all. We shall see.
> **Chief Seattle**, Suqwamish/Duwamish leader. Speech, circa 1860. Attributed by a reporter.

The world is white no longer, and it will never be again.
> **James Baldwin**, writer, educator. *Notes of a Native Son*, 1955

the reign of the white race is ending on earth
and the reign of the peoples in the universe is beginning.
> **Paul Laraque**, Haitian poet. From poem "Reign of the Peoples,"
> circa 1979

Chapter 4

"Middle Passages"

Slavery, Reparations for Slavery, Restitution for Past Wrongs

By the rivers of Babylon, there we sat down
Yeeah we wept, when we remembered Zion.
When the wicked
Carried us away in captivity
Required from us a song
Now how shall we sing the lord's song in a strange land

From song "Rivers of Babylon," adapted from the Bible

No man can put a chain about the ankle of his fellowman, without at last finding the other end of it about his own neck.

Frederick Douglass, slavery abolitionist, political theorist. In *The Life and Times of Frederick Douglass,* 1881

This question of reparations has been demonized only where African Americans are concerned. Jews, quite rightly, have received billions of dollars in reparations for World War II, as have Korean women who were forced into prostitution by the Japanese. [Native] Canadians have received reparations from the Canadian government. Aborigines have received reparations from the Australian government... [Slavery] is America's holocaust, and our country hides from it.

Randall Robinson, activist and writer. Interview, *Black World Today*, 2000

The concept is this, basically: The whole black nation has to be put together as a black army and we're going to walk on this nation. We're going to walk on this racist power structure. And we're going to say to the whole damn government, 'Stick 'em up, motherfucker! This is a hold-up! We come for what's ours!'

Bobby Seale, co-founder, Black Panther Party. Speech, circa 1968

I would have been able to free a thousand more slaves if I could only have convinced them that they were slaves.

Harriet Tubman, Underground Railroad conductor. Attributed.

None are more hopelessly enslaved than those who falsely believe they are free.

> **Johann Wolfgang von Goethe**, German playwright, poet. Attributed.

The slave master will not teach you knowledge of self, as there would not be a master-slave relationship any longer.

> **Elijah Muhammad**, former leader of the Nation of Islam. *Message to the Black Man in America,* 1965

This country couldn't call us Africans because if it had, we would have understood some things about ourselves.

> **Sonia Sanchez**, educator, poet, writer. Attributed.

When The Slave Master holds the monopoly on story-telling, the slave will find himself celebrating slavery, and in the process of his own genocide, he will actually collaborate quite blindly.

> **Author unknown**

Emancipate yourselves from mental slavery
none but ourselves can free our minds

> **Bob Marley**, Jamaican reggae singer. From song "Redemption Song," 1980

When you've taken something from somebody, and they're still there looking at you, it's got to be hard. We haven't disappeared. The land is here and we're still here. Their feet are always moving, but they're not going anywhere, and they're saying, "We'll do this and that with this program," and we're just saying "You have our land."

> **Oren Lyons**, educator, Chief of the Turtle Clan of the Onondaga Nation. *Esquire*, February 1994

When millions of people have been cheated for centuries, restitution is a costly process... Justice so long deferred has accumulated interest and its cost for this society will be substantial in financial as well as human terms.

> **Martin Luther King, Jr.**, civil rights leader. *A Testament of Hope*, 1986

There was one of two things I had a right to, liberty or death. If I could not have one, I would have the other, for no man should take me alive.

> **Harriet Tubman**, Underground Railroad conductor. In *Harriet, the Moses of her People*, 1869

Remember that if I must die I die in trying to liberate a few of my poor and oppressed people from my condition of servitude which God in his Holy Writ has hurled his most bitter denunciations against.

> **John Copeland**, member of the anti-slavery guerrilla band of John Brown which attacked Harper's Ferry. From letter to his parents before his execution, 1859

On slave ships.
hurling ourselves into oceans.
Slitting the throats of our captors.
We took their whips.
And their ships.
Blood flowed in the Atlantic—
and it wasn't all ours.

> **Assata Shakur**, former Black Panther, in exile in Cuba. From poem, "The Tradition," 1987

Our brethren of the South should not be called slaves, but prisoners of war.

> **Robert Johnson**, at a Boston, MA protest against the Fugitive Slave Law. *Liberator*, December 1852

"U.S. Slave System" by Ricardo Levins Morales

My father was a slave, and my people died to build this country, and I'm going to stay and have a piece of it just like you.

> **Paul Robeson**, activist, scholar, athlete. Statement before the House Un-American Activities Committee, 1956

You might as well expect the rivers to run backward as that any man who was born a free man should be contented when penned up and denied liberty to go where he pleases.

> **Chief Joseph**, Nez Perce leader, on reservation life. Statement, Washington, DC. *North American Review*, 1879

Oh, freedom! Oh, freedom!
Oh, freedom over me!
And before I'd be a slave, I'll be buried in my grave,
And go home to my Lord and be free

> **From African-American spiritual**, 1800s

Have you got to learn that human rights are mutual and reciprocal, and if you take my liberty and life, you forfeit your own liberty and life?

> **Jermain Wesley Loguen**, runaway African slave who became involved in the Underground Railroad upon gaining freedom. From letter to his former mistress, 3/28/1860

I must own, to the shame of my own countrymen, that I was first kidnapped and betrayed by some of my own complexion; but if there were no buyers, there would be no sellers.

> **Ottobah Cugoano**, Ghanaian man kidnapped and sold into slavery in England, where he later became a writer and slavery abolitionist. "Thoughts and Sentiments on the Evils of Slavery," 1787

No chains around my feet, but I'm not free
I know I am bound here, in captivity

> **Bob Marley**, Jamaican reggae singer. From song "Concrete Jungle," 1972

The youth of today both white and black had nothing to do with the decisions of our ancestors in the past, this nation was fucked up from the beginning and now we're all left to clean up the mess.

> **Post on the Dead Prez internet message board**, 2004

And I suggest you don't fuck wit us

Cracka you stuck wit us
>   **Goodie Mob**, hip hop group. From song "The Coming," 1995

The white man's happiness cannot be purchased by the black man's misery.
>   **Frederick Douglass**, slavery abolitionist, political theorist.
>   Speech, 1849

A relationship that white people can have with our struggle is to go to their granddaddies and daddies and say "y'all still owe reparations to our community because even though the chains is taken off the blacks we never received the wealth that was stolen." [Then] we got something in common and we can work towards getting the government to acknowledge that... White people let's work together on that cuz it'll be a shame if we just gotta come take it.
>   **Stic.man**, of hip hop group Dead Prez. *Reactmag.com*, June
>   2004

The answer to the race problem is simple—it's give and take. If they don't give, we're going to take it.
>   **Dick Gregory**, activist, nutritionist, comedian. *What's Happening*,
>   1965

They think because they hold us in their infernal chains of slavery, that we wish to be white, or of their color—but they are dreadfully deceived—we wish to be just as it pleased our Creator to have made us.
>   **David Walker**, slavery abolitionist, writer. "Appeal," 1829

In their time the great wars came and went, the little wars came and went; the white slavers came and went, they took away the heart of our race; they bore away the mind and muscle of our race. The city fell and was rebuilt, the city fell and our people trudged through mountain and forest to found a new home.
>   **Wole Soyinka**, Nigerian playwright, educator. From play set in
>   the last days of the Yoruba kingdom of Old Oyo, "Death and the
>   King's Horseman," 1975

Chapter 5

"Basta Ya!"

Indigenous Peoples Struggle

I am a part of this Creation as you are, no more than, no less than each and every one of you within the sound of my voice. I am the generation of generations before me, and of generations to come. I am not a citizen of the United States or a ward of the federal Government. I have a right to continue my cycle in this Universe undisturbed.

> **Anna Mae Pictou Aquash**, American Indian Movement activist, murdered in 1975. Attributed.

We, those who are the color of the earth. Guariji'o. Here, no longer shame for the color of our skin. Huasteco. Language. Huave. Clothing. Kikapu.' Dance. Kukapa.' Song. Mame. Size. Matlatzinca. History. Mixteco. Here, no longer embarrassment. Nahuatl. Here the pride of our being the color we are of the color of the earth.

> **Zapatista National Liberation Army**, Mexico. Speech as Zapatista marchers arrived in Mexico City, March 2001

You force me to follow laws that are not my own, and lifestyles that I don't know; you try to force me to mimic your behavior, which I don't know properly, and it will make me foolish, impoverished and sick, because I am only a tourist in your worlds; you evict me from my own land by force; you don't even buy it. You don't give me water in return, you don't give me food in return. Nothing; you force me to go to town and search for work, or to sit at home and wait for your handouts of maize as if I were the criminal.

> **Lesikar Ole Ngila**, Tanzanian Maasai activist. Message to the United Nations on the topic of Indigenous Peoples. "Reflections of a Maasai Warrior," March 2004

Dear President Bush: Please send your assistance in freeing our small nation from occupation. This foreign force occupied our lands to steal our rich resources ... As in your own words, 'The occupation and overthrow of one small nation is one too many.'
Yours sincerely,
An American Indian.

> **From a letter** criticizing President George Bush Sr.'s justification for attacking Iraq in 1990. *The Guardian*, April 10, 2003

Zapatista commandante in a liberated area in the highlands of Chiapas, Mexico, 1998.
Photo by Bill Hackwell

I am an Indian. This is not my country, but it is my land.
> **Cherríe Moraga**, writer, educator. In *The Vinyl Project*, from the
> Freedom Archives, 2003

Proclamation to the Great White Father and all his People: we feel that this
so-called Alcatraz Island is more than suitable for an Indian Reservation,
as determined by the white man's own standard. By this we mean that
this place resembles most Indian reservations in that: It is isolated from
modern facilities…no fresh running water…inadequate sanitation…no oil
or mineral rights…no industry…unemployment…no healthcare facilities…
soil is rocky and unproductive…no educational facilities…population has
always been held as prisoners.
> **Indians of All Tribes**, a coalition that took over Alcatraz Island
> and its abandoned prison in San Francisco Bay for 19 months
> beginning in 1969. Statement to press.

That which we called independence was not independence for the Indian
but independence for the criollo, for the heirs of the conquerors who

continue to infamously abuse and cheat the oppressed Indian.

Antonio Díaz Soto y Gama, advisor to Mexican revolutionary
Emiliano Zapata, circa 1914

Where today are the Pequot? Where are the Narragansett, the Mohawks, the Pocanokets, and many other once powerful tribes of our race? They have vanished before the avarice and the oppression of the white men, as snow before a summer sun.

Tecumseh, Shawnee leader, warrior. From speech to members of
the Choctaw and Chickasaw nations, in an appeal for unity against
white settler invasion, September 1811

We don't want power, we don't want to be congressmen, or bankers...we want to be ourselves. We want to have our heritage, because we are the owners of this land and because we belong here. The white man says there is freedom and justice for all. We have "freedom and justice," and that is why we have been almost exterminated. We shall never forget this.

Statement by Grand Council of American Indians, 1927. *Blu
Magazine*, 1999

What hurts Indians most is that our costumes are considered beautiful, but it's as if the person wearing it didn't exist.

Rigoberta Menchú Tum, Guatemala Mayan human rights
activist. *I, Rigoberta Menchu*, 1983

Our religion and ceremonies have become fads, and a fashionable pastime among many whites seeking for something that they hope will give meaning to their empty lives... After macrobiotics, Zen, and channeling, the "poor Vanishing Indian" is once more the subject of "deep and meaningful conversation" in the high rises.

Mary Brave Bird, writer. *Ohitika Woman*, 1993

The joke used to be that in every Indian home, there is the mother, father, children, grandparents, and the anthropologist.

Elizabeth Cook-Lynn, writer. *From the River's Edge*, 1991

It has seemed so strange to me that the larger culture, with its own absence of spirit and lack of attachment for the land, respects these very things about Indian traditions, without adopting those respected ways themselves.

Linda Hogan, writer. "The Sacred Seed of the Medicine Tree,"
1990

We are not myths of the past, ruins in the jungle, or zoos. We are people and we want to be respected, not to be victims of intolerance and racism.

> **Rigoberta Menchú Tum**, Guatemalan Mayan human rights activist. Interview, 1992

Where are the warriors today? Who slew them? Where are our lands? Who owns them? What white man can say I ever stole his lands or a penny of his money? Yet they say I am a thief. What white woman, however lonely, was ever when a captive insulted by me? Yet they say I am a bad Indian.

> **Sitting Bull**, Teton Lakota leader, warrior. *Life of Sitting Bull and History of the Indian War of 1890-1891*, 1891

These white people think this country belongs to them—they don't realize that they are only in charge right now because there's more of them than there are of us. The whole country changed with only a handful of raggedly-ass pilgrims that came over here in the 1500s. And it can take a handful of raggedy-ass Indians to do the same, and I intend to be one of those raggedy-ass Indians.

> **Anna Mae Pictou Aquash**, Mi'kmaq activist with the American Indian Movement, circa 1975

We are the Original People. We are one of the fingers on the hand of humankind. Why is it we are underrepresented in our own lands, and without a seat—or many seats—in the United Nations? Why is it we're allowed to send our delegates only to prisons and to cemeteries?

> **Leonard Peltier**, writer, U.S. political prisoner. *Prison Writings*, 1999

Now your way of life is no longer working, and so you are interested in our way. But if we tell you our way, then it will be polluted, we will have no medicine, and we will be destroyed as well as you.

> **Buffalo Tiger**, Miccasukee leader, late 1800s. In *Gaia Atlas of First Peoples*, 1990

I am an Indian man. My only desire is to live like one.

> **Leonard Peltier**, writer, U.S. political prisoner. *Prison Writings,* 1999

In the case of my country, Guatemala, 65% of the inhabitants are indigenous. The constitution speaks of protection for the indigenous. Who authorized a minority to protect an immense majority? ... The human being is to be

respected and defended, not protected like a bird or a river.
> **Rigoberta Menchú Tum**, Guatemala Mayan human rights activist. Interview, 1992

Resistance means staying close
to the land. Herding sheep. Planting
corn. Singing prayers. The rest
is doing everything we can to protect
the right of the oldest cultures to seed the future
> **Ann Filemyr**, educator, poet, activist. From poem, "Seeding the Future, *for Ingrid Washinawatok*," 2000

My ancestors…would have showed better judgement if they had not let your's land.
> **Will Rogers**, writer, actor, comedian. *Will Rogers, a Biography*, 1962

The farther man's feet are removed from the earth, the less respect he has for living, growing things, and sooner or later it will mean less respect for mankind.
> **Apache proverb**, conveyed by Stalking Wolf, an Apache elder. In *The Search,* 1980

They sent the Indians to Oklahoma. They had a treaty that said, "You shall have this land as long as grass grows and water flows." It was not only a good rhyme but looked like a good treaty, and it was 'till they struck oil. Then the government took it again. They said the treaty only refers to "water and grass, it don't say anything about oil."
> **Will Rogers**, writer, actor, comedian. Essay, February 1928

This is the only treaty I will make!
> **Osceola**, Seminole diplomat, warrior. Stated as he stuck a dagger into a treaty document presented by U.S. officials, 1835. Attributed.

Members of the Native Youth Movement and two high ranking police officers during demonstration demanding freedom for Mumia Abu-Jamal, Philadelphia, PA 2001. Photo by Hans Bennet

They made us many promises, more than I can remember, but they never kept but one; they promised to take our land, and they took it.
> **Sign painted on Bureau of Indian Affairs building**, Washington, D.C., 1970. Quoting Red Cloud, 1822-1909.

Sometimes they have to kill us, because they cannot break our spirit.
> **John Trudell**, poet, activist, former chairman of the American Indian Movement. Attributed.

But there is beauty in all life. And the beauty is that this Guahibo tribe, as the U'wa, and as other tribes all over, are survivors. They are strategists and they are warriors. But in Colombia, being a "warrior" means positioning yourself very delicately. It means occupying this church with all your tribe, even the children. This single act of protest, signifies that their spirit has not been broken, and will not be broken.
> **Ana MarÃ-a Murillo**, U'wa Defense Project, Colombia, 7/23/03

Someone once said that you can measure the stature of a man by the size of his enemy... With that in mind, I say to our people, "We have been and still are at odds with the most dangerous, well-funded, strongest military and political organization in the history of the world." If you sometimes feel overwhelmed, as I sometimes am, then remember Geronimo, Crazy Horse, Sitting Bull, Osceola, Tecumseh and a host of others—you are in good company. I am proud to be a Native American because my people before me stood up against overwhelming odds so that I might have a chance to exist. They were successful, as I am living proof.

> **Leonard Peltier**, writer, U.S. political prisoner. Statement to supporters, December 2003

What does it really mean to listen to Native people? I see so many people who want to "borrow" their clothes, their art, their rituals, their secrets, their spirituality and absorb it into Western thinking. But this is not listening to and respecting their input. This is stealing. This is conning. In order to listen to Native people, it is necessary to see and respect their world view as viable and necessary. We need to heed the wisdom so that the human race and the planet will continue not only to grow and evolve but to survive.

> **Harvey Arden**, writer, activist. From message in solidarity with Leonard Peltier, June 2004

The history books are wrong when they talk about "the last Indian wars." They have never stopped!

> **Janet McCloud**, activist. Statement after a "Fish-in" confrontation in Washington State, late 1960s

Who will speak for the Native American or Mexican, who has been persecuted continually since the white man discovered this side of the planet? Laws shaped and formed to benefit those in control and not those who were here first. All my life I have feared the persecution of the white man in this country, and now I sit here feeling the full force of racism and arrogance of society.

> **Fernando Caro**, prisoner on California's death row as of 2000. Interview, *Blu Magazine*, 1999

But, in America, when we speak of liberation, what can it mean? We must ask ourselves, in America, who are the people of the land? And the answer is—and can only be—the first Americans, the Native Americans, the American Indian. In the United States of America, when you speak of liberation, or when you speak of freeing the land, you are automatically speaking of the American Indians, whether you realize it or not.

> **Kwame Toure**, formerly Stokely Carmichael, civil rights and Black power activist. Speech, Yellow Thunder demonstrations, South Dakota, 1982

Red Power means we want power over our own lives… We simply want the power, the political and economic power, to run our own lives in our own way.

Vine Deloria, educator, writer. *The New Indians*, 1968

RED POWER is the spirit to resist, RED POWER is pride in what we are, RED POWER is love for our people, RED POWER is our coming together to fight for liberation, RED POWER is now!!!!!!!

From the Red Power e-mail server, 2003

Chapter 6

"The Purse-Seine"

Civilization and Progress

Textbook authors seem not to have encountered the trick question, "Which came first, civilization or the wilderness?" The answer is civilization, for only the "civilized" mind could define the world of Native farmers, fishers, and gatherers and hunters, coexisting with forests, crops, and animals, as a "wilderness."

> **James W. Loewen**, historian. *Lies My Teacher Told Me*, 1995

Civilization is not mere advance in technology and in the material aspects of life. We should remember it is an abstract noun and indicates a state of living and not things.

> **Chakravarti Rajagopalachari**, Indian political leader, 1878-1972. In *Woman, Native, Other*, 1989

Only to the white man was nature a "wilderness" and only to him was the land "infested" with "wild" animals and "savage" people. To us it was tame. Earth was bountiful and we were surrounded with the blessings of the Great Mystery. Not until the hairy man from the East came and with brutal frenzy heaped injustices upon us and the families that we loved was it "wild" for us. When the very animals of the forest began fleeing from his approach, then it was that for us the "Wild West" began.

> **Luther Standing Bear**, Lakota leader, writer. *Land of the Spotted Eagle*, 1933

You gotta say this for the white race—its self-confidence knows no bounds. Who else could go to a small island in the South Pacific where there's no poverty, no crime, no unemployment, no war and no worry, and call it a "primitive society?"

> **Dick Gregory**, activist, nutritionist, comedian. *From the Back of the Bus*, 1962

The West didn't get wild until the white people got there. There's no such word as *wild* in the Indian languages. The closest we can get to it is the word *free*. We were free people.

> **Oren Lyons**, educator, Chief of the Turtle Clan of the Onondaga Nation. *Esquire*, February 1994

Civilized men arrived in the Pacific, armed with alcohol, syphilis, trousers, and the Bible.

Havelock Ellis, English writer. *The Dance of Life*, 1923

Growth for the sake of growth is the ideology of the cancer cell. Cancer has no purpose but growth; but it does have another result—the death of the host.

Edward Abbey, writer. *One life at a Time, Please*, 1988

You can't say civilization isn't advancing: in every war they kill you in a new way.

Will Rogers, writer, actor, comedian. Attributed.

Perhaps, if this was a Nazi army, history may have instructed us to understand—the Nazis were often brutal in their repression. If this were a Roman army, history may have taught us the lessons from the ashes of Carthage. But this is the 21st Century and—long live racism—nothing has been learned. There is no civilization.

Firas Al-Atraqchi, Canadian writer. "Racism At Heart of POW Abuse," referring to photos of Iraqi prisoners being abused by U.S. soldiers in Iraq, 5/1/2004

You speak finally of 'duty,' 'humanity' and 'civilization!' What is this duty?... It is markets, competition, interests, privileges. Trade and finance are things which express your 'humanity.' Taxes, forced labour, excessive exploitation, that is the summing up of your civilization!

Ho Chi Minh, Vietnamese political leader, poet. Essay, "Open Letter to M. Leon Archimbaud," 1923

"Civilization" has been thrust upon me since the days of the reservations, and it has not added one whit to my sense of justice, to my reverence for the rights of life, to my love for truth, honesty, and generosity, or to my faith in Wakan Tanka, God of the Lakotas.

Luther Standing Bear, Lakota leader, writer, 1868-1939

The crash of glass and children's screams.
We see the mushroom clouds again.
Now you can appreciate the genius of our civilization.

David Roberts, English poet. From poem "A Message from Tony Blair to the People of Iraq," 2003

"Coffin-nails" are of the white man's inception, along with his multitudinous diseased adjuncts of civilization: whiskey, beer, wine and opium with attending crimes and ills. And to cap the irony of it all, he brings the "glad tidings" of an endlessly burning hell where we are roasted for emulating his "superior" example.
> **Mourning Dove**, Cogewea writer, 1927

A civilization that proves incapable of solving the problems it creates is a decadent civilization.
A civilization that chooses to close its eyes to its most crucial problems is a stricken civilization.
A civilization that uses its principles for trickery and deceit is a dying civilization.
> **Aimé Césaire**, Martiniquen poet, political leader. *Discourse on Colonialism*, 1955

They tell us they want to civilize us. They lie. They want to kill us.
> **Crazy Horse**, Lakota leader, warrior, 1876

We are now in the terminal phase of this culture which has come to dominate the whole world. As it reaches its end point, its contradictions become more extreme, as in the ever-widening gulf of wealth between rich and poor, and in the increasingly obvious insanity of the fixation on unlimited economic growth on a finite planet.
> **Alan Watson Featherstone**. Essay, "Planetary Healing," 2003

There must be something in their [American Indian's] social bond, something singularly captivating, and far superior to anything to be boasted among us; for thousands of Europeans are [now] Indians, and we have no examples of even one of those Aborigines having from choice become Europeans.
> **Michel-Guillaume-Jean de Crèvecoeur**, agriculturist. *Letters From an American Farmer,* 1782

Long before I heard of Christ or saw a white man...I knew God. I perceived what goodness is. I saw and loved what is really beautiful. Civilization has not taught me anything better!
> **Ohiyesa, a.k.a. Charles Eastman**, Lakota physician, writer, 1858-1939. Attributed.

Much has been said of...what you term "civilization" among the Indians... You say, "Why do not the Indians till the ground and live as we do?" May

we not ask, "Why do not the white people hunt and live as we do?
    Old Tassel, Cherokee leader, 1780's

The Northern Cheyenne count as "progress" their ability to maintain environmental quality, rather than the development of their coal resources.
    LaDonna Harris. In *The Native American Reader*, 1990

[Man's] own past is full of clear and somber warnings—vanished civilizations buried, like dead flies in lacquer, beneath their own dust and mud.
    Paul Sears. *Deserts on the March*, 1947

Chapter 7

"The Matrix"

Technology, Artificialism

Technology can relieve the symptoms of a problem without affecting the underlying causes. Faith in technology as the ultimate solution to all problems can thus divert our attention from the most fundamental problem—the problem of growth in a finite system—and prevent us from taking effective action to solve it.

> **Donella H. Meadows**, et al. *The Limits to Growth*, 1972

The aboriginal peoples of Australia illustrate the conflict between technology and the natural world succinctly, by asking, 'What will you do when the clever men destroy your water?' That, in truth, is what the world is coming to.

> **Winona LaDuke**, activist, writer. *A Gathering of the Spirit*, 1984

The society that performs miracles with machinery has the capacity to make some miracles for men—if it values men as highly as it values machines.

> **Martin Luther King, Jr.**, civil rights leader. In *Great Labor Quotations,* 2000

The danger of the past was that men became slaves. The danger of the future is that men may become robots.

> **Erich Fromm**, German-American psychologist, socialist. *The Sane Society*, 1955

It's not that the technology should go away. It will not go away from its own voluntary will; we won't let it. I know we won't. It is not being used as a healing thing. It is a destructive thing the way that it is now. It must be used to heal; we make that choice.

> **John Trudell**, poet, activist, former chairman of the American Indian Movement. Interview, *Overthrow*, December 1983

We can use the internet for anything. It is man that put what is in the net, not the net telling us what to do.

> **Mutabaruka**, Jamaican poet, activist. Internet forum, 2003

It's easier, and thus "more fun," to use oil for almost everything. Raking leaves, for instance. By 1987 Americans alone had paid more than a hundred million dollars to buy electric leaf blowers—machines that blow leaves

around a yard, thereby replacing the rake.
> **Bill McKibben**, writer. *The End of Nature*, 1989

Conservative people are undoubtedly right in their distrust and hatred of science, for the scientific spirit is the very spirit of innovation and adventure—the most reckless kind of adventure into the unknown. And such is it's aggressive strength that its revolutionary activity can neither be restrained nor restricted within its own field.
> **Jean-Paul Sartre**, French writer. *Existentialism*, 1947

Our cities are a wilderness of spinning wheels instead of palaces; yet the people have not clothes. We have blackened every leaf of English greenwood with ashes, and the people die of cold; our harbors are a forest of merchant ships, and the people die of hunger.
> **John Ruskin**, English artist, writer. *The Crown of Wild Olive*, 1866

It seems as if we are now living inside of a machine; days and events move with a hard reasoning of their own. We live amid swarms of people, yet there is a vast distance between people, a distance that words cannot bridge. No longer do our lives depend upon the soil, the sun, the rain, or the wind; we live by the grace of jobs and the brutal logic of jobs.
> **Richard Wright**, writer. *12 Million Black Voices*, 1941

The white man's advanced technological capacity has occurred as a result of his lack of regard for the spiritual path and for the way of all living things. The white man's desire for material possessions and power has blinded him to the pain he has caused Mother Earth by his quest for what he calls natural resources.
> **Thomas Banyacya**, Hopi elder. In *Gaia Atlas of First Peoples*, 1990

Technology feeds on itself. Technology makes more technology possible.
> **Alvin Toffler**, technology analyst. *Future Shock*, 1970

The unleashed power of the atom has changed everything save our modes of thinking, and we thus drift toward unparalleled catastrophes.
> **Albert Einstein**, physicist. *New York Times Magazine*, August 1964

Biotechnology is the ultimate in corporate vertical integration, where control begins with the gene and ends at the supermarket.

> **Richard Nilsen**. Speech, Third World Biotechnology Conference, 1987

Do you not see the prodigious mechanization, the mechanization of man; the gigantic rape of everything intimate, undamaged, undefiled that, despoiled as we are, our human spirit has still managed to preserve.

> **Aimé Césaire**, Martiniquen poet, political leader. *Discourse on Colonialism*, 1955

Chapter 8

"A Lexus or Justice"

Consumer Culture, Materialism, Advertising, Waste

A commercial world, a corporate world, is not the natural state of things, even though corporations and the media would have us believe that. If it was the natural state, we wouldn't need to be constantly bombarded with advertisements.

> **Nell Geizer**. In *Global Uprising,* 2001

The advertising media in this country continuously informs the American male of his need for indispensable signs of his virility.

> **Frances Beal**, writer, activist. In *Sisterhood is Powerful,* 1970

After all, in this society, if something isn't for sale, it might as well not exist—and it's almost impossible to think of anything to do with something of value besides market it.

> **CrimethInc. Worker's Collective**. *Days of War, Nights of Love,* 2000

Advertising enjoins everyone to consume, while the economy prohibits the vast majority of humanity from doing so. The command that everybody do what so many cannot becomes an invitation to crime.

> **Eduardo Galeano**, Uruguayan historian, educator. *Upside Down,* 1998

We used to be hunter-gatherers, now we're shopper-borrowers.

> **Robin Williams**, actor. *ABC TV,* 1990

The junk merchant doesn't sell his product to the consumer, he sells the consumer to the product. He does not improve and simplify his merchandise. He degrades and simplifies the client.

> **William Burroughs**, writer, poet. *Naked Lunch,* 1959

To us, as to other spiritually-minded people in every age and race, the love of possessions is a snare, and the burdens of a complex society a source of needless peril and temptation.

> **Ohiyesa, a.k.a. Charles Eastman**, Lakota physician, writer, 1858-1939

It is not the destiny of Black America to repeat white America's mistakes. But we will, if we mistake the trappings of success in a sick society for the signs of a meaningful life.

Audre Lorde, educator, activist, poet. In *Black Women Writers at Work*, 1983

All that 'bling bling' shit comes from Black people not having nothing. We ain't never had shit. People say these rappers aren't talking about nothing, but that comes from the generation and the class before that talked about pulling yourself up by your bootstraps. This whole, 'I got to get my hair done, my nails and get my suit just to fit in with the crackers...' If we want to have diamonds or gold, I'm not promoting that, 'cause I don't know what we're gonna do with it but wear it. Let's have things that are beneficial to us, like *land*.

Stic.man, of hip hop group Dead Prez. Interview, *BET.com,* circa 2002

Whoever doesn't have, isn't. He who has no car or doesn't wear designer shoes or imported perfume is only pretending to exist. Importer economy, imposter culture: we are all obliged to take the consumer's cruise across the swirling waters of the market.

Eduardo Galeano, Uruguayan historian, educator. *Upside Down*, 1998

With the breakdown of community at all levels, human beings have become more like what the traditional model of *Homo Economicus* described. Shopping has become the great national pastime. The one place one can be assured of a welcome is in a store. Status attaches to finding unusual goods and unusual prices.

Herman E. Daly and John B. Cobb, Jr. *For the Common Good,* 1989

Don't gain the world and lose your soul
wisdom is better than silver and gold

Bob Marley, Jamaican reggae singer. From song "Zion Train," 1980

Some of our landfills are now richer in resources than some of our mines.

Denis Hayes, environmental activist. Speech, Museum of Natural History, 1989

With disposable diapers, the first lesson a child learns is that when you make a mess, you throw it into the garbage and it goes away. That message

is fundamentally wrong.
> **Patricia Greenstreet**, writer. *New York Times Magazine*, September 1990

Live simply so that others may simply live.
> **Bumper sticker**

Everybody used to believe in the Trash Fairy—put your trash on the curb and it's gone.
> **Natalie Roy**, writer. *Washington Post,* 2/23/1991

We are overwhelmed by the amount of shit society offers us. We look around us and see our lives displayed in neon lighting. In one city block there is a McDonalds, a Chevron, a couple of banks, and a Taco Bell. Two massive car dealerships glow in the short distance, the new SUV's proudly displayed in the front. We can even see the old Wal-Mart which apparently wasn't large enough or new enough to satiate a growing population of consumers. Everything must be new, and it must be big. Even the highway passing through town isn't big enough. And there is nothing unique about this specific location. This is life in North America. This is becoming everywhere.
> **Earth Liberation Front** saboteurs of a Wal-Mart construction site. From anonymous communiqué, October 2003

An Innu hunter's prestige comes not from the wealth he accumulates but from what he gives away. When a hunter kills caribou or other game he shares with everyone else in the camp.
> **Daniel Ashini**, Innu nation Spokesman. In *The Gaia Atlas of First Peoples*, 1990

Would you rather have a Lexus or justice
a dream or some substance
a beamer, a necklace—or freedom
> **Dead Prez**, hip hop group. From song "Hip Hop," 2000

Chapter 9

"Gaia"

The Earth, the Environment, Ecology, Natural Resources

Here's a story that you may not understand,
But the parking lots will crack and bloom again.
>   **Dana Lyons**, singer. From song "Willy Says," circa 2000

You yourself don't know that the forest controls the river flow? That without the forest we will not have river flow? If you don't, then you see the forest being destroyed, and you do nothing. You see the forest being privatized, and you do nothing. You see a school that does not have a windbreak and you do nothing.
>   **Wangari Maathai**, Kenyan environmental/political activist, educator. *Guerrilla News Network*, October 2004

The earth is the first condition of our existence. To make it an object of trade was the last step towards making human beings an object of trade. To buy and sell land is an immorality surpassed only by the immorality of selling oneself into slavery.
>   **Friedrich Engels**, German political theorist. *Outlines of a Critique of Political Economy*, 1844

Biocentrism, is the belief that nature does not exist to serve humans. Rather, humans are part of nature, one species among many... Biocentrism is a law of nature, that exists independently of whether humans recognize it or not.
>   **Judi Bari**, environmental activist. Speech, June, 1996

The insufferable arrogance of human beings to think that Nature was made solely for their benefit, as if it was conceivable that the sun had been set afire merely to ripen men's apples and head their cabbages.
>   **Savinien de Cyrano de Bergerac**, French playwright, 1656

The logic that led to slavery and segregation in the Americas, colonization and Apartheid in Africa, and the rule of white supremacy throughout the world is the same one that leads to the exploitation of animals and the ravaging of nature... People who fight against white racism but fail to connect it to the degradation of the earth are anti-ecological—whether they know it or not. People who struggle against environmental degradation but do not incorporate in it a disciplined and sustained fight against white supremacy are racists—whether they acknowledge it or not. The fight for justice cannot be segregated but must be integrated with the fight for life in all its forms.

> **James H. Cone**, educator, writer. Essay, "Whose Earth is It Anyway?" 2000

You cannot seriously address the destruction of wilderness without addressing the society that is destroying it. It's about time for the ecology movement to stop considering itself as separate from the social justice movement. The same power that manifests itself as resource extraction in the countryside manifests itself as racism, classism, and human exploitation in the city.

> **Judi Bari**, environmental activist. Speech, June 1996

Every time we have objected to the use of the land as a commodity, we have been told that progress is necessary to American life. Now the laugh is ours.

> **Vine Deloria**, educator, writer. *We Talk, You Listen,* 1970

A day will come in your lifetime when the earth, your mother, will beg you, with tears running, to save her. Ho, if you fail to help her, you [Lakota] and all people will die like dogs. Remember this.

> **Hollow Horn**, Lakota medicine man. Prophecy made upon completing a Sun Dance ceremony, 1929

We are like rats fighting the elephants. People who are struggling for the land are being killed for it, but the word is more important than violence. Europe needs to know what is the tremendous effect of Climate Change in Papua New Guinea… We the people are going to make a big hole for the elephant to fall in.

> **Stanis Kaka**, Papua New Guinean attendee of an international climate change conference, Barcelona, Spain, 2002

I understand that every living thing comes from one mother, and that is our Mother Earth. It has been said by the old people that only the white man rapes his mother.

> **Russell Means**, activist, actor, former leader in the American Indian Movement. Testimony in U.S. District Court, Lincoln, Nebraska, 1974

You ask me to plow the ground. Shall I take a knife and tear my mother's bosom? Then when I die she will not take me to her bosom to rest. You ask me to dig for stones! Shall I dig under her skin for her bones? Then when I die I cannot enter her body to be born again.

You ask me to cut grass and make hay and sell it, and be rich like the white man, but how dare I cut my mother's hair?

Smohalla, Wanapum medicine man. Speech, late 1800s. Attributed.

In America today you can murder land for private profit. You can leave the corpse for all to see, and nobody calls the cops.

Paul Brooks, writer. *The Pursuit of Wilderness*, 1971

You can be charged with manslaughter for running a child over with your car, but not for polluting the water/air/soil and killing twelve children and their parents by giving them leukemia.

Kristin Reid, activist, 1/16/2004

If you pave over nature, drive death machines called cars, and contribute to the greenhouse effect in this society you are considered responsible, normal, good. If you ride the bus, hitchhike, walk on the street in a poor neighborhood, or do not own a car, you are considered suspicious, if not an outright bum.

William Upski Wimsatt, writer, activist. *No More Prisons*, 1999

We are dying because of oil and because of gas. Our people are being shot in the street, communities are being wiped out, people have been arrested, jailed, tried in kangaroo courts methods and hanged, and we have a responsibility to ask for justice and we are doing so now.

Oronto Douglas, Nigerian environmental activist. Interview, *CorpWatch*, May 2001

Imagine each mountain to be a World Trade Centre built by nature over millennia. Think of how many tragedies bigger than what the world experienced on Sept 11th are taking place to provide raw material for insatiable industry and markets.

Vandana Shiva, Indian scientist, activist. Essay, "Solidarity Against All Forms of Terrorism," 2001

For the World Bank and the WTO, our forests are a marketable commodity. But for us, the forests are a home, our source of livelihood, the dwelling of our gods, the burial ground of our ancestors, the inspiration of our culture. We do not need you to save our forests. We will not let you sell our forests. So go back from our forests and our country.

From letter by Indian Adivasi activists, delivered as they occupied World Bank offices in New Delhi and plastered its walls with cow dung, November 1999. In *We Are Everywhere*, 2003

Sell a country! Why not sell the air, the great sea, as well as the earth? Didn't the Great Spirit make them all for the use of his children?
Tecumseh, Shawnee leader, warrior 1768-1813. Attributed.

Man makes war on the peaceful forests, and each day the shadows on the mountains retreat. Nothing will remain for us of the mystic refuges where we could garner thought and love.
Victor de Laprade, French poet, 1844. Attributed.

Nothing the Great Mystery placed in the land of the Indian pleased the white man, and nothing escaped his transforming hand. Wherever forests have not been mowed down, wherever the animal is recessed in their quiet protection, wherever the earth is not bereft of four-footed life—that to him is an "unbroken wilderness."
Chief Joseph, Nez Perce leader, 1840-1904

The human mind is a product of the Pleistocene age, shaped by wilderness that has all but disappeared. If we complete the destruction of nature, we will have succeeded in cutting ourselves off from the source of sanity itself.
David Orr. *Adbusters,* September/October 2002

You cannot affirm the power plant and condemn the smokestack, or affirm the smoke and condemn the cough.
Wendell Berry, writer, farmer. *The Gift of Good Land*, 1981

The air [in Manchester, England] is so polluted that you wake up in the morning listening to the birds cough.
Anonymous French letter writer. *Le Monde*, August 1982

I have become an environmentalist, because it is over the environment that the last of the Indian Wars will be fought.
Mary Brave Bird, writer. *Ohitika Woman*, 1993

How can the spirit of the earth like the White man? Everywhere the White man has touched, it is sore.
Anonymous Wintu man. In *Freedom and Culture*, 1959

I cannot accept money for the Black Hills because land is sacred to me…[the whites] are trying to change our value system. To be a traditional person is to believe in our own culture, is to believe in yourself as a Lakota person; then you cannot sell the land.

Severt Young Bear. In *Black Hills White Justice*, 1991

For a long time historically, for example, black people in the south were not even allowed to visit state parks, because of Jim Crow and segregation. And somehow we were blamed for not having appreciation for state parks. I mean, it wasn't our faults, we couldn't go to them! So we're finding as the more urban folks get to visit parks and wilderness areas and are able to appreciate that these are national treasures and not just treasures for people that have money to visit them.

Robert Bullard, environmental justice activist. Interview, *Earth First! Journal*, July 1999

Environmental sustainability takes place when people have a stake and a share in the rewards of the conserved resource. If people have the ability to drink water from a well, and look after that well, and will suffer the consequences of contamination, they will not contaminate that well. People who pollute a well or a river are the ones who don't have to drink from it.

Vandana Shiva, Indian scientist, activist. Interview, *In Motion Magazine*, 3/28/2004

There are two separate languages now—the language of economics and the language of ecology, and they do not converge. The language of economics is attractive, and remains so, because it is politically appealing. It offers promises. It is precise, authoritative, aesthetically pleasing. Policy-makers apply the models, and if they don't work there is a tendency to conclude that it is reality that is playing tricks. The assumption is not that the models are wrong but that they must be applied with greater rigour.

Manfred Max-Neef, Chilean economist, educator. Attributed.

Coal versus nuclear is not a Hobson's choice. It's a false choice. We must not solve global warming by creating a nuclear garrison state. We must not approach problems with such single-minded tunnel vision.

Denis Hayes. Speech, Museum of Natural History, 1989

Let me ask you this—why are there only 8 inches of top-soil left in America, when there once were some 18 inches at the time of the Declaration of Independence in 1776? Where goes our sacred earth?

Hobart Keith, Lakota man. In *Gaia Atlas of First Peoples*, 1990

Let the people walk. Or ride horses, bicycles, mules, wild pigs—anything—but keep the automobiles and the motorcycles and all their motorized relatives out. We have agreed not to drive our automobiles into cathedrals, concert halls, art museums, legislative assemblies, private bedrooms and other sanctums of our culture; we should treat our national parks with the same deference, for they, too, are holy places.

> **Edward Abbey**, writer. *Desert Solitaire*, 1971

Suburbia is where the developer bulldozes out the trees, then names the streets after them.

> **Bill Vaughn**. *The Portable Curmudgeon*, 1987

If people destroy something replaceable made by mankind, they are called vandals; If they destroy something irreplaceable made by God, they are called developers.

> **Joseph Wood Krutch**, naturalist, writer. *Mother Earth News,*
> 1990

Grab this land! Take it, hold it, my brothers, make it, my brothers, shake it, squeeze it, turn it, twist it, beat it, kick it, kiss it, whip it, stomp it, dig it, plow it, seed it, reap it, rent it, buy it, sell it, own it, build it, multiply it, and pass it on—can you hear me? Pass it on!

> **Toni Morrison**, writer, educator. *Song of Solomon*, 1977

We will look upon the earth and her sister planets as being *with* us, not *for* us. One does not rape a sister.

> **Mary Daly**, theologian, educator. *Beyond God the Father*, 1973

According to tribal legend these hills were a reclining female figure from whose breasts flowed life-giving forces and to them the [Teton] went as a child to its mother's arms.

> **Edward Lazarus**, referring to the Black Hills of South Dakota and
> the Teton American Indian Nation. *Black Hills White Justice*, 1991

Capitalism, first of all, is based on the principle of private property—of certain humans owning the earth for the purpose of exploiting it for profit. At an earlier stage, capitalists even believed they could own other humans. But just as slavery has been discredited in the mores of today's dominant world view, so do the principles of biocentrism discredit the concept that humans can own the earth.

> **Judi Bari**, environmental activist. Speech, June, 1996

I say, work at whatever you're passionate about; then we don't have to attack "environmentalists" who only care about nature and we don't have to attack "social activists" for only caring about people.

> **Julia Butterfly Hill**, environmental activist. Interview, *Satya* magazine, May 2002

No white men's roads through black men's homes!

> **Sammie A. Abbott**, activist. Slogan in fight against a proposed highway through a Washington, DC neighborhood, 1965

At first, the people talking about ecology were only defending the fishes, the animals, the forest, and the river. They didn't realize that human beings were in the forest—and that these humans were the real ecologists, because they couldn't live without the forest and the forest couldn't be saved without them.

> **Osmarino Amancio Rodrigues**, Brazilian environmental and union activist. In *The Burning Season,* 1990

Environmental Racism and the prison-industrial complex are poisoned fruit with the same toxic root: a philosophy of violence against our society's disposable people.

> **Simon Finger**. Essay *"Prisons as Environmental Racism,"* 2001

The environmental movement isn't only about middle class white people worrying about the preservation of trees and animals and pretty flowers. It's also about people of color preserving the integrity of their communities and the land where they work.

> **Richard Moore**, activist. *Buzzworm,* 1990

The oceans are the planet's last great living wilderness, man's only remaining frontier on earth, and perhaps his last chance to prove himself a rational species.

> **John L. Cullney**. *Wilderness Conservation*, 1990

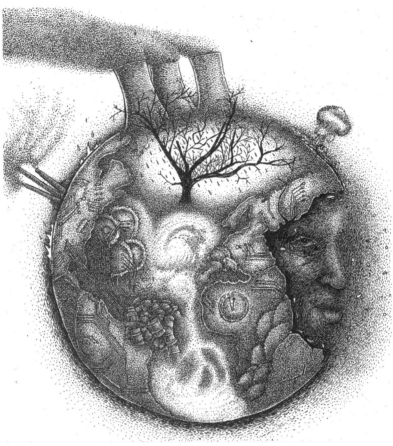

"Earth in Peril" by Mac McGill

Drift-net fishing is strip-mining the seas.
Bumper sticker

For us, it's a dam of tears. We don't have water to drink, nor rice to eat. And we can't eat tear drops.
Paw Lert, Thai activist working against the Bhumipol Dam which displaced his village. In *We Are Everywhere*, 2003

There is good water here, but you must pay for it. If you can see the way we live, you can see that we cannot pay.
Nolulama Makhiwa, resident of Shakashead, South Africa. *New York Times*, 5/29/2003

Water flows uphill towards money.
Proverb from the American West

The earth we abuse and the living things we kill will, in the end, take their revenge; for in exploiting their presence we are diminishing our future.
Marya Mannes. *More in Anger,* 1958

We've tried to play Noah. We've found our Ark is too small. Now, we're playing God, deciding which species may live.
Norman Myers, English scientist. "Can the Elephant Be Saved?" *WBGH-TV*, 1990

Let us open our eyes to the sacredness of Mother Earth, or our eyes will be opened for us.
Grandfather David Monongye, activist, letter to the United Nations General Assembly, circa 1982

Earth gives life and seeks the man who walks gently upon it.
Hopi proverb

The earth is the mother of all people, and all people should have equal rights upon it.
Chief Joseph, Nez Perce leader, 1840-1904

You forget that the fruits belong to all and that the land belongs to no one.
Jean-Jacques Rousseau, French philosopher. Attributed.

Oh, I don't object, of course, to cutting wood from necessity, but why destroy the forests? The woods of Russia are trembling under the blows of the axe. Millions of trees have perished. The homes of the wild animals and birds have been desolated; the rivers are shrinking, and many beautiful landscapes are gone forever. And why?
Anton Chekhov, Russian playwright. *Uncle Vanya,* 1897

In early life, I was deeply hurt as I witnessed the grand old forests of Michigan, under whose shades my forefathers lived and died, falling before the cyclone of civilization as before a prairie fire.
Simon Pokagon, Potawatomi writer, 1830-1899

It took a couple of million years for this land to evolve to the state it is in today, and it took 48 hours to destroy it. One of the things that bothers me the most is that we get up in arms over destruction of the rain forest, when the natural habitats in North America have been all but eliminated.

> **Buzz Hoagland**, on the plowing of the largest remaining stretch of virgin prairie in northeast Kansas. *New York Times*, November 1990

Too much emphasis is put on the difficulty of survival. It's as easy as living in your own home. Nature provides everything. All you have to do is look and take it. Nature takes very good care of you. All you have to do is respect her, but she'll eat you alive if you don't.

> **Tom Brown**, wilderness educator. *The Search*, 1980

There are more humans than all of the rabbits on earth. There are more of us than all the wildebeests, than all the rats, than all the mice. We are the most numerous mammal on the planet. But because we're not like rabbits or rats or mice we have technology, we have a consumptive appetite, we have a global economy.

> **David Suzuki**, Canadian environmentalist. Interview, *PBS*, 8/29/2003

Chapter 10

"The Creatures of the Earth"

Animals and Animal Liberation

There is not one world for man and one for animals, they are part of the same one and lead parallel lives.

> **Rigoberta Menchú Tum**, Guatemala Mayan human rights activist. *I, Rigoberta Menchu, 1983*

As far back as I can remember, the origin of my revolt against the powerful was my horror at the tortures inflicted on animals. I used to wish animals could get revenge, that the dog could bite the man who was mercilessly beating him, that the horse bleeding under the whip could throw off the man tormenting him.

> **Louise Michel**, French anarchist rebel leader in the 1871 Paris Commune. *Mémoires*, 1886

It can no longer be maintained by anyone but a religious fanatic that man is the special darling of the whole universe, or that other animals were created to provide us with food, or that we have divine authority over them, and divine permission to kill them.

> **Peter Singer**, Australian educator. *Animal Liberation*, 1975

We come here...speaking the truth on behalf of people, of the world, of the four-footed, of the winged, of the fish that swim. Someone must speak for them. I do not see a delegation for the four-footed. I see no seat for the eagles.

> **Oren Lyons**, educator, Chief of the Turtle Clan of the Onondaga Nation. Speech, United Nations, Geneva, Switzerland, 1977

Zoos are becoming facsimiles—or perhaps caricatures—of how animals once were in their natural habitat. If the right policies toward nature were pursued, we would need no zoos at all.

> **Michael Fox**, writer. *Sierra*, November/December 1990

In the false country of the zoo
Grief is well represented there.

> **Jean Garrigue**, poet. From poem, "False Country of the Zoo," 1947

I don't eat fish, because I can't afford to take a life to save 1 life, and a fish love 'im life just like I love mine.

> **Prof I, Rastafarian man**, Jamaica. In *The Red X Tapes, 1992*

The animals had rights—the right of man's protection, the right to live, the right to multiply, the right to freedom, and the right to man's indebtedness—and in recognition of these rights the Lakota never enslaved an animal, and spared all life that was not needed for food and clothing.

Luther Standing Bear, Lakota leader, writer, 1868-1939

"Mass Production" by Nicole Schulman.

The tragedy of the blue whale is in the reflection of an even greater one, that of man himself. What is the nature of a species that knowingly and without good reason exterminates another?

George Small. *The Blue Whale*, 1971

We have enslaved the rest of the animal creation, and have treated our distant cousins in fur and feathers so badly that beyond a doubt, if they were able to formulate a religion, they would depict the Devil in human form.

William Ralph Inge, English writer. *Outspoken Essays*, 1922

DEDICATED
TO THE LAST WISCONSIN
PASSENGER PIGEON
SHOT AT BABCOCK, SEPT. 1899
THIS SPECIES BECAME EXTINCT
THROUGH THE AVARICE AND

THOUGHTLESSNESS OF MAN
From monument erected by the Wisconsin Society for Ornithology, 1947

Support the right to arm bears.
Bumper Sticker

The Lakota could despise no creature, for all were of one blood, made by the same hand, and filled with the essence of the Great Mystery.
Chief Joseph, Nez Perce leader, 1840-1904

The most cruel environmental threat comes from the environmental movement itself as we see the animal rights laws systematically destroy our way of life and violate our right as aboriginal peoples to our traditions and values.
Rhoda Inuksu, Inuk spokeswoman. Testimony at World Commission on Environment and Development, May 1986

When the Buffalo went away the hearts of my people fell to the ground, and they could not lift them up again.
Plenty Coups, Crow leader, 1849-1932

Chapter 11

"Still I Rise"

Resistance, Struggle, Rebellion

Rise like Lions after slumber
In unvanquishable number!
Shake your chains to earth like dew
Which in sleep had fallen on you -
Ye are many; they are few!

> **Percy Bysshe Shelley**, English writer, political activist, poet.
> From poem "The Mask of Anarchy," 1819

It seems to me that if it were not for resistance to degrading conditions, the tendency of our whole civilization would be downward; after a while we would reach the point where there would be no resistance, and slavery would come.

> **Eugene Debs**, activist, labor organizer, socialist. From court statement following arrest during the Pullman Strike, 1894

There will always be small-minded, narrow-minded, power-driven, power-hungry people who will try to set limits, who will try to give you constraints. And the human spirit to refuse such constraints. The willingness to take risks and to vindicate your humanity.

> **Hanan Mikhail-Ashrawi**, Palestinian human rights activist, educator. Interview, Conversations With History series, UC Berkeley, April 2000

Contrary to popular belief, conventional wisdom would have one believe that it is insane to resist this, the mightiest of empires... But what history really shows is that today's empire is tomorrow's ashes, that nothing lasts forever, and that to not resist is to acquiesce to your own oppression. The greatest form of sanity that anyone can exercise is to resist that force that is trying to repress, oppress, and fight down the human spirit.

> **Mumia Abu-Jamal**, journalist, U.S. political prisoner

I hate having to struggle. I honestly do because I wish I had been born into a world where it was unnecessary. This context of struggle and being a warrior and being a struggler has been forced on me by oppression. Otherwise, I would be a sculptor, or a gardener, a carpenter. I would be free to be so much more.

> **Assata Shakur**, former Black Panther, in exile in Cuba. Interview,

Blu Magazine, 2000

It isn't the rebels that cause the troubles of the world—it's the troubles that cause the rebels.

Carl Oglesby, activist with Students for a Democratic Society. Attributed.

The highest expression of dignity can be summed up in a single word: 'No.'

Dai Qing, Chinese activist working to stop the Three Gorges Dam, Hubei province, China. In *We Are Everywhere*, 2003

We were born into an unjust system; we are not prepared to grow old in it.

Bernadette Devlin, Irish civil rights leader. *The Price of My Soul*, 1969

Down here we hear relaxed, matter-of-fact conversations centering around how best to kill all the nation's niggers and in what order. It's not the fact that they consider killing me that upsets. They've been "killing all the niggers" from nearly half a millennium now, but I am still alive. I might be the most resilient dead man in the universe. The upsetting thing is that they never take into consideration the fact that I am going to resist.

George Jackson, writer, Black Panther member, killed by prison guards in 1971. *Soledad Brother*, 1970

The only way to live on this planet, with any human dignity, at this time, is to struggle.

Assata Shakur, former Black Panther, in exile in Cuba. Interview, *Blu Magazine*, 2000

The right to rebellion, to defy those who oppress us with various alibis (always the gods of Power and Money with different masks), is universal.

Subcomandante Marcos, Mexican Zapatista revolutionary, writer. Statement, Mexico, April 2003

Pray for the dead and fight like hell for the living.

Mother Jones, union organizer, activist. Attributed.

Beneath the yoke of barbarism one must not keep silence; one must fight. Whoever is silent at such a time is a traitor to humanity.

Stefan Zweig, Austrian writer. Statement after his books were burned by Nazi students, 1933

We must interrupt America's corrupt plan
And become abrupt and erupt here and there to take back our land
Unify with others who have also been denied their existence
To discover the magnitude of our collective resistance
>**Welfare Poets**. From poem, "In the Shadow of Death," circa 1999

The buffets and blows of this have and have-not society have engendered in me a flame that will live, will live to grow, until it either destroys my tormentor or myself.
>**George Jackson**, writer, Black Panther member, killed by prison guards in 1971. Letter to father from prison, 1965

If there is no struggle there is no progress. Those who profess to favor freedom and yet deprecate agitation, are men who want crops without plowing up the ground, they want rain without thunder and lightning. They want the ocean without the awful roar of its many waters.
>**Frederick Douglass**, slavery abolitionist, political theorist. Speech, Canandaigua, NY, 8/4/1857

"Hands Raised" by Rini Templeton.

The tap root of power lies below the surface. It is obedience, cooperation, collusion: the social glue that ensures that each day proceeds much like the last. Every single one of us has the power to give or withhold our willing participation. To 'reproduce' or reshape society.
Alex Begg, writer. *Empowering the Earth*, 2000

The reasons aren't well known to science but rebellion is contagious.
Subcomandante Marcos, Mexican Zapatista revolutionary, writer. *Letter to Jóse Saramago*, 12/1/1999

Resistance is the secret of joy.
Alice Walker, writer, poet. *Possessing the Secret of Joy,* 1991

The choice, as every choice, is yours: to fight for freedom or be fettered, to struggle for liberty or be satisfied with slavery, to side with life or death.
Mumia Abu-Jamal, journalist, U.S. political prisoner

Chapter 12

"Ain't No Power Like the Power of the People"

Political Movements, Social Change Work, Activism

Within the humblest and most fragile of men there is concealed a weapon more potent, more powerful, more mighty than is encapsulated in the most complex technological device the mind can conceive, more tremendous than the atom bomb, stronger than the strongest steel. Man's spirit. While that spark remains...no force can prevail against it.

> **Harrison E. Salisbury**, writer. Introduction to 1971 ed. of *The Prison Diary of Ho Chi Minh,* 1942

When a human being acts in accordance with her or his innermost principles, that person is very powerful. Almost invincible. There is great power when you have no doubt or conflict with what you are doing. We must discover our real, basic values, because once we are working within those values, nothing can stop us.

> **Severn Cullis-Suziki**, activist. In *Global Uprising,* 2001

The eternal struggle for freedom, justice and sanity in the world begins deep within the human heart.

> **Author unknown**

I do not ask that you place your hands upon the tyrant to topple him over, just that you support him no longer. Then you will behold him, like a colossus whose pedestal has been pulled away, fall of his own weight and break into pieces.

> **Etienne de la Boétie**, French writer, judge. "The Politics of Obedience: Discourse on Voluntary Servitude," 1548

Agitators are inevitable. They are as necessary to social organism as blood is to animal organism. Revolution follows as a matter of course.

> **T. Thomas Fortune**, journalist, activist, publisher. Attributed.

If it had not been for this thing I might have lived out my life talking at street corners to scorning men. I might have died, unmarked, unknown, a failure. Now we are not a failure. This is our career and our triumph. Never in our full life could we hope to do such work for tolerance; for justice, for man's understanding of man, as we do by accident.

> **Bartolomeo Vanzetti**, Italian immigrant, anarchist, sentenced to

death with Nicola Sacco on fraudulent charges. From statement
before execution, 1927

I am in the world to change the world.
   Käthe Kollwitz, German artist, activist, 1867-1945. Attributed.

You must be the change you want to see in the world.
   Mahatma Gandhi, Indian activist, political leader. Attributed.

Once social change begins, it cannot be reversed. You cannot uneducate the
person who has learned to read. You cannot humiliate the person who feels
pride. You cannot oppress the people who are not afraid anymore.
   César Chávez, union and labor organizer. Speech, San Francisco,
   CA, 11/9/1984

We think that counterpower is something that the state can't control. It is a
power that comes up from below, from the neighborhoods, the assemblies
and within each person, each subject.
   Nekka, Argentinean activist from the Solano unemployed workers
   movement. In *We Are Everywhere,* 2003

I march because once I thought I was alone. I thought that the world was
sitting on my neck. The jobs I get are hard; the roads I travel are rocky. The
foods I eat are course; the bed I sleep in is hard; the house I live in is old and
infested; my expenses are so high that I cannot afford to live; and my friends
are poor, which makes me too poor to die.
   Soul Brother #44 (Ernest White), activist. *Why We March,* 1969

I knew someone had to take the first step and I made up my mind not to
move.
   Rosa Parks, civil rights activist, whose refusal give up her bus
   seat to a white passenger helped precipitate the Montgomery Bus
   Boycott, 1955. Attributed.

I had no epiphany, no singular revelation, no moment of truth, but a steady
accumulation of a thousand slights, a thousand indignities, a thousand
unremembered moments, produced in me an anger, a rebelliousness, a desire
to fight the system that imprisoned my people. There was no particular day
on which I said, From henceforth I will devote myself to the liberation of my
people; instead, I simply found myself doing so, and could not do otherwise.
   Nelson Mandela, South African political leader and former
   political prisoner. *Long Walk to Freedom,* 1995

Political activity does not only happen in political parties or in organized groups; it happens as soon as you are conscious of your actions and your decisions.

Julieta Ojeda, Bolivian activist with Mujeres Creando (Women Creating). Interview, *Z Magazine*, June 2002

Activists demonstrate in San Francisco, CA in solidarity with protests against a meeting of the International Monetary Fund in Montreal, Canada, 2000. Photo by Bill Hackwell

All I ask is that, in the midst of a murderous world, we agree to reflect on murder and to make a choice. After that, we can distinguish those who accept the consequences of being murderers themselves or the accomplices of murderers, and those who refuse to do so with all their force and being.

Albert Camus, French writer. Attributed.

Take sides. Neutrality helps the oppressor, never the victim. Silence encourages the tormentor, never the tormented.

Elie Wiesel, Romanian writer, survivor of a Nazi concentration camp, 1986

Soon their broad roads will pass over the graves of your fathers, and the place of their rest will be blotted out forever. The annihilation of our race is at hand unless we unite in one common cause against the common foe. Think not, brave Choctaws and Chickasaws, that you can remain passive and indifferent to the common danger, and thus escape the common fate.

> **Tecumseh**, Shawnee leader, warrior. From speech to members of the Choctaw and Chickasaw nations, in an appeal for unity against white settler invasion. *History of the Choctaw, Chickasaw and Natchez Indians*, 1899

You can't be neutral on a moving train.

> **Howard Zinn**, historian, educator. Title of his memoir, 1995

When a cause comes along and you know in your bones that it is just, yet refuse to defend it, at that moment you begin to die. And I have never seen so many corpses walking around talking about justice.

> **Mumia Abu-Jamal**, journalist, U.S. political prisoner

Take a look around and be for or against
But you can't do shit if you ridin' the fence

> **The Coup**, hip hop group. From the song "Ride the Fence," 2001

We may talk of occupying neutral ground, but on this subject, in its present attitude, there is no such thing as neutral ground. He that is not for us is against us, and he that gathereth not with us, scattereth abroad. If you are on what you suppose to be neutral ground, the South look upon you as on the side of the oppressor.

> **Angelina Grimké Weld**, women's rights activist, slavery abolitionist. From her last public speech, delivered as pro-slavery crowds attacked the hall where she spoke and later burned it to the ground. Philadelphia, PA, May 1838

The world is a dangerous place, not because of those who do evil, but because of those who look on and do nothing.

> **Albert Einstein**, physicist, socialist, 1879-1955. Attributed.

To wish the victims success is not enough, the thing is to share their fate, to join them in death or victory.

> **Ernesto "Che" Guevara**, Argentinean-Cuban revolutionary and military leader. Essay, "Two, Three, Many Vietnams," 1967

Philosophers have only interpreted the world in various ways; the point is
to change it.
> **Karl Marx**, German political theorist. *Theses on Feuerbach,*
> 1845

In a participatory universe there are no neutral observers.
> **Tee shirt**, March 2004

If it iz to be war
Let it be war
& let us
choose sidez accordingly
> **Martin Wiley, a.k.a. KOT**, poet. From poem "If It Iz To Be War,"
> circa 2001

Washing one's hands of the conflict between the powerful and the powerless
means to side with the powerful, not to be neutral.
> **Paulo Freire**, Brazilian educator. Attributed.

The minute you stand up and say I am going to do something, even a small
thing, you win right in that moment. You become a human being, you have
a self. You have a purpose; you have a reason to live.
> **Melody Ermachild Chavis**, private investigator, journalist,
> referring to the Revolutionary Association of the Women of
> Afghanistan. Interview, *Guerrilla News Network*, 8/25/2003

The time is always right to do what's right. Social justice will go on with us
or without us. No matter how they confine your body, don't never let them
imprison your soul.
> **Shujaa Graham**, former U.S. political prisoner. Speech, political
> prisoners conference, 3/16/2003

The only way we will be free is if each and every one of us is directing all
of our energies to only one cause—the freedom of the people. There is one
truth—if your people are oppressed and you are not making an effort to help
your people get out of their oppression, by your very act of inaction you are
against your people.
> **Kwame Toure**, formerly Stokely Carmichael, civil rights and
> Black power activist. Speech, 1997

It is easy enough to shout slogans, to sign manifestos, but it is quite a
different matter to build, manage, command, spend days and nights seeking

the solution of problems.

> **Patrice Lumumba**, Congolese political leader. *Congo, My Country*, 1961

Action is the antidote to despair.

> **Joan Báez**, singer, activist. *Rolling Stone*, 1983

I've always thought that the best solution for those who feel helpless is for them to help others. I think then they will start feeling less helpless themselves.

> **Aung San Suu Kyi**, Burmese human rights activist. Interview, *Shambala Sun*, January 1996

Be ashamed to die until you have won some victory for humanity.

> **Horace Mann**, educator. Official motto of Antioch College, Yellow Springs, OH

Be realistic and do the impossible, because if we don't do the impossible, we face the unthinkable.

> **Murray Bookchin**, writer, educator. Attributed.

No one person can do everything, but everyone can do something.

> **Adage on social change**

Dare to struggle and dare to win.

> **Mao Tse-Tung**, Chinese revolutionary, political theorist. Attributed.

When I look at the world with lucidity I feel very sad, because everything is going bad and it makes me very sad, but it makes me strong because we have to fight, we have to change that, it's our only opportunity. If you feel resignated, you dead.

> **Manu Chao**, French singer, activist. In *The Vinyl Project*, from the Freedom Archives, 2003

We have been blamed for being agitators. I thank God for being one. Whatever little we have gained, we have gained by agitation, while we have uniformly lost by moderation.

> **Daniel O'Connell**, Irish political leader, 1776-1847. Attributed.

Our apologies, good friends, for the fracture of good order, the burning of paper instead of children, the angering of the orderlies in the front parlor of the charnal house.

Daniel Berrigan, U.S. Catholic priest, comment after entering a draft office and burning records during the Vietnam war. *Meditation*, 1967

By John Jonik

Every daring attempt to make a great change in existing conditions, every lofty vision of new possibilities for the human race, has been labeled Utopian.

Emma Goldman, activist, writer, anarchist. Speech, 1912

First they ignore you, then they laugh at you, then they fight you, and then you win.

Mahatma Gandhi, Indian activist, political leader

At best, those who romanticize "everyday resistance" or "cultural politics" read the evolution of political movements teleologically; they presume that those conditions necessarily, or even typically, lead to political action. They don't... This idealism may stem from a romantic confusion, but it's also an evasive acknowledgment of the fact that there is no real popular political movement. Further, it's a way of pretending that the missing movement is not a problem, that everyday, apolitical social practices are a new, maybe even more "authentic," form of politics.

> **Adolph Reed**. Essay, "Why Is There No Black Political Movement?" 1999

Perhaps the worst thing that can be said about social indignation is that it so frequently leads to the death of personal humility. Once that has happened, one has ceased to live in that world of men which one is striving so mightily to make over. One has entered into a dialogue with that terrifying deity, sometimes called History, previously, and perhaps again, to be referred to as God, to which no sacrifice in human suffering is too great.

> **James Baldwin**, writer, educator. Essay, "The Crusade of Indignation," July 1956

I do not know of any salvation for society except through eccentrics, misfits, dissenters, people who protest.

> **William O. Douglas**, U.S. Supreme Court Justice. In *The Power of Reason*, 1964

[On social service:] A palliative invented by the upper-class, administered by the bright offspring of the middle-class to ease the pains of the working-class to keep them from ousting the upper-class.

> **George Schuyler**, writer. *The Messenger*, February 1927

Who can fight the United States and their military? Who can fight the mighty United States today, except the will of the people.

> **Elias Rashmawi**, activist, educator. Speech, 5/17/2003

Where else could power be in world affairs but in the people? The question is whether or not the people will choose to exercise that power.

> **Ramsey Clark**, human rights activist, former U.S. Attorney General. Speech, 5/17/2003

The entire world is in dispute between two projects of globalization. Globalization from above, which globalizes conformity, cynicism, stupidity, war, destruction, death, and forgetting, and globalization from below, which globalizes rebellion, hope, creativity, intelligence, imagination, life, memory, and the construction of a world with room for many worlds.

Subcomandante Marcos, Mexican Zapatista revolutionary, writer. Tape recorded message played at anti-World Trade Organization protest in Cancun, Mexico, 9/9/2003

The greatest threat to corporate power, interestingly enough, is globalization —grassroots globalization. It's what those in power fear the most. We can turn their own actions and mechanisms, their own empowerment, against them.

Amy Goodman, radio reporter. Interview, *Guerrilla News Network*, 2004

The great are only great because we are on our knees. Let us rise!

Max Stirner, German anarchist. *The Ego and His Own*, 1845

And it's known that people create the situations they live in. But man must change living in a systematic world that is controlled by rules that are made by man.

Iriel Sayeed, activist, poet. Essay, "Food: The Famine and The Feast," 2003

If you are trying to transform a brutalized society into one where people can live in dignity and hope, you must begin with the empowering of the most powerless. You build from the ground up.

Adrienne Rich, writer, poet. *Blood, Blood and Poetry*, 1986

Who is this middle class that we so often worry about alienating? I'm afraid it is made up of people who are often not our natural allies, and who in fact are more invested in maintaining their privilege than other classes of people who potentially have a lot more to offer to social change movements, but who we have a pattern of ignoring.

Cynthia Peters, writer. Essay, "Courting the Middle Class?" 7/9/2003

Right-wing grassroots efforts—to close abortion clinics, kill affirmative action, and put gays and lesbians back into the closet—have never bothered with stop signs at all. Perhaps they know something that we forgot. Good organizing issues are deeply felt, controversial. Our problem is that the gap from the "small and winnable" to the large and significant is often unbridgeable.

Gary Delgado, community organizer, writer. Essay, "The Last Stop Sign," 1998

We in the UK are dependent on your movement in the United States because you, unlike us, are in the belly of the beast, and we need you so very much.

Selma James, founder, Global Women's Strike. Anti-war meeting, Philadelphia, PA, 2003

We are gathered here in the largest demonstration in the history of this nation. Let the nation and the world know the meaning of our numbers. We are not a pressure group, we are not an organization or a group of organizations, we are not a mob. We are the advance guard of a massive moral revolution for jobs and freedom.

A. Philip Randolph, President, Brotherhood of Sleeping Car Porters. Speech at the March on Washington, 1963

If what we want does not exist, we can talk about its absence, we can argue for its legalization—or we can make it happen. Structural change does not happen from the exterior, it starts from the grassroots. The first fugitive slaves in this country did not spend their lives asking for manumission, they claimed their lives as they knew they should be lived. When the Zapatistas declared war on the Mexican government, they did not come to San Cristobal from meeting halls. They came from the mountains of Chiapas where they had already formed their rebel army. Even the so-called forefathers who came and took over this land called America did not wait to be given England's blessing before they did it.

Fran Harris. "Cutting the System Strings," *Blu Magazine*, 2001

It has been proven that a little old lady in Kansas can bring the Interior Department to its knees.

Anonymous federal official, on the requirements of the National Environmental Policy Act, 1972

The individual can compel the establishment, can say to it, You are accountable to me. The individual can expose the dark machinations of any regime in the world, in any sphere, by means of civil disobedience. An action like mine teaches citizens that their own reasoning, the reasoning of every individual, is no less important than that of the leaders. They use force and sacrifice thousands of people on the alter of their megalomania. Don't follow blindly.

Mordechai Vanunu, Israeli scientist who exposed Israel's possession of nuclear weapons and was sent to prison for treason.

I don't know what your destiny will be, but one thing I know: the only ones among you who will be really happy are those who will have sought and found how to serve.

> **Albert Schweitzer**, German philosopher, musician, physician. Attributed.

Power generally consists of having a lot of money or a lot of people. Citizen organizations tend to have people, not money. Thus, our ability to win depends on our being able to do with people, what the other side is able to do with money.

> **Kim Bobo, Jackie Kendall, Steve Max**. *Organizing for Social Change,* 1991

The forces in a developing social struggle are frequently buried beneath the visible surface and make themselves felt in many ways long before they burst out into the open... In the United States, it is our weakness to confuse the numerical strength of an organization and the publicity attached to its leaders with the germinating forces that sow the seeds of social upheaval in our community.

> **M.S. Handler**, journalist. Introduction, *The Autobiography of Malcolm X*, 1964

Never doubt that a small group of thoughtful, committed citizens can change the world. Indeed, it's the only thing that ever has.

> **Margaret Mead**, cultural anthropologist, 1901-1978. Attributed.

If you think you are too small to make a difference, try sleeping in a small room with a mosquito.

> **Proverb**, West Africa

The real portrait of an activist, after all, is just a mirror.

> **Jennifer Baumgardner and Amy Richards**, writers, activists. *Grasssroots*, 2005

Chapter 13

"The Ones We've Been Waiting For"

Leaders

Most people don't wanna be the King
or the queen for that matter
people want freedom

> **Ras Baraka**, poet, Deputy Mayor of Newark, NJ. From poem,
> "Why Mumia must live and go free," circa 1996

It's not that I was born a heroine. It was a question of growing up in a company town where people were going without food and children were going without health services.

> **Genora Dollinger**, labor organizer. In *Striking Flint*, 1995

No single person can liberate a country. You can only liberate a country if you act as a collective.

> **Nelson Mandela**, South African political leader and former
> political prisoner. In *How to Get White Men Out of Office*, 2004

There is a saying in community organizing that leadership is developed, not found. There are very few "natural leaders" sitting around not doing anything but waiting for you to call.

> **Kim Bobo, Jackie Kendall, Steve Max**. *Organizing for Social
> Change*, 1991

Too many so-called leaders of the movement have been made into celebrities and their revolutionary fervor destroyed by mass media…the task is to transform society; only the people can do that—not heroes, not celebrities, not stars.

> **Huey P. Newton**, co-founder, Black Panther Party. *Revolutionary
> Suicide*, 1973

I don't want you to follow me or anyone else. If you are looking for a Moses to lead you out of the capitalist wilderness, you will stay right where you are. I would not lead you into this Promised Land, if I could, because if I could lead you in, someone else could lead you out.

> **Eugene Debs**, activist, labor organizer, socialist. In *Great Labor
> Quotations*, 2000

The idea of saviors has been built into the entire culture, beyond politics. We have learned to look to stars, leaders, experts in every field, thus surrendering our own strength, demeaning our own ability, obliterating our own selves. But from time to time, Americans reject that idea and rebel.

> **Howard Zinn**, historian, educator. *A People's History of the United States*, 1980

There's no such thing as liberators, the people will liberate themselves.

> **Ernesto "Che" Guevara**, Argentinean-Cuban revolutionary, military leader. Attributed.

Labor rally during a series of mass actions against a meeting of the World Trade Organiztion, Seattle, WA 1999. Banner shows Emiliano Zapata. Photo by Hans Bennet

Hungry people with no jobs will not continue to go hungry without reacting. They will soon take action and follow anyone who can give them jobs—or even promises to do so.

> **Kwame Nkrumah**, Ghanaian political leader. *Letter to Patrice Lumumba*, 1960

If we are not serious representatives of the people, we will wind up on the side of our enemies. And no matter the piles of glittering resources a society might have, remember the people are its most precious resource.

> **Amiri Baraka**, poet, educator. Speech, Johannesburg, South Africa, July 1995

Strong people don't need strong leaders.

> **Ella Baker**, civil rights activist. Attributed

Who ever walked behind anyone to freedom?
Hazel Scott, musician. *Ms* magazine, November 1974

The *Priistas* say...that they have killed the Zapatista leader of this community. But they lie. They lie because the Zapatistas have no leaders. They think that by killing our leaders they can destroy the movement, but this is not so. It is true that there are people who command and people who obey, but those who command do it for those who obey, and those who obey do it out of pure will, out of service to the people. There are no Zapatista leaders, only Zapatistas.
Moisés, Mexican poet, songwriter. In *We Are Everywhere*, 2003

To imagine that a leader's personal charisma and a c.v. of struggle will dent the Corporate Cartel is to have no understanding of how Capitalism works, or for that matter, how power works. Radical change will not be negotiated by governments; it can only be enforced by people.
Arundhati Roy, Indian writer, activist. Speech, World Social Forum, 1/16/2004

Deep inside that T-shirt where we have tried to trap him, the eyes of Che Guevara are still burning with impatience.
Ariel Dorfman, Argentinean-born writer, educator. Essay, "Che Guevara," *Time* magazine online, June 1999

Most of my heroes don't appear on no stamps
Public Enemy, hip hop group. From song "Fight The Power," 1990

One of the things blacks are saying is that the black community is not going to let the white community define who their heroes are.
Richard Majors, of the National Council of African American Men, regarding Million Man March, Washington, DC 1995. *CNN. com*, 10/16/1995

I tell the presidents of the Arab and Muslim countries to wake up! Wake up please! We are being killed, we are refugees from our houses, our children have nothing—not even shoes to wear! Wake up! Wake up! Stop being traitors! Be human beings and not the dummies of the Americans!
Mohammad Ali, Iraqi man from the city of Falluja who survived a three week U.S. attack. Dahr Jamail's *Iraq Dispatches*, 11/23/2004

These Uncle Tom leaders do not speak for the Negro majority; they don't speak for the black masses. They speak for the "black bourgeoisie," the brainwashed, white-minded, middle-class minority who are ashamed of black, and don't want to be identified with the black masses.

> **Malcolm X**, Black nationalist leader. Speech, "God's Judgment of White America," 12/4/1963

We are the ones we've been waiting for.

> **June Jordan**, poet, educator. Attributed.

Chapter 14

"Whose Streets? Our Streets!"

Direct Action, Civil Disobedience

Don't be hesitant to represent
Yeah, you wanna act hard
You wanna talk…
So what about a little civil unrest
Against this government in defense of your people?
> **Welfare Poets**. From poem "No Taxation," circa 1999

There is a time when the operation of the machine becomes so odious, makes you so sick at heart, that you can't take part; you can't even passively take part, and you've got to put your bodies upon the gears and upon the wheels, upon the levers, upon all the apparatus, and you've got to make it stop. And you've got to indicate to the people who run it, to the people who own it, that unless you're free, the machine will be prevented from working at all.
> **Mario Savio**, Free Speech Movement activist. From speech before sit-in at University of California at Berkeley, 1964

Individuals have international duties which transcend the national obligations of obedience. Therefore [individual citizens] have the duty to violate domestic laws to prevent crimes against peace and humanity from occurring.
> **From Nuremberg War Crime Tribunal** following World War II, 1950

Noncooperation with evil is as much a duty as is cooperation with good.
> **Mahatma Gandhi**, Indian activist, political leader. Speech, 1922

When laws, customs or institutions cease to be beneficial to man, they cease to be obligatory.
> **Henry Ward Beecher**, slavery abolitionist, clergyman. *Life Thoughts*, 1858

I am not defying the government. I am obeying God.
> **Desmond Tutu**, South African archbishop. Comment on call to boycott elections in South Africa. *New York Times*, September 1988

If the injustice has a spring, or a pulley, or a rope, or a crank, exclusively for itself, then perhaps you may consider whether the remedy will not be worse than the evil; but if it is of such a nature that it requires you to be the agent of injustice to another, then, I say, break the law. Let your life be a counter-friction to stop the machine.

> **Henry David Thoreau**, writer, philosopher. *Civil Disobedience*, 1849

A lot of people are confusing non-violence with actually being controlled. It's time for people to open up their minds about non-cooperation. That is really what we are talking about. We can non-cooperate in a non-violent manner.

> **John Trudell**, poet, activist, former chairman of the American Indian Movement. Interview, *Overthrow*, December 1983

If you conduct your protest activities in a manner which is sanctioned by the state, the state understands that the protest will have no effect on anything. You can gauge the effectiveness—real or potential at least—of any line of activity by the degree of severity of repression visited upon it by the state. It responds harshly to those things it sees as, at least incipiently, destabilizing. So you look where they are visiting repression: that's exactly what you need to be doing.

> **Ward Churchill**, educator, activist. Interview, *Satya* magazine, April 2004

Working-class sabotage is aimed directly at "the boss" and at his profits, in the belief that that is the solar plexus of the employer, that is his heart, his religion, his sentiment, his patriotism. Everything is centered in his pocket book, and if you strike that you are striking at the most vulnerable point in his entire moral and economic system.

> **Elizabeth Gurley Flynn**, labor activist. "The Conscious Withdrawal of the Workers' Industrial Efficiency," 1916

For us, sabotage may not be a means to change any world but our own, as an expression of our feelings toward this society. We strike for ourselves, out of our own frustrations, and rage and despair...as a means of therapy and adventure. Because to not act, or to resign oneself to such an impoverished life of working and consuming is not good enough for us. We are not content and we intend to express this.

> **Earth Liberation Front**, from anonymous communiqué by saboteurs of a Wal-Mart construction site, 2003

I regret nothing for myself, I am sorry only for those who are perpetually blind to the cruel side of the world, those who never feel stirred to fight for something infinite, for humanity itself.

> **Bill Ayers**, educator, former member of the Weather Underground organization which bombed U.S. government and military sites in the 1970s. *Fugitive Days*, 2001

Monkey wrenching is an American tradition. Look at the Boston Tea Party—it's celebrated on a postage stamp. Someday we'd like to see tree-spiking celebrated that way.

> **Mike Roselle**, environmental activist. *Utne Reader,* May-June 1987

There [has been] much romanticization of frontline action. Some [perceive] frontliners as being 'hard-core' activists. The true reality tells us that it is equally demanding to incorporate the struggle into one's everyday life. We aren't trying to criticize those at the frontlines, but we need to take a deeper look at the glorification that we give those frontline actions.

> **Jen Chang, Bethany Or, Eloginy Tharmendran, Emmie Tsumura, Steve Daniels, Darryl Leroux**, editors of *Resist!*, 2001

The purpose of direct action is to create a situation so crisis-packed that it will inevitably open the door to negotiation.

> **Martin Luther King, Jr.**, civil rights leader. "Letter from Birmingham City Jail," 4/16/1963

When the speedup comes, just twiddle your thumbs.
Sit down! Sit Down!
And, when the boss won't talk, don't take a walk.
Sit down! Sit down!

> **Labor sit-down chant**, early 1900s

With our bodies, with what we are, we came to defend the rights of millions—dignity and justice—even with our lives. In the face of the total control of the world which the owners of money are exercising, we have only our bodies for protesting and rebelling against injustice.

> **Don Vitaliano**, Italian priest. In *We Are Everywhere*, 2003

Chapter 15

"By Any Means Necessary"

Violence, Non-Violence, Pacifism, Self-Defense

I think that we live in a pornographic age. And that there's a pornography of violence, there's this kind of sado-masochistic voyeurism. And that is part and parcel of our contemporary culture.

> **Cornel West**, theologian, writer, educator. *National Public Radio*, March 2004

I think it is fair to say that right now the world is in a state of crisis. Violence has become the dominant means of global powers to solve conflict; the threat of violence is the means to preclude conflict and maintain global hegemony.

> **Dawn Peterson**, sister of 9/11/01 World Trade Center attack victim Davin Peterson. Speech, Ferrara, Italy, 5/28/2003

You cannot put new ideas into a man's head by chopping it off; neither can you infuse a new spirit into his heart by piercing it with a dagger. Violent acts create bitterness in the survivors and brutality in the destroyers.

> **Mahatma Gandhi**, Indian activist, political leader. Attributed.

[A] society that becomes accustomed to using violence to solve its problems, both large and small, is a society in which the roots of human relations are diseased.

> **Ignacio Martín-Baró**, Salvadorian social psychologist. "Writings for a Liberation Psychology," 1994

Look upon your mother, wife and children, and answer God Almighty; and believe this, that it is no more harm for you to kill a man, who is trying to kill you, than it is for you to take a drink of water when thirsty.

> **David Walker**, slavery abolitionist, writer. "Appeal," 1829

What though before us lies the open grave?
Like men we'll face the murderous, cowardly pack,
Pressed to the wall, dying, but fighting back!

> **Claude McKay**, poet. From poem "If We Must Die," 1917, in response to mass white-on-black killings.

Dakotas, must we starve like buffaloes in the snow? Shall we let our blood freeze like the little stream? Or shall we make the snow red with the blood

of the white braves?
> **Lion Bear**, Dakota leader. Speech, late 1800s

I, John Brown, am now quite certain that the crimes of this guilty land will never be purged away but with blood.
> **John Brown**, anti-slavery guerrilla leader. From last writing before his execution, 1859

In the face of death, there is no political correctness.
> **Nidal Sakr**, human rights activist.

We say it's no longer a question of violence or nonviolence. We say it's a question of resistance to fascism or nonexistence within fascism.
> **Fred Hampton**, Black Panther leader, assassinated by Chicago police in December 1969. Speech, Northern Illinois University, November 1969

It's important to remember that the term "pacifism" doesn't mean "passive" as in sit back and let things happen to you. It stems from the world "pacific," which is to be peaceful. Think of the Pacific Ocean, which is giant and even with its gentleness it can drown hatred and turn it into something that replenishes and regenerates. When we think of pacifism, we have to think of it more in terms of the power, strength, and unity of the ocean.
> **Michael Franti**, lyricist for music group Spearhead. Interview, *Insubordination* magazine, 4/4/2003

In a world built on violence, one must be a revolutionary before one can be a pacifist. In such a world a non-revolutionary pacifist is a contradiction in terms, a monstrosity.
> **A. J. Muste**, labor and socialist activist. Essay, "Pacifism and Class War," 1928

The naked truth of decolonization evokes for us the searing bullets and bloodstained knives which emanate from it. For if the last shall be first, this will only come to pass after a murderous and decisive struggle between the two protagonists.
> **Franz Fanon**, Martiniquen psychiatrist, writer. *The Wretched of the Earth*, 1963

There is not a single example of people in the Third World being able to achieve qualitative economic and social change by peaceful means. Not in

Chile, not in India, not in the Congo, not in South Africa, not in Palestine. Nowhere. Imperialism has too much of a stake in the current economic order and is willing to use force and violence wherever needed.

> **David Gilbert**, writer, U.S. political prisoner. *No Surrender*, 2004

Our army is very different from others, because its proposal is to cease being an army. A soldier is an absurd person who has to resort to arms in order to convince others, and in that sense the movement has no future if its future is military.

> **Subcomandante Marcos**. Interview, *New Left Review*, May-June 2001

Violence in the colonies does not only have for its aim the keeping of these enslaved men at arm's length; it seeks to dehumanize them. Everything will be done to wipe out their traditions, to substitute our language for theirs and to destroy their culture without giving them ours.

> **Jean-Paul Sartre**, French writer. Introduction, *The Wretched of the Earth*, 1963

Soldiers were sent out in the winter, who destroyed our villages. Then "Longhair" [General Custer] came in the same way. They say we massacred him, but he would have done the same to us had we not defended ourselves and fought to the last.

> **Crazy Horse**, Oglala Lakota leader who lead the annihilation of General George Custer's U.S. Army forces at the battle of the Little Big Horn, 1876. Statement on his deathbed, September 1877

We did not go out of our own country to kill them. They came to kill us and got killed themselves.

> **Sitting Bull**, Lakota leader and warrior. Statement after battle of the Little Big Horn, in which all U.S. Army forces were killed, 1876

What we should be most concerned about is not some natural tendency toward violent uprising, but rather the inclination of people faced with an overwhelming environment of injustice to submit to it. Historically, the most terrible things—war, genocide, and slavery—have resulted not from disobedience, but from obedience.

> **Howard Zinn**, historian, educator. *Declarations of Independence*, 1991

The fact is that as man has advanced in civilization he has become increasingly, not less, violent and warlike. The violences that have been attributed to his original nature have, in fact, been acquired predominantly within the relatively recent period of man's cultural evolution.

> **Ashley Montagu**, English social scientist. *The Human Revolution*, 1965

People respect the expression of strength and dignity displayed by men who refuse to bow to the weapons of oppression. Though it may mean death, these men will fight, because death with dignity is preferable to ignominy. Then, too, there is always the chance that the oppressor will be overwhelmed.

> **Huey P. Newton**, co-founder, Black Panther Party. *Revolutionary Suicide*, 1973

I define violence as physical force directed at a sentient being or natural creation. I do not believe that violence can be committed against something inanimate whose sole purpose is the destruction of innocent life and natural creation.

> **Rod Coronado**, animal rights and environmental activist, serving a four year sentence for arson of an animal testing laboratory at the time of interview. *Satya* magazine, May 1997

Defining violence in terms of property—that basically nullifies the whole notion that life is sacred.

> **Ward Churchill**, educator, activist, on whether property destruction for political purposes can be defined as violence. Interview, *Satya* magazine, April 2004

I think violence really marginalizes and brutalizes women. It depoliticizes things. It's undemocratic in so many ways. But at the same time, when you look at the massive amount of violence that America is perpetrating in Iraq, I don't know that I'm in a position to tell Iraqis that you must fight a pristine, feminist, democratic, secular, non-violent war. I can't say.

> **Arundhati Roy**, Indian writer, activist. Interview, San Francisco, CA 8/16/2004

Armed struggle must be a movement intended to hit at the symbols of oppression and not to slaughter human beings.

> **Nelson Mandela**, South African political leader and former political prisoner, May 1994

We have a right to resist, to expropriate money and arms, to kill the enemy of our people, to bomb and do whatever else aids us in winning and we will win.

> **Kuwasi Balagoon**, former Black Panther and Black Liberation Army member. *A Soldier's Story,* 2001

Now, if it is deemed necessary that I should forfeit my life for the furtherance of the ends of justice, and mingle my blood further with the blood of my children, and with the blood of millions in this slave country whose rights are disregarded by wicked, cruel, and unjust enactments, I submit: so let it be done!

> **John Brown**, anti-slavery guerrilla leader. Speech at his trial after armed attack at Harper's Ferry, 1859

We will protect ourselves from the force and violence of the racist police and the racist military, by whatever means necessary.

> **Black Panther Party platform**, 1966

Concerning nonviolence: it is criminal to teach a man not to defend himself when he is the constant victim of brutal attacks.

> **Malcolm X**, Black nationalist leader. Speech, 3/12/1964

Peaceably If We Can: Forcibly If We Must.

> **Slogan during the labor movement for an eight-hour work day**, 1870s

I knew that I could never again raise my voice against the violence of the oppressed in the ghettos without having first spoken clearly to the greatest purveyor of violence in the world today—my own government.

> **Martin Luther King, Jr.,** civil rights leader. Speech, "Beyond Vietnam," New York, NY 4/4/1967

Political power grows out of the barrel of a gun.

> **Mao Tse-Tung**, Chinese revolutionary, political theorist. "Problems of War and Strategy," 1938

Unorganized violence is like a blind man with a pistol.

> **Chester Himes**, writer. Attributed.

Violence is as American as cherry pie.

> **H. "Rap" Brown**, Black power leader. *Die Nigger Die!,* 1969

Self-Defense is not a violent act. A violent act is to teach a man or women not to defend themselves when they are the constant victims of brutal attacks.
Author unknown

Self defense is not fear.
Proverb, Kenya

Since you have decided that the dye is cast, I have the pleasure of saying farewell like the Roman gladiators who were about to fight in the arena: Hail Cesar, those who are about to die salute you! My only regret is that I would not even see your face because in that case you would be thousands of miles away while I shall be in the frontline to die fighting in defense of my homeland.
Fidel Castro, Cuban revolutionary, political leader. Message to George W. Bush on possibility of U.S. military action against Cuba. Speech, 5/14/2004

National liberation, national renaissance, the restoration of nationhood to the people, commonwealth: whatever may be the headings used or the new formulas introduced, decolonization is always a violent phenomenon.
Franz Fanon, Martiniquen psychiatrist, writer. *The Wretched of the Earth,* 1963

I think it's pretty easy to define self-defense in connection with preservation of one's life. Life is very precious. It's a social contract. We're guaranteed through the Constitution a right to defend ourselves against unjust, perpetrated violence, and a right to human dignity. Certainly, the self-defense of the victim is not the same as the violence of the oppressor.
David Hilliard, activist, writer, former Black Panther. Interview, *Satya* magazine, April 2004

Nonviolence is not a garment to be put on and off at will. Its seat is in the heart, and it must be an inseparable part of our very being.
Mahatma Gandhi, Indian activist, political leader. *Non-violence in Peace and War*, 1948

The only thing that's been a worse flop than the organization of nonviolence has been the organization of violence.
Joan Báez, singer, activist. *Daybreak,* 1968

We…need some clarity about violence. It's simple. The state has a monopoly of it. What that means is that there is no way for the public, most particularly

in developed first world societies, to compete on the field of violence with their governments. That ought to be utterly and blatantly obvious. Our strong suit is information, facts, justice, disobedience, and especially numbers.
    Michael Albert, writer. activist. Essay, *"New Targets,"* 2001

Having been a person who was beaten into submission, quieted, stunned and made mute by terror, I know that there comes a time when you get people back, because that's survival. It's an organic part of what violence does. So I don't believe in the perpetration of it anymore.
    Eve Ensler, playwright. Interview, *Salon.com*, 11/26/2001

We are not offensive. We don't go out attacking anybody, but if someone attacks us then we certainly believe in the principle of self defense. That is the law, the true law, the law of life, the law of Mother Nature. There's not one species on the face of this earth that doesn't defend itself when attacked.
    Ramona Africa, activist, MOVE Organization member. Interview, *Insubordination* magazine, May 2002

If every Negro said "I'm nonviolent," white folks would love it. But if we had to fight Russia and we said we're nonviolent and don't believe in killing nobody, we'd be hauled off to a concentration camp.
    Dick Gregory, activist, nutritionist, comedian. Interview, *Playboy*, August 1964

We permit the police, Klan and Nazis to terrorize whatever sector of the population they wish without repaying them back in kind. In short, by not engaging in mass organizing and delivering war to the oppressors we become anarchists in name only.
    Kuwasi Balagoon, former Black Panther and Black Liberation Army member. *A Soldier's Story,* 2001

I would never tell someone who is living in a village being attacked by the U.S. military: 'Don't pick up arms to defend yourself.' They're dealing with their last line of defense. Here in the U.S., we have many other lines of defense up to that point—our use of the media, culture, art, music, our voices, word of mouth, direct action and civil disobedience. There are many steps until that final one of taking up arms and engaging in physical confrontation with someone.
    Michael Franti, lyricist for music group Spearhead. Interview, *Insubordination* magazine, 4/4/2003

A Winchester rifle should have a place of honor in every home. When the white man...knows he runs as great a risk of biting the dust every time his Afro-American victim does, he will have a greater respect for Afro-American life.

> **Ida B. Wells**, journalist, activist. In *When and Where I Enter,* 1984

I believe in the armed struggle as the only solution for those people who fight to free themselves.

> **Ernesto "Che" Guevara**, Argentinean-Cuban revolutionary, military leader. *Letter to parents*, 1965

There is nothing in our book, the Koran, that teaches us to suffer peacefully. Our religion teaches us to be intelligent. Be peaceful, be courteous, obey the law, respect everyone; but if someone puts his hand on you, send him to the cemetery.

> **Malcolm X**, Black nationalist leader. Speech, "Message to the Grassroots," November 1963

If we enter a revolution out of reactionaryism, the revolutionary has to become more violent than the oppressor to take it away from the oppressor, and in the process...the violence stays.

> **John Trudell**, poet, activist, former chairman of the American Indian Movement. Interview, *Blu Magazine*, 2000

Non-violence does not mean making peace. On the other hand, it means fighting bravely and sincerely for truth and doing what is just. Like all fights, there will be a terrible loss and pain.

> **Mahatma Gandhi**, Indian activist, political leader. Attributed.

Violence breeds violence, repression breeds retaliation, and only a cleansing of our whole society can remove this sickness from our souls.

> **Author unknown**. *No More Prisons* music compilation, 1999

Chapter 16

"U.N.I.T.Y"

Unity, Solidarity, Coalition Building

The most dangerous word in any human tongue is the word for brother. It's inflammatory.
> **Tennessee Williams**, playwright. Play, *Camino Real*, 1953

If we know, then we must fight for your life as though it were our own—which it is—and render impassable with our bodies the corridor to the gas chamber. For, if they take you in the morning, they will be coming for us that night.
> **James Baldwin**, writer, educator. "An Open Letter to My Sister, Angela Davis," November 1970

In Germany the Nazis came for the Communists, and I didn't speak up because I was not a Communist. Then they came for the Jews and I didn't speak up because I was not a Jew. Then they came for the trade unionists and I didn't speak up because I was not a trade unionist. Then they came for the Catholics and I was a Protestant so I didn't speak up. Then they came for me. By that time there was no one to speak up for anyone.
> **Martin Niemöller**, German pastor, 1892-1984

It's not good enough to be right. Sometimes, if only in order to test our resolve, it's important to win something. In order to win something, we need to agree on something. That something does not need to be an over-arching pre-ordained ideology into which we force-fit our delightfully factious, argumentative selves... It could be a minimum agenda.
> **Arundhati Roy**, Indian writer, activist. Speech, World Social Forum, 1/16/2004

If you tremble with indignation at every injustice, then you are a comrade of mine.
> **Ernesto "Che" Guevara**, Argentinean-Cuban revolutionary and military leader. Attributed.

Injustice anywhere is a threat to justice everywhere. We are caught in an inescapable network of mutuality, tied in a single garment of destiny.
> **Martin Luther King, Jr.**, civil rights leader. "Letter from Birmingham City Jail," 4/16/1963

If you have come to help me you are wasting your time. But if you have come because your future is bound up with mine, then let us work together.
> **Attributed by Lilla Watson** to a group of Australian Aboriginal activists in Queensland, 1970s

Self-interest is the only principle upon which individuals or groups will act as if they are the same.
> **A. Philip Randolph**, civil right leader, union organizer, 1919

Wouldn't It Be Loverly? If you find yourself humming this tune as you think about building a coalition, beware! Coalitions are not built because it is good, moral, or nice to get everyone working together. Coalitions are about building power.
> **Kim Bobo**, Jackie Kendall, Steve Max. *Organizing for Social Change,* 1996

Every organization says they have a correct line. Everyone also claims to be humble and open to learning, but when you are in an organization it's not that simple, people want you to get with their line.
> **Stic.man**, of hip hop group Dead Prez. Interview, *People's War* magazine, 2003

The world is big but it's smaller when we fight as one.
> **Mohammed Saoli**, Moroccan attendee of an international climate change conference in Barcelona, Spain, 2002

You can't deal with racial categories when you're talking about freeing somebody. The system don't deal with categories when they deal with us. They'll take a black one, a white one, a Puerto Rican one to use against us. The system will use anything they can to fight us. We should use anything that we can to defend ourselves.
> **Mike Africa, Jr.**, Move Organization member, on why racial diversity is important to the movement to free U.S. political prisoner Mumia Abu-Jamal. Interview, March 2000

Some people say you fight fire best with fire, but we say you put fire out best with water. We say you don't fight racism with racism—we're gonna fight racism with solidarity. We say you don't fight capitalism with no black capitalism; you fight capitalism with socialism.
> **Fred Hampton**, Black Panther leader, assassinated by Chicago police in December 1969. Speech, Chicago, IL, 1969

A democratic society needs multiple voices but one goal.

> **Paul Laraque**, Haitian poet. Speech, Woodstock, NY, January 2003

Gathered tonight in this room are people from all walks of life; and for that reason, this is a very dangerous meeting for the powers that be. They would like to see us divided.

> **Cynthia McKinney**, former U.S. Congresswoman. Speech, Harlem, NY 8/6/2003

I'm not trying to imply that the struggle for freedom has been the same for all people in America, only that freedom is dependent on all people being willing to fight tooth and nail to achieve it for all people.

> **Hakim Greene**, of hip hop group Channel Live. Coalition of Artists and Activists press release, 7/28/2003

"If They Take You" by Ricardo Levins Morales

I'm trying hard to find common denominators. Because I seriously doubt there will be any world here if we don't find some way to talk to people we disagree with.

Pete Seeger, folk singer, activist. In *Great Labor Quotations*, 2000

The great mistake of politics throughout history has been to unite people by dividing them from other people.

William Upski Wimsatt, activist. *Bomb The Suburbs*, 1994

When you unite, that is the power of God. God love love, which is unity.

Bob Marley, Jamaican reggae singer. Interview with Mumia Abu-Jamal, 1979

I feel as if I'm gonna keel over any minute and die. That is often what it feels like if you're really doing coalition work. Most of the time you feel threatened to the core and if you don't, you're not really doing no coalescing.

Bernice Johnson Reagon, educator, activist, singer. In *Home Girls*, 1983

We all have a fundamentalist in us, a place that's hardened our heart to other people, a part of us that thinks, my way is the way. We all have to work on that.

Melody Ermachild Chavis, private investigator, journalist. Interview, *Guerrilla News Network*, August 2003

There are a lot of Stalinists out there. A lot of people like to feel that they're right. That's okay. You can feel that you're right. But don't get too comfortable. Unless you're really born of the Virgin Mary, I think we should chill a little bit.

June Jordan, poet, educator. Interview, *Z Magazine*, March 2001

Life will not be a pyramid with the apex sustained by the bottom. But it will be an oceanic circle whose centre will be the individual always ready to perish for the village, the latter ready to perish for the circle of villages, until at last the whole becomes one life composed of individuals…the outermost circumference will not wield power to crush the inner circle but will give strength to all within and derive its strength from it.

Mahatma Gandhi, Indian activist, political leader. In *Essential Writings of Mahatma Gandhi*, 1990

Unity in diversity is an ecological term used to describe the elegant web of inter-dependant inter-relationships which make up a natural habitat. Ecology teaches that the most resilient natural systems are made up of biologically diverse communities.

Ann Filemyr, educator, poet, on building coalitions. Essay, "Unity in Diversity," 1996

The easiest people for a government to oppress are the groups most vilified by society and the press: gangs, prostitutes, street vendors, gays, lesbians, community activists. Once a government knows it can repress those of us who have been marginalized, they will begin oppressing the rest of society.

Magdaleno Rose-Avila, gang nonviolence organizer, Los Angeles, CA. *Blu Magazine*, 2000

The problem becomes what we lose when we as people of color join ranks with the community of people who in large part have failed to acknowledge the issues and concerns that we face on a daily basis. We lose our perspective and our inclination to fight and organize from that perspective. So many of us have decided to continue to do the work without you. We will not forsake our struggle to add some color and multicultural spice to your otherwise pale marches and bland rallies.

Ewuare Osayande, educator, activist, poet. Speech, 4/3/2003

There can be no black-white unity until there is first some black unity. There can be no workers' solidarity until there is first some racial solidarity. We cannot think of uniting with others, until after we have first united among ourselves.

Malcolm X, Black nationalist leader. Speech, New York, NY 3/12/1964

If white men in the U.S. Congress can be friends yet disagree on a multitude of items, Black men can and must do the same.

Marvin X, poet, educator. From letter, 2004

Brothers,—My people are brave and numerous; but the white people are too strong for them alone. I wish you to take up the tomahawk with them. If we all unite, we will cause the rivers to stain the great waters with their blood. Brothers,—If you do not unite with us, they will first destroy us, and then you will fall an easy prey to them. They have destroyed many nations of red men because they were not united, because they were not friends to each other.

> **Tecumseh**, Shawnee leader and war strategist who worked for unity against white settler invasion. Speech to members of the Osage nation, winter 1811-1812

The insidious colonial tendencies we have internalized—and that express themselves in sadistic competition for money and attention, political cannibalism, and moral distrust—must be overcome. We must realize that we are not each other's enemies and that the true enemy is currently enjoying our divisiveness.

> **Guillermo Gómez-Peña**, performing artist, writer. *Warrior for Gringostroika*, 1993

This kind of action is a prevalent error among oppressed peoples. It is based upon the false notion that there is only a limited and particular amount of freedom that must be divided up between us, with the largest and juiciest pieces of liberty going as spoils to the victor or the stronger. So instead of joining together to fight for more, we quarrel between ourselves for a larger slice of the one pie.

> **Audre Lorde**, educator, activist, poet. *Sister Outsider*, 1984

Hopefully, we can learn from the 60s that we cannot afford to do our enemies work by destroying each other.

> **Audre Lorde**, educator, activist, poet. Attributed.

The longing for a better world will need to arise at the imagined meeting place of many movements of resistance, as many as there are sites of enclosure and exclusion. The resistance will be as transnational as capital. Because enclosure takes myriad forms, so shall resistance to it.

> **Iain Boal**, historian. *First World, Ha Ha Ha!*, 1995

We need to work like the Zapatistas do, like ants who go everywhere no matter which political party the other belongs to. Zapatistas proved people can work together in spite of differences.

> **Anna Esther Ceceña**, of the FZLN, the Mexican support committee of the Zapatistas. In *We Are Everywhere*, 2003

Critics of African unity often refer to the wide differences in culture, language and ideas in various parts of Africa. This is true, but the essential fact remains that we are all Africans, and have a common interest in the independence of Africa. The difficulties presented by questions of language, culture and different political systems are not insuperable.

Kwame Nkrumah, Ghanaian political leader. *Neo-Colonialism,* 1965

We...realize that we have to be united and make our small voices (no matter what color, age, gender, and more) into one that's large and powerful enough to awaken this sleeping giant of the American people so that we can decide the future of this country.

Willie Baptist, activist, of Kensington Welfare Rights Union. Interview, *Dissident Voice*, June 2003

Herb? Herb is the healing of the nation, seen? Once you smoke herb, you all must think alike. Now if you thinking alike, dat mean we 'pon the same track. If we 'pon the same track, that mean we gonna unite. Some say "don't smoke herb." Dey don't want us to unite, right, so they say, "don't smoke herb."...it's true!

Bob Marley, Jamaican reggae singer. Interview with Mumia Abu-Jamal, 1979

In our movements for liberation we often see the 'this group won't work with that group because their ideologies are too different' behavior, which keeps us from being stronger. If we really want to bring this system down, we have to come at all levels.

Mario Hardy Ramirez, activist, educator. Speech, January 31, 2003

Work for unity. But avoid uniformity. Look instead for ways to connect. And don't look for unity to shine down like a light from above. Unity is born from within. Not everybody in the world is going to have the same vision. There will always be divisive issues; we won't all be liberated in the same way. But even if we disagree with each other, we need to respect each other's viewpoints. After all, we're all trying to work for a better future.

Assata Shakur, former Black Panther, in exile in Cuba. Interview, *Blu Magazine*, 2000

We can hang together, or hang separately.

An adage on unity

The only thing that's worse than fighting with your allies is fighting without them.

An adage on unity

In a nutshell, we have to get our act together. The state of the world does not allow for personality conflicts, egos, obstructions or distractions. My distaste for fascism, a police state and world domination by the few over the many overrules any distaste for any persons or group of people's hang-ups, complexes or neurosis. In the scope of things it is all very trivial and we cannot allow our personal feelings to allow us to be distracted or rendered ineffective. It is going to take all of us, so get over it and get on with it.

> **Shafiq El-Amin**, of Minority Xperience Network. At anti-war meeting, Philadelphia, PA June 2003

If we get down, and we quarrel every day
We're singing prayers to the devil I say

> **Bob Marley**, Jamaican reggae singer. From song "Positive Vibration," 1976

Chapter 17

"Freedom Train"

Freedom, Justice, Equality, Liberation, Independence, Self-Determination, Human Rights

this freedom, this liberty, this beautiful
and terrible thing, needful to man as air
> **Robert Earl Hayden**, poet. From poem "Frederick Douglass,"
> 1985

I am not interested in picking up crumbs of compassion thrown from the table of someone who considers himself my master. I want the full menu of rights.
> **Desmond M. Tutu**, South African bishop, anti-apartheid activist.
> *NBC*, January 1985

We are not rebels and revolutionaries, but humans who will no longer be denied our humanity.
> **Marcus Garvey**, Jamaican Black nationalist leader. Attributed.

I believe once people get a taste of freedom, they will figure out how to get it.
> **Stic.man**, of hip hop group Dead Prez. Interview, *People's War
> Magazine*, summer 2003

Only one thing's sadder than remembering you once were free, and that's *forgetting* you once were free. That would be the saddest thing of all.
> **Mathew King**, Lakota spiritual elder. In *Prison Writings*, 1999

Among the myriad freedoms claimed by the U.S. government are the freedom to murder, annihilate, and dominate other people. The freedom to finance and sponsor despots and dictators across the world. The freedom to train, arm, and shelter terrorists. The freedom to topple democratically elected governments. The freedom to amass and use weapons of mass destruction—chemical, biological, and nuclear. The freedom to go to war against any country whose government it disagrees with. And, most terrible of all, the freedom to commit these crimes against humanity in the name of "justice," in the name of "righteousness," in the name of "freedom."
> **Arundhati Roy**, Indian writer, activist. Essay, "The Loneliness of
> Noam Chomsky," 8/24/2003

When you start looking at freedom as a goal, you are no longer free.
> **Wise Intelligent**, of hip hop group Poor Righteous Teachers.
> Interview, *Blu Magazine*, 1999

Freedom cannot be taken by any goddam judge's opinion.
> **John Africa**, founder, MOVE Organization, circa 1980

Wanting to be free is to begin being free.
> **Ramón Emeterio Betances**, Puerto Rican physician, slavery
> abolitionist. Attributed.

Liberty is within us, like the dawn is within the night.
> **Otto René Castillo**, Guatemalan revolutionary fighter, poet.
> Attributed.

To change masters is not to be free.
> **José Martí**, Cuban political theorist, poet. Attributed.

In your struggle for freedom, justice and equality I am with you. I came to Louisville because I could not remain silent while my own people, many I grew up with, many I went to school with, many my blood relatives, were being beaten, stomped and kicked in the streets simply because they want freedom, and justice and equality in housing.
> **Muhammad Ali**, champion boxer, activist, speaking alongside
> Martin Luther King, Jr. to protestors demanding fair housing in
> Ali's hometown of Louisville, KY, 1967

There's something contagious about demanding freedom.
> **Robin Morgan**, writer. *Sisterhood is Powerful*, 1970

Crowns will fall, thrones will tremble, kingdoms will disappear, the divine right of kings and the divine right of capital will fade away like the mists of the morning when the Angel of Liberty shall kindle the fires of justice in the hearts of men.
> **Mary Elizabeth Lease**, political activist, writer. Speech, Women's
> Christian Temperance Union, circa 1890

We know through painful experience that freedom is never voluntarily given by the oppressor; it must be demanded by the oppressed.
> **Martin Luther King, Jr.**, civil rights leader. "Letter from
> Birmingham City Jail," 4/16/1963

Youth of the MOVE Organization rally for political prisoners Mumia Abu-Jamal and the
MOVE 9, Philadelphia, PA 2002. Photo by Hans Bennet

Freedom is not something that anybody can be given; freedom is something
people take and people are as free as they want to be.
> **James Baldwin**, writer, educator. *Nobody Knows My Name*, 1961

We have dared to be free; let us dare to be so by ourselves and for
ourselves.
> **Jean Jacques Dessalines**, Haitian revolutionary leader, Emperor
> of Haiti. "Proclamation," 1804

We will never win as long as we allow ourselves to doubt that justice exists
only when people are willing to defend it.
> **Cecilia Rodríguez**, activist, representative of the Zapatistas.
> *Current Biography*, May 1999

You cannot expect the same people who took your freedom from you to
give it back to you. You got to take it from them.
> **John Africa**, founder, MOVE Organization, circa 1980

Justice is like a snake: it only bites the barefooted.

Monsignor Oscar Arnulfo Romero, Archbishop of San Salvador, El Salvador, Assassinated in 1980. Attributed.

A man is either free or he is not. There cannot be any apprenticeship for freedom.

Amiri Baraka, poet, activist. Essay, "Tokenism: 300 Years for Five Cents," 1962

Freedom is never voluntarily given by the oppressor; it must be demanded by the oppressed.

Martin Luther King, Jr., civil rights leader. *Why We Can't Wait*, 1964

Men and women of Cochabamba, rights cannot be begged for, they must be fought for. No one is going to fight for ours. We will fight together for what is just or we will tolerate the humiliation of bad government.

La Coordinadora for the Defense of Water and Life, Cochabamba, Bolivia, during struggle against privatization theft of the city's water, 2000

Man is born free, and everywhere he is in fetters.

Jean Jacques Rousseau, French philosopher. *The Social Contract*, 1762

You know the lovers of freedom by their scars.

Muti Ajamu-Osagboro, activist, U.S. political prisoner held in Pennsylvania

Any people searching for independence must remember that it can't be achieved without suffering.

Ali Abdul Khadar Khalil, Palestinian human rights activist. *Time* magazine, 1988

Liberty means responsibility. That is why most men dread it.

George Bernard Shaw, Irish playwright, writer. *Maxims for Revolutionists*, 1903

The price of liberty is eternal vigilance.

Frederick Douglass, slavery abolitionist, political theorist. Speech, 1889

If you're not ready to die for it, put the word "freedom" out of your vocabulary.

Malcolm X, Black nationalist leader. *Chicago Defender*, November 1962

It is our duty to fight for our freedom. It is our duty to win. We must love each other and support each other. We have nothing to lose but our chains.

> **Assata Shakur**, former Black Panther, in exile in Cuba. From radio broadcast "To My People," taped in prison, 7/4/1973

The day comes when justice arms the weak and puts the giants to flight.

> **Pedro Albizu Campos**, Puerto Rican revolutionary leader. Attributed.

What makes equality such a difficult business is that we only want it with our superiors.

> **Henry Becque**, French dramatist. *Querelles Littéraires*, 1980

Only oppression should fear the full exercise of freedom.

> **José Martí**, Cuban political theorist, poet. Attributed.

Freedom is that cold road seldom traveled by the multitude.

> **Aceyalone**, hip hop MC. From song "Mumia 911," 1999

Once a man is forced to surrender his natural human freedom
The value of a man is less than that of a pig.

> **Ho Chi Minh**, Vietnamese political leader, poet. *The Prison Diary of Ho Chi Minh*, 1942

Policies change, and programs change, according to time. But the objective never changes. You might change your method of achieving the objective, but the objective never changes. Our objective is complete freedom, complete justice, complete equality, by any means necessary.

> **Malcolm X**, Black nationalist leader. Speech, 12/20/1964

Chapter 18

"The Blood Red Flower"

Revolution and Revolutionaries

I may need to call upon the whirlwind
and the flame
because some things cannot be washed away
some things must burn

> **Richard Cammarieri**, poet, community organizer. From poem "Domestic Policy," circa 1996

Revolutions are not made: they come. A revolution is as natural a growth as an oak. It comes out of the past. Its foundations are laid far back.

> **Wendell Phillips**, slavery abolitionist. Speech, 1852

They will end by understanding that our ideal is the only one that guarantees the inviolability of human dignity.

> **Ricardo Flores Magón**, Mexican writer, organizer, rebel leader. In *Flores Magón*, 1977

All men recognize the right of revolution; that is, the right to refuse allegiance to, and to resist, the government, when its tyranny or its inefficiency are great and unendurable.

> **Henry David Thoreau**, writer, philosopher. *Civil Disobedience*, 1849

No doubt some of you are disconcerted by my use of the term "revolution." It's telling that some people who claim with pride to be proud Americans would disclaim the very process that made such a nationality possible... Why was it right for people to revolt against the British because of "taxation without representation," and somehow wrong for truly underrepresented Africans in America to revolt against America? For any oppressed people, revolution, according to the Declaration of Independence, is a right.

> **Mumia Abu-Jamal**, journalist, U.S. political prisoner. Graduation speech to students at Evergreen State College class of 1999, via audio tape from death row, 6/11/1999

In this world, [revolution] means changing from the inhumane to the humane. It means that everybody has a right to live, to eat, to have a house, an education, to be free from torture, from repression. Maybe 20 years ago I thought that to change the structure in any given country was enough. Now

I know it means changing the human being who's going to live in that future to be prepared to live with others.

> **Assata Shakur**, former Black Panther, in exile in Cuba. Interview, *BET.com*, 2001

To be revolutionary is to be original, to know where we came from, to validate what is ours and help it to flourish, the best of what is ours, of our beginnings, our principles, and to leave behind what no longer serves us.

> **Inés Hernández-Ávila**, writer, activist. *Columbia Book of Quotations by Women*, 1996

True revolution means a total change, a complete separation and disassociation from everything that is causing the problems you're revolting against.

> **Delbert Africa**, U.S. political prisoner from the MOVE Organization. Essay, "Application Don't Need No Conversation," 2000

The hard painstaking work of changing ourselves into new beings, of loving ourselves and our people and working with them to create a new reality; this is the first revolution, that internal revolution.

> **Safiya Buhkari**, activist, former Black Panther member. "Reflections, Musings and Political Opinions," 1997

The state is not something that can be destroyed by a revolution, but is a condition, a certain relationship between human beings, a mode of human behavior; we destroy it by contracting other relationships, by behaving differently.

> **Gustav Landauer**, German philosopher, 1870-1919. Attributed.

Oh, the revolution... I'm beginning to find out that it's tough. Before you start jumping on anybody else and telling them how they got to change, you really got to change yourself. And I know if you've changed yourself you've already made the world a much better place.

> **Umar Bin Hassan**, poet, activist. Interview, *Blu Magazine*, 1999

All revolutions must be social revolutions, based upon fundamental changes in society; otherwise it is not a revolution, but merely a change in government.

> **Chingling Soon**, Chinese political leader. *The People's Tribune*, 1927

I want a revolution that changes the very nature of how power is structured and perceived, that challenges all systems of domination and control, that nurtures the empowerment of individuals and the collective power we can wield when we act together in solidarity.

Starhawk, activist, writer. Essay, "Quebec City: Beyond Violence and Nonviolence," 2001

The ultimate end of all revolutionary social change is to establish the sanctity of human life, the dignity of man, the right of every human being to liberty and well-being.

Emma Goldman, activist, writer, anarchist. *My Further Disillusionment*, 1924

Settle your quarrels, come together, understand the reality of our situation, understand that fascism is already here, that people are dying who could be saved, that generations more will die or live poor butchered half-lives if you fail to act. Do what must be done, discover your humanity and your love in revolution. Pass on the torch. Join us, give up your life for the people.

George Jackson, writer, Black Panther member, killed by prison guards in 1971. *Soledad Brother*, 1970

My name is Assata Shakur (slave name Joanne Chesimard), and I am a revolutionary. A Black revolutionary. By that I mean that I have declared war on all forces that have raped our women, castrated our men, and kept our babies empty-bellied.

Assata Shakur, former Black Panther, in exile in Cuba. Radio broadcast "To My People," taped in prison, 7/4/1973

If we are extremists we are not ashamed of it. In fact, the conditions that our people suffer are extreme, and an extreme illness cannot be cured with a moderate medicine.

Malcolm X, Black nationalist leader. Attributed.

A desperate disease requires a dangerous remedy.

Guy Fawkes, English revolutionary. Statement at his interrogation in the "gunpowder plot," 1605

They can do anything they want to to us. We might not be back, I might be in jail, I might be anywhere, but when I leave you can know I said, with the last words on my lips, that I am—a revolutionary. And you're gonna have to keep on sayin that. You're gonna have to say that I am a proletariat. I am the people, I am not the pig.

Fred Hampton, Black Panther leader, assassinated by Chicago police in December 1969. Speech, circa 1969

A revolutionary is any enemy of the capitalist state.
> **Audience member**, political prisoners supporters conference, Philadelphia, PA, March 2003

Revolutionaries do not make revolutions! The revolutionaries are those who know when power is lying in the street and when they can pick it up.
> **Hannah Arendt**, German educator, political analyst. *Crises of the Republic*, 1972

A revolution is a struggle to the death between the future and the past.
> **Fidel Castro**, Cuban revolutionary, political leader. Speech, January 1961

Revolution always unfolds inside an atmosphere of rising expectations.
> **June Jordan**, poet, educator. *Technical Difficulties*, 1992

The fundamental premise of a revolution is that the existing social structure has become incapable of solving the urgent problems of development of the nation.
> **Leon Trotsky**, Russian revolutionary theorist. In *History of the Russian Revolution*, 1932

The Negro has always been a revolutionary, not because he is black but because he is a man.
> **Adam Clayton Powell, Jr.**, Congressman, writer. *Marching Blacks*, 1945

Our only hope today lies in our ability to recapture the revolutionary spirit and go out into a sometimes hostile world declaring eternal hostility to poverty, racism, and militarism.
> **Martin Luther King, Jr.**, civil rights leader. Speech, 4/4/1967

When reform becomes impossible, revolution becomes imperative.
> **Kelly Miller**, educator. *The Negro in the New World Order*, 1919

So much energy has been spent thinking about ways to tear down the system, but when it's gone, what will you eat, what will you wear? We have to start building our own solutions, take care of our own needs, so we don't have to rely on this system and so we can be ready for real change.
> **Walidah Imarisha**, activist, poet. Philadelphia, PA 7/27/03

Mass demonstration against U.S. War with Iraq, Washington, DC, 2002.
Photo by Hans Bennet.

Revolutionary movements are routinely slandered in the bourgeois media. That reality has led radical movements to automatically rally behind any left movement fighting the power structure. Sadly, such a direct, simple response isn't adequate. The examples of Stalin in the Soviet Union and Pol Pot in Cambodia painfully demonstrate that some regimes that claim to be revolutionary end up committing atrocities and even genocide. Our loyalty is not to the "left" label but rather to humankind.

David Gilbert, writer, U.S. political prisoner. *No Surrender*, 2004

I cannot give you the answer you are clamoring for. Go home and think! I cannot decree your pet, text-book revolution. I want instead to excite general enlightenment by forcing all the people to examine the condition of their lives... I don't want to foreclose it with catchy, half-baked orthodoxy. My critics say: There is no time for your beautiful educational program; the masses are ready and will be enlightened in the course of the struggle. And they quote Fanon on the sin of betraying the revolution. They do not realize that revolutions are betrayed just as much by stupidity, incompetence, impatience, and precipitate action as by doing nothing at all.

Chinua Achebe, Nigerian writer, educator. *Anthills of the Savannah*, 1987

We don't say others should do what Cuba has done. Every people has to choose its path and decide if it wants to change its society or not. A lot of people don't like Cuban society. Young people have decided to leave and we can't blame them. It's not easy. I tell you sincerely, it's not easy.

> **Aleida Guevara**, Cuban political leader, daughter of Ernesto "Che" Guevara. Interview, *AFP*, 6/14/2003

We can neither export revolution nor can the United States prevent it.

> **Fidel Castro**, Cuban revolutionary, political leader. Interview, *Newsweek*, 1/9/1984

You can jail a revolutionary, but you can't jail a revolution. You can run a freedom fighter all around the country but you can't run freedom fighting out of the country. You can murder a liberator but you can't murder liberation.

> **Fred Hampton**, Black Panther leader, assassinated by Chicago police in December 1969. Speech, in *The Roots of Resistance*, from the Freedom Archives, 2002

Wherever a Puerto Rican is, the duty of a Puerto Rican is to make revolution.

> **Gloria González**, educator, former Young Lords member. *Blu Magazine*, 2000

The black revolution is much more than a struggle for the rights of Negroes. It is forcing America to face all of its interrelated flaws—racism, poverty, militarism and materialism. It is exposing evils that are rooted deeply in the whole structure of our society.

> **Martin Luther King, Jr.**, civil rights leader. *A Testament of Hope*, 1986

U.S.' greatest fear of revolution and greatest desire of empire will one day come to a climax. Progressives of whatever color will join hands and fight the mutual enemy. We must remember Malcolm's quote: 'I believe there will ultimately be a clash between the oppressed and those who do the oppressing. I believe there will be a clash between those who want freedom, justice and equality for everyone, and those who want to continue the system of exploitation. I believe there will be that kind of a clash, but I don't think it will be based on the color of the skin.'

> **Yuri Kochiyama**, activist, writer. Interview, *The Objector*, September 2003

When you talk of revolution, you never talk of the day after.
   Margaret Storm Jameson, English writer. *The Clash*, 1922

Revolutions do not take place in velvet boxes. They never have. It is only the poets who make them lovely.
   Carl Oglesby, activist, singer. Speech, November 1965

The only solution is revolution. It is the responsibility of every African to unite and fight to end racism and oppression of our people worldwide. Reformation is not the answer and will never be the answer.
   Naomi Beverly, activist. *Black Star* newspaper, 2002

"Progress" affects few. Only revolution can effect many.
   Alice Walker, writer, poet. *Ms.* magazine, August 1979

A revolution is not a dinner party, or writing an essay, or painting a picture, or doing embroidery; it cannot be so refined, so leisurely and gentle, so temperate, kind, courteous, restrained and magnanimous. A revolution is an insurrection, an act of violence by which one class overthrows another.
   Mao Tse-Tung, Chinese revolutionary, political theorist, March 1927

The revolution will not be televised.
   Gil Scott Heron, poet, musician. From poem "The Revolution Will Not Be Televised," 1970

Revolution is not a word but an application; it is not war but peace; it does not weaken, but strengthens. Revolution does not cause separation, it generates togetherness.
   John Africa, founder, MOVE Organization. circa 1980

The foundation of the revolution must rest upon the bones of the oppressors.
   Kuwasi Balagoon, former Black Panther and Black Liberation Army member. *A Soldier's Story*, 2001

Let the ruling classes tremble at a Communist revolution. The proletarians have nothing to lose but their chains. They have a world to win.
   Karl Marx and Friedrich Engels, German political theorists. *The Communist Manifesto*, 1848

I know I am a pawn in this movement to liberate life. I was thrust into this revolution by a power higher than all. To win is consistency, to stay strong, never bow down, and fight for what's right.

> **Pam Africa**, activist, MOVE Organization member. At political prisoner's conference, March 2003

The dreamer is the designer of tomorrow. The practical man, the sensible, cold head, can laugh at the dreamer; they do not know that he, the dreamer, is the true dynamic force that pushes the world forward. Suppress the dreamer, and the world will deteriorate toward barbarism. Despised, impoverished, the dreamer opens the way for his race, sowing, sowing, sowing the seeds which will be harvested, not by him, but by the practical men, the sensible, cold heads of tomorrow, who will laugh at the sight of another indefatigable dreamer seeding, seeding, seeding.

> **Ricardo Flores Magón**, Mexican writer, organizer, rebel leader. *Epistolario Revolucionario*, 1921

We are realists. We dream the impossible.

> **Ernesto "Che" Guevara**, Argentinean-Cuban revolutionary and military leader. Attributed.

Chapter 19

"Each One, Teach One"

Education, Political Awareness, Information

Don't tell me to leave you alone.
Death's working like a dog
> **Ferruccio Brugnaro**, Italian poet. From poem "Don't Tell Me Not to Bother You."

I, for one, believe that if you give people a thorough understanding of what it is that confronts them, and the basic causes that produce it, they'll create their own program; and when the people create a program, you get action.
> **Malcolm X**, Black nationalist leader. Speech, New York, NY 12/20/1964

People do not like to think. If one thinks, one must reach conclusions. Conclusions are not always pleasant.
> **Helen Keller**, educator, socialist activist. In *Lies My Teacher Told Me*, 1995

Information is in the ability to inform, and when you have no information to give, you can only *mis*inform...when you do not have a solution, all you can offer is the problem.
> **MOVE Organization**. *20 Years On The MOVE*, 1991

It would be better not to know so many things than to know so many things that are not so.
> **Felix Okoye**, educator. *The American Image of Africa,* 1971

In the end, we conserve only what we love. We will love only what we understand. We will understand only what we are taught.
> **Baba Dioum**, Senegalese poet. In *A Dictionary of Environmental Quotations,* 1992

The power of a movement lies in the fact that it can indeed change the habits of people. This change is not the result of force but of dedication, of moral persuasion.
> **Stephen Biko**, South African anti-apartheid leader, killed by police in 1977. Interview, July 1976. In *Biko*, 1978

We have to give ourselves the responsibility of constructing a vision of the world that is truly ours, not a colonized vision of the world. An independent, liberated view of reality. If we paint a more humanistic world to live in, we

will construct that world. If we paint a nightmare, we'll live in a nightmare.
> **Alurista** (Alberto Baltazar Urista), writer, activist. *Chicano Authors*, 1980

For coloured people to acquire learning in this country, makes tyrants quake and tremble on their sandy foundation. Why, what is the matter? Why, they know that their infernal deeds of cruelty will be known to the world.
> **David Walker**, slavery abolitionist, writer. "Appeal," 1829

Students, parents, teachers and community activists begin a hunger fast in front of Oakland City Hall to demand education funding after California Governor Arnold Schwarzenegger refused to meet with them. Photo by David Bacon

All rational education is at bottom nothing but the progressive immolation of authority for the benefit of liberty, the final object of education necessarily being the formation of free men full of respect and love for the liberty of others.
> **Mikhail Bakunin**, Russian anarchist writer, circa 1890, statement
> in the prospectus for the International School For the Children of

Political Refugees, opened by Louise Michel. In *Louise Michel*, 2004

If you plan for a year, plant rice. If you plan for ten years, plant trees. If you plan for 100 years, educate your children.
Proverb, China

If you give me a fish, you have fed me for a day. If you teach me to fish, then you have fed me until the river is contaminated or the shoreline seized for development. But if you teach me to ORGANIZE, then whatever the challenge, I can join together with my peers...and we will fashion OUR OWN SOLUTION!
Ricardo Levins Morales, artist, activist, writer. Revision of a traditional proverb.

What was so unique about the [activist] soldiers back in the 60s was the ability to transform a gangster mentality into a revolutionary mentality. You could go to a dope dealer who's turning over a $1000—back then that was a lot of money—and convince him that that was the wrong path and have him join the movement for change. We seem to have had the uncanny ability to do that. That was very important because those are the lumpen elements or the illegitimate capitalists who our enemies would use to cause dissension within our communities.
Geronimo "Ji Jaga" Pratt, activist, former Black Panther and political prisoner. Interview, *Blu Magazine*, 2000

I think there is a difference in do people think the system is broken and what people will do to make money. For some people just because they know the system is broken doesn't mean 'well, let's fix the problem.' It means 'well, what that gotta do with me?'
M-1, of hip hop group Dead Prez. Interview, *Allhiphop.com*, 2003

People in the reform world system are blind, paranoid, driven aimlessly, recklessly toward so-called solutions that are never there, becomin' more frustrated, more desperate with each failure, strikin' out again and again, only to be repeatedly struck down by the absence of clarity, tryin' to look through mud for the answer to your problems, runnin,' searchin,' attemptin' to solve your problems by leanin' heavily on your problematical references, the same reference that caused the problem, runnin,' searchin' for answers, drivin' still harder, and findin' nothin,' and gettin frustrated and seein' still less, lookin' in schools, lookin' in books, lookin' in churches, lookin' in monasteries, lookin' in synagogues, lookin' in mosques, lookin' in politics, arithmetic and hat tricks, at science, sickness and decay, at breakdowns, psychiatrists and crack-ups, at medicine, misfits and doctors, at technology, tumors and cancer, lookin' to the west and seein nothin,' lookin' to the east and seein' less, lookin' at me lookin' at you, lookin' at the problems and lookin' on, runnin,' drivin,' searchin' for answers to your problems when all you have to do is STOP!

Delbert Africa, MOVE member, U.S. political prisoner. Essay "Application Don't Need No Conversation," 2000

If those in charge of our society—politicians, corporate executives, and owners of press and television—can dominate our ideas, they will be secure in their power. They will not need soldiers patrolling the streets. We will control ourselves.

Howard Zinn, historian, educator. *Declarations of Independence,* 1991

The most potent weapon in the hands of the oppressor is the mind of the oppressed.

Stephen Biko, South African anti-apartheid leader, killed by police in 1977. Speech, Cape Town Conference on Inter-Racial Studies, 1971

I wouldn't send my children to school any more than I'd send them to Jeffrey Dahmer Daycare. School has become a normalized condition—like black eyes…'that means he loves me.' The biggest damage school does to us is learning that *we can't believe our own experience.*

Asiba Tupahache, former public school teacher who became a homeschooler. In *No More Prisons,* 1999

By John Jonik

When I think back on all the crap I learned in high school
It's a wonder I can think at all
>   **Paul Simon**, singer. From song "Kodachrome," 1973

Education is a system of imposed ignorance.
>   **Noam Chomsky**, political analyst, linguist. In *The Vinyl Project*,
>   from the Freedom Archives, 2003

The political elite loves to kiss babies when they run for office, or even to offer empty words about 'our children' when discussing them, but from coast to coast, 'from sea to shining sea,' urban public schools are places not of learning, nor of refuge, but of societal rejection and dismissal.
>   **Mumia Abu-Jamal**, journalist, U.S. political prisoner. Essay, "In
>   the Shadows of Brown," 4/29/2004

When the cruise missiles fly at 400 per day, that is 400 times $1.3 million in self-destructing technology? 30 days of this is $15.6 billion in cruise missiles alone. This is great news for Raytheon and Lockheed-Martin, but it is bad news for public schools.

> **Stan Goff**, writer, former U.S. Army sergeant. *Guerrilla News Network*, 3/17/2003

Schools run by federal bureaucrats produce little bureaucrats.

> **Phillip Martin**, Choctaw leader. In *Tribal Assets*, 1990

The end of all education should surely be service to others. We cannot seek achievement for ourselves and forget about the progress and prosperity of our community. Our ambitions must be broad enough to include the aspirations and needs of others for their sake and for our own.

> **César Chávez**, union and labor organizer. *Americanos*, 1999

You go to school and gotta fight a tank to get in
Instead of phonics, hooked on prison economics
Incarcerate you, make a bigger profit

> **C Rayz Walz**, hip hop MC. From song "AWOL," 2001

There is a fringe of exception, but for the most part, educated intellectuals are subservient to power, and there is nothing new to that. It goes all through history.

> **Noam Chomsky**, political analyst, linguist. Interview, *Guerrilla News Network*, 12/17/2003

I am a threat to the degree that I'm trying to tell the truth about America.

> **Cornel West**, theologian, writer, educator. Attributed.

The intellectual tradition is one of servility to power, and if I didn't betray it I'd be ashamed of myself.

> **Noam Chomsky**, political analyst, linguist. Interview, *BBC*, 11/25/1992

Arise ye prisoners of your mind-set

> **Allen Ginsberg**, poet. From poem "Fifth Internationale," 1994

How much it gonna cost to
buy you outa buyin' into a reality
that originally bought you?

> **Saul Williams**, hip hop MC, activist. From song, "Penny for a Thought," 2001

It is being educated in the English way that makes you a big man. That is what I disagree with. My message was: "Think African. Make students read African history." The people listened, but the government did not. That was when my confrontation with the government started.

> **Fela Kuti**, Nigerian singer. *Los Angeles Times*, July 1989

The master's tools will never dismantle the master's house. They may allow us temporarily to beat him at his own game, but they will never enable us to bring about genuine change.

> **Audre Lorde**, educator, activist, poet. Speech, Second Sex Conference, 9/29/1979

I believe that one of the primary duties of African intellectual institutions is really not merely to question the system of thought of Europe, but to question the *value of* these systems... The deliberate suppression of facts, of historical facts, which are dug up by anthropologists; the biased, the very dishonest selectiveness of material, which then becomes the basis of supposedly rigid structuralism in analyzing social systems; the habit of ignoring or merely treating as curious the systems, the metaphysical systems, the philosophical ideas of African society.

> **Wole Soyinka**, Nigerian playwright, educator. Interview, *Black World*, August 1975

The reality, the depth, and the persistence of the delusion of white supremacy in this country causes any real concept of education to be as remote, and as much to be feared, as change or freedom itself.

> **James Baldwin**, writer, educator. In film, "The Price of the Ticket," 1990

'What I believe' is a process rather than a finality. Finalities are for gods and governments, not for the human intellect.

> **Emma Goldman**, activist, writer, anarchist. "What I Believe," 1908

Good and evil are not qualities born in man:
More often than not, they arise from our education.

> **Ho Chi Minh**, Vietnamese political leader, poet. *The Prison Diary of Ho Chi Minh*, 1942

You can't punish the student for doing what the teacher has taught them. That

is not to condone what they've done, but we need to get to the root of it.
> **Ramona Africa**, activist, MOVE Organization member. Interview,
> *Urban Spectrum*, March 2004

Who could bear to hold privilege that meant the suffering and death of others if they had not been trained from early childhood to see these others as not real? Who would tolerate, for even an hour, the inhuman conditions imposed by the privileged, if they had not been trained from early childhood to feel themselves not fully entitled to life?
> **Aurora Levins Morales**, historian, activist, writer. *Medicine Stories,* 1998

If we have lost touch with what our forefathers discovered and knew, this has been due to the system of education to which we were introduced. This system of education prepared us for a subservient role to Europe and things European. It was directed at estranging us from our own cultures in order the more effectively to serve a new and alien interest.
> **Kwame Nkrumah**, Ghanaian political leader. Speech, Accra, 1962

We're educated to destroy ourselves
To piece by piece dismantle true self
> **Mystic**, hip hop MC. From song "Ghetto Birds," 2001

I don't have to enter the mainstream of politics. I can have a program, which is much more productive than entering the system, which would mean that I agree with that system. We can never win, so I will educate instead.
> **Fela Kuti**, Nigerian singer. *New African*, September 1989

Maybe I cannot change narrow-minded thinking. Maybe I cannot broaden a thousand ways of thinking or a hundred, but at least I can broaden one. And I hope one way will broaden another and more, until what we believe will not destroy us anymore.
> **Mercy Fajarina**. In *Global Uprising,* 2001

There are only two positions; either you support multiculturalism in American education, or you support the maintenance of white supremacy.
> **Molefi Asante**, educator, historian. *Newsweek*, 12/24/1990

Upper class means a certainty of belonging, an assumption of one's importance in the world... Take away black studies, women's studies, ethnic studies, Jewish studies, labor history, Chicano studies, Native American studies: what is left is what has passed for history with no qualifying objective, the story of those whose belonging was never disputed.

Susanna J. Sturgis, writer. *Out the Other Side,* 1988

My mission is to take you
lyrically break you
lyrically assassinate you
lyrically incinerate your body and recreate you
to destroy the power that mentally incarcerates you

Immortal Technique, hip hop MC. From song "Revolutionary," Viper Records, 2001

Chapter 20

"Speaking Truth to Power"

Speaking Out, Freedom of Speech, Censorship

Nothing is more dangerous to a system that depends on misinformation than a voice that obeys its own dictates and has the courage to speak out.
Jonathan Jackson, Jr., writer, nephew of George Jackson, 1994

Family members of people killed or unjustly imprisoned by police speak at a rally, Philadelphia, PA 2000. Photo by Ohn Taliaferro

There will be a time when our silence will be more powerful than the voices you strangle today!
August Spies, anarchist convicted after a railroad trial for his alleged role in the Haymarket Affair bombing of 1886. Statement just before execution, 11/11/1887

Censorship is more depraving and corrupting than anything pornography can produce.
Tony Smythe, British National Council for Civil Liberties. *The Observer*, September 1972

A dictatorship, especially that one, hated very much books and education and the people who deal in books and education.

> **Amir Nayef al-Sayegh**, Iraqi translator, referring to Saddam Hussein's regime. *Guerrilla News Network,* 7/22/2003

I bet these lyrics got 'im really vexed
But to be damned by the Devil is to be truly blessed

> **Will Villainova**, hip hop MC. From "Devils in a Blue Dress," a song about police brutality in New York, NY, 2000

At times to be silent is to lie.

> **Miguel Unamuno**, Spanish philosopher, educator, circa 1936

My poetry is a sacred obligation that does not require the approval of the FBI... I will not ask for my right to speak, as that right has been given to me by the Most High.

> **Amir Sulaiman**, poet. Statement, "The High Cost of Free Speech," detailing his harassment by the FBI for poetry they told him was "anti-American," 2004

The long history of anti-obscenity laws makes it very clear that such laws are most often invoked against political and life-style dissidents.

> **Gloria Steinem**, activist, writer. *Ms. Magazine,* October 1973

Not by our mouths will we let fear silence us.

> **Author unknown.**

The only way to make sure people you agree with can speak is to support the rights of people you don't agree with.

> **Eleanor Holmes Norton**, former U.S. Congresswoman. *New York Post*, 1970

I disapprove of what you say, but will defend to the death your right to say it.

> **S.G. Tallentyre**. *The Friends of Voltaire*, 1906

You can't burn an argument. Ideas do not need visas. You can't keep it out.

> **Arundhati Roy**, Indian writer, activist, on the burning of copies of her book condemning a dam project by the dam's supporters, India. Interview, *Satya* magazine, April 2000

Where they have burned books, they will end in burning human beings.

> **Heinrich Heine**, German poet, playwright. From play "Almansor," 1821

In the "free" market, free speech has become a commodity like everything else: justice, human rights, drinking water, clean air. It's available only to those who can afford it.

Arundhati Roy, Indian writer, activist. Essay, "The Loneliness of Noam Chomsky," 8/24/2003

Freedom of the press is limited to those who own one.

A.J. Liebling. Attributed.

I am not one of those who shy away from protesting injustice and oppression, arguing that they are expected in a military regime. The military do not act alone. They are supported by a gaggle of politicians, lawyers, judges, academics and businessmen, all of them hiding under the claim that they are only doing their duty, men and women too afraid to wash their pants of urine.

Ken Saro-Wiwa, Nigerian Ogoni writer, human rights/environmental activist. From his closing statement at Nigerian military tribunal prior to his execution, 1995

Listen well: We are the colour of the earth! Without us, money would not exist, and we know well how to live without the colour of money. But do not be concerned. We have not come to exploit anyone, so we shall not engage in competition with you...lower your voice and listen, because there is now another voice which has not come to steal or to impose, but something more serious: to take your place. This voice is ours. The voice of those who are the colour of the earth.

Representative of the Zapatista National Liberation Army (EZLN), Speech, Mexico City, March 2001

Those of us who speak out are moved by a deep sense of the fragility of our self-worth. It is the determination to protect our sense of who we are that leads us to risk criticism, alienation, and serious loss while most others, similarly harmed, remain silent.

Derrick Bell, educator, activist. In *Race in America*, 1993

People who know me, ask me how I can stand in front of a TV camera and know that I am speaking to the people of the world. Seven weeks ago I would not have been able to do so. But seven weeks ago there was no need to do so.

Michael Berg, father of Nick Berg, a U.S. contractor in Iraq beheaded on video by insurgents, in a statement in which he calls for world peace and places blame for the death on President George Bush.

A time comes when silence is betrayal.
Martin Luther King Jr., civil rights leader. Speech, 4/4/1967

If the government just came in and shut us all down, it would be more apparent who the enemy is, and we could adjust accordingly. But censorship by omission is worse, because in effect it's a way of leaving the door open, letting you think freedom of expression is possible in certain instances, when really the (corporate executives who control radio, TV and the record industry) have made up their minds to make that impossible.
Paris, hip hop MC. *Oakland Tribune*, 4/21/03

When society is threatened, that's when you need to be able to speak out without fear of intimidation or fear of losing rights or being imprisoned. And if you can't guarantee those rights when times are tough then what the hell's the point of saying that we are a democracy, blah, blah, blah. People go to war and die for those rights.
David Suzuki, Canadian environmentalist. Interview, *PBS*, 8/29/2003

Chapter 21

"Mightier Than the Sword"
Words, Writing, Language

we fear language
an electric cattle prod
to drive us into corners
where we cower
for fear of being called
terrorists or communists or
criminals

> **Marilyn Buck**, U.S. political prisoner, convicted of conspiracy
> in the prison escape of Assata Shakur. From poem, "For Fear of
> Being Called," 1996

It is not only by shooting bullets in the battlefields that tyranny is overthrown, but also by hurling of ideas of redemption, words of freedom and terrible anathema's against the hangman that people bring down dictators and empires.

> **Emiliano Zapata**, Mexican revolutionary, 1914

In this land, they wield words like weapons
Lobbing grenades behind my back

> **Quincy Tran**, poet. From untitled poem, 2000

If the word has the potency to revive and make us free, it has also the power to blind, imprison and destroy.

> **Ralph Ellison**, writer, educator. Essay, "Twentieth-Century
> Fiction and the Black Mask of Humanity," 1946

Derogatory terms do not mean; they assault. Their intention is not to communicate but to harm. Thus they are not discursive signs or linguistic statements but modes of aggression. They express a structure of power and domination, a hierarchy that contextualizes them and gives them their force. As gestures of assault they reflect their users status as a member of the dominant group. The derogatory term does more than speak; it silences.

> **Steve Martinot and Jared Sexton**. Essay, "The Avant-garde of
> White Supremacy," 2002

How smooth must be the language of the whites, when they can make right look like wrong, and wrong like right.

Black Hawk, Sauk leader, warrior, late 1800s. In *The Wisdom of Native Americans,* 1999

I like fighting with words. My words whoop people's asses many a day before I have to use my fists.
Cheryl Wright, activist. Philadelphia, PA, 2002

What are the words you do not yet have? What do you need to say? What are the tyrannies you swallow day by day and attempt to make your own, until you will sicken and die of them, still in silence?
Audre Lorde, educator, activist, poet. *Sister Outsider,* 1984

I detest writing. The process itself epitomizes the European concept of "legitimate" thinking; what is written has an importance that is denied the spoken. My culture, the Lakota culture, has an oral tradition, so I ordinarily reject writing. It is one of the white world's ways of destroying the cultures of non-European peoples, the imposing of an abstraction over the spoken relationship of a people.
Russell Means, activist, actor, former leader in the American Indian Movement. Speech, Black Hills International Survival Gathering, July 1980

The white people must think that paper has some mysterious power to help them in the world. The Indian needs no writings; words that are true sink deep into his heart, where they remain. He never forgets them. On the other hand, if the white man loses his papers, he is helpless.
Four Guns, Lakota judge, late 1800s. In *The Wisdom of Native Americans,* 1999

Rastafarianism is word power. In words we have seen the power of creation. One is not op-pressed, but down-pressed. We do not have under-standing: with wisdom comes over-standing. The emphasis is on the positive.
D. Harris, Jamaican educator. In *Dreads*, 1997

[Literature] can make us identify with situations and people far away. If it does that, it's a miracle. I tell my students, it's not difficult to identify with somebody like yourself, somebody next door who looks like you. What's more difficult is to identify with someone you don't see, who's very far away, who's a different color, who eats a different kind of food. When you begin to do that then literature is really performing its wonders.
Chinua Achebe, Nigerian writer, educator. Interview, *Atlantic online*, August 2000

Beneath the rule of men entirely great, the pen is mightier than the sword.
Edward Bulwer-Lytton, English writer, 1803-1873

It does not require many words to speak the truth.
Chief Joseph, Nez Perce leader. Statement, Washington, DC. *North American Review*, 1879

The liberation of language is rooted in the liberation of ourselves.
Mary Daly, theologian, educator. *Beyond God the Father*, 1973

I have heard talk and talk, but nothing is done. Good words do not last long unless they amount to something. Words do not pay for my dead people. They do not pay for my country, now overrun by white men. They do not protect my father's grave.
Chief Joseph, Nez Perce leader. Statement, Washington, DC. *North American Review*, 1879

The fact that I write at all reveals the utter failure of their intimidation tactics—as does the fact that you read.
Mumia Abu-Jamal, journalist, U.S. political prisoner. From message to his supporters and readers, circa 2001

Sit down and read. Educate yourself for the coming conflicts.
Mother Jones, union organizer, activist. Attributed.

Chapter 22

"Until Lions Write Books"

History

history is a living weapon in yr hand
& you have imagined it, it is thus that you
"find out for yourself"
history is the dream of what can be, it is
the relation between things in a continuum
of imagination.

    Diane Di Prima, poet. From poem "Rant," 1990

History, depending on how it is told, can be used as a weapon to divide us further or as a vehicle to seek truths that might bring us to greater mutual understanding.

    Yuri Kochiyama, activist, writer. *Blu Magazine*, 2001

The struggle we engage in is over whose story will triumph, the rapist's story or the raped woman's, the child abuser's or the child's, the stories of bigoted police officers or those of families of color whose children are being murdered...the stories of the abused are full of dangerous, subversive revelations that undermine the whole fabric of inequality.

    Aurora Levins Morales, historian, activist, writer. *Medicine Stories,* 1998

Either we're gonna tell our own history or our oppressors will make a history for us.

    Assata Shakur, former Black Panther, in exile in Cuba, on why she wrote her autobiography. Interview, *BET.com*, 2001

In order to create an alternative an oppressed group must at once shatter the self-reflecting world which encircles it and, at the same time, project its own image onto history.

    Sheila Rowbotham, historian, educator. *Women's Consciousness, Man's World*, 1973

I am certain that the seed we have surrendered into the worthy conscience of thousands and thousands of Chileans, will not be able to be reaped at one stroke. They have the power, they can make us their vassals, but can not stop the social processes, neither by crime nor by force. History is ours and is made by the people.

    Salvador Allende, Chilean President, physician, from last speech hours before his death as his government was overthrown in a rightwing coup, Santiago, Chile, 9/11/1973

We are not makers of history. We are made by history.
> **Martin Luther King, Jr.**, civil rights activist. *Strength to Love*, 1963

Power recalls the past not to remember but to sanctify, to justify the perpetuation of privilege by right of inheritance.
> **Eduardo Galeano**, Uruguayan historian, educator. *Upside Down*, 1998

The mainstream is so polluted with lies
Once you get wet, it's so hard to get dry
We're all taught how to justify history as it passes by
And it's your world that comes crashing down
When the big boys decide to throw their weight around
> **Ani DiFranco**, singer. From song "Roll With It," 1991

No historian would accept accounts of Nazi officials as to what happened in Nazi Germany because those accounts were written to justify that regime. Yet American historians are still subjective about their own history with a few exceptions.
> **Roxanne Dunbar Ortiz**, educator. Testimony before U.S. District Court, Lincoln, Nebraska, 1974

As long as someone controls your history
The truth shall remain just a mystery
> **Ben Harper**, singer. From song, "People Lead," 1995

The books you read were written by men who conquered this place. Look with care at the reasons they put on their pages, because if you accept them without question, you will not understand the truth of the land, but rather the truth of men.
> **Ermilo Abreu Gómez**, Mexican writer. *Canek,* 1979

People who imagine that history flatters them (as it does, indeed, since they wrote it) are impaled on their history like a butterfly on a pin and become incapable of seeing or changing themselves, or the world. This is the place in which it seems to me, most white Americans find themselves. Impaled. They are dimly, or vividly, aware that the history they have fed themselves is mainly a lie, but they do not know how to release themselves from it, and they suffer enormously from the resulting personal incoherence.

James Baldwin, writer, educator. *Ebony,* August 1965

Until lions write books, history will always glorify the hunter.

Proverb, South Africa

For the rich and the privileged it's easy to pretend that history doesn't exist. On the other hand, for the people at the wrong end of the guns, they have a way of paying attention to what actually happens in the world and they remember and draw conclusions from it.

Noam Chomsky, political analyst, linguist. Interview, *Guerrilla News Network,* 12/17/2003

World history would indeed be very easy to make if the struggle were taken up only on condition of infallibly favorable chances.

Karl Marx, German political theorist. Letter, 1878

Chicano history predates Plymouth Rock and Jamestown... When we start relating to what we are and where we come from we will start becoming proud of ourselves.

Rodolfo "Corky" Gonzales, activist, writer. *A War of Words,* 1985

Those who cannot remember the past are condemned to repeat it.

George Santayana, Spanish educator, poet. *The Life of Reason,* 1905

History is a light that illuminates the past, and a key that unlocks the door to the future.

Runoko Rashidi, historian, writer.

Human history is a history not only of cruelty but also of compassion, sacrifice, courage, kindness. What we choose to emphasize in this complex history will determine our lives.

Howard Zinn, historian, educator. Essay, "The Optimism of Uncertainty," September 2004

When you know the beginning well, the end will not trouble you.

Proverb, origin unknown

As the future ripens in the past, so the past rots in the present.
>   **Tariq Ali**, English historian, writer. Essay, "New Labour, New
>   Bombs," 2001

Knowledge of history must go hand in hand with a rich appreciation for the diverse cultures of Africa. We must see our ancestors as the initiators of world history, and not as its victims. The art, the literature, the song, the dance, can create a litany of healing and reconciliation. The power of a people with a firm grasp of its history is formidable, and we Africans have the wealth of all history behind us.
>   **Ayanna Gillian**, writer, speaking to Africans in the African
>   Diaspora. Essay, "Our World Was Never Wrenched From Its True
>   Course," 2004

History will one day have its say; it will not be the history taught in the United Nations, Washington, Paris, or Brussels…but the history taught in the countries that have rid themselves of colonialism and its puppets.
>   **Patrice Lumumba**, Congolese political leader. From letter to his
>   wife, January 1961

What passes for identity in America is a series of myths about one's heroic ancestors.
>   **James Baldwin**, writer, educator. "A Talk to Teachers," 1963

The history of an oppressed people is hidden in the lies and the agreed-upon myth of its conquerors.
>   **Meridel Le Sueur**, writer. *Crusaders,* 1955

The muse of history, dipping her iron pen in the generous blood of the Negro, has written large across the page of that Preamble and the face of the Declaration of Independence the words, "sham," "hypocrisy."
>   **Archibald Henry Grimké**, attorney, activist. *The Shame of*
>   *America or the Negro's Case Against the Republic,* 1924

Neither morality nor immorality can simply be conferred upon us by history. Merely being part of the United States, without regard to our own acts and ideas, does not make us moral or immoral beings. History is more complicated than that.
>   **James Loewen**, historian. *Lies My Teacher Told Me,* 1995

The African in America will look for his history in Africa. That's where it begins. If you don't begin your history in Africa, you will never have history, you just have slave history.

> **Kwame Toure**, formerly Stokely Carmichael, civil rights and Black power activist. Speech, 1997

You cannot subjugate a man and recognize his humanity, his history and his personality; so, systematically, you must take this away from him. You begin by telling lies about this man's role in history.

> **John Henrik Clarke**, historian. Speech, New York City, 1969

Textbooks should show history as contingent, affected by the power of ideas and individuals. Instead, they present history as a "done deal."

> **James Loewen**, historian. *Lies My Teacher Told Me*, 1995

Let's start with the past, which people often want to avoid. It's history, they say. Get over it—don't get stuck in the past. But this advice to forget history is selective; many of the same folks who tell indigenous people not to get stuck in the past are also demanding that schoolchildren get more instruction in the accomplishments of the Founding Fathers.

> **Robert Jensen**, writer. Essay "What the 'Fighting Sioux' Tells Us About Whites," 2003

Anything is possible! We as a people hold the power of a raging ocean, together there is no measure to our depths. We are the masters of this universe and for some reason we tend to allow that 'power' to fall into the wrong hands...

> **Iriel Sayeed**, activist, poet. Essay, "A World Called Me!" 2004

Considering that virtually none of the standard fare surrounding Thanksgiving contains an ounce of authenticity, historical accuracy, or cross-cultural perception, why is it so apparently ingrained? Is it necessary to the American psyche to perpetually exploit and debase its victims in order to justify its history?

> **Michael Dorris**. Essay, "Why I'm Not Thankful for Thanksgiving," 1978

And you, are you so forgetful of your past, is there no echo in your soul of your poets' songs, your dreamers' dreams, your rebels' calls?

> **Emma Goldman**, activist, writer, anarchist. Attributed.

Because I have the power to resurrect the past

train it like a pit bull
and sic it on your ass!
> **Turiya Autry and Walidah Imarisha**, activists, poets. From
> poem "Supa Soul Sistas," 2000

There is nothing more powerful than an idea whose time has come.
> **Victor Hugo**, French writer, poet. Attributed.

Everyone needs to identify with their own history. If they know their history, they can construct their future.
> **Assata Shakur**, former Black Panther, in exile in Cuba. Interview,
> "From Exile With Love," 2001

In this great future, you can't forget your past.
> **Bob Marley**, Jamaican reggae singer. From song "No Woman,
> No Cry," 1974

Our history is stolen from us. We are stripped of our names. We are made into caricatures in a burlesque written by those who despise us or know nothing at all of us.
> **Aurora Levins Morales**, historian, activist, writer. *Medicine
> Stories,* 1998

If the warriorz that made it through the battle don't tell their story, then how will the truth ever get documented? If the truth never gets documented how will we know if we're being lied to? If we don't know we're being lied to then we can easily be led astray.
> **J.P. Ablo**, activist. Essay, "Banned for Life," *Blu Magazine,*
> 2001

From broken promises
of the past
People learn that surety
is found only
in their own firm grasp
> **Michele Gibbs**, poet, writer. From poem "it's simple/but not
> easy," 1996

Chapter 23

"The Long Haul"

Political Commitment and Perseverance

I have been unable to live an uncommitted or suspended life. I have not hesitated to declare my affiliation with an extremely unpopular cause.

> **Edward Said**, writer, literary critic, educator, referring to his work supporting self-determination for his homeland, Palestine. *Out of Place*, 2000

By John Jonik

I don't see it as a supreme effort, it's a way of life: if you believe in freedom, if you believe in justice, if you believe in democracy, if you believe in people's rights, if you believe in the harmony of all humankind, I don't know if you have any other choice than to be there for as long as it takes.

> **Harry Belafonte**, actor, singer, activist, on why he supports the

Cuban Revolution. Interview, *Cuba Now*, 10/25/2003

I used to think we struggle some years, we win and then it's over. But I realize this planet is so twisted and raped and violated, that it will take lifetimes to make this place livable, to deal with the needs of people. For me, my lifestyle has to always incorporate struggle, that revolution is not around the corner, that I'm in this for the long haul.

> **Assata Shakur**, former Black Panther, in exile in Cuba. Interview, *BET.com*, 2001

Men fight and lose the battle, and the thing that they fought for comes about in spite of their defeat, and then it turns out not to be what they meant, and other men have to fight for what they meant under another name.

> **William Morris**, English writer, poet. "News From Nowhere," 1890

People who are involved in this revolution should make up their minds here and now that this is a life long commitment. It's not something that's going to end in five or ten years. It should be our life, not just some part-time extra-curricular activity that we're involved in, because it is serious. It is a life and death situation... People need to do this for themselves. Not for Ramona, not for MOVE, not for Mumia, not for Leonard Peltier, but for themselves and their families.

> **Ramona Africa**, activist, MOVE Organization member. Interview, *Insubordination* magazine, May 2002

I am a Sun Dancer. I took a vow for my people. I chose to seek the Creator's will and to follow it to the best of my ability. I WILL NOT STAND DOWN FROM THAT VOW. I will continue to speak, write and organize until Grandfather himself quiets my life. If I can do this in prison, I have no doubt you can do much better from where you stand. I encourage you to do your best, be kind to one another, seek harmony and balance with all natural life, enjoy what freedom you have left, and most of all, never, never give up.

> **Leonard Peltier**, writer, U.S. political prisoner. "Anniversary Statement," 1/23/2004

The passion for truth and justice is not a sprint. It's a long-distance run that requires a different kind of training, a different degree of commitment. Our eye must be on a goal that we know we will never reach in our lifetimes. Faith is the name of believing in the transcendent, often despite all evidence to the contrary.

> **Richard Thieme**, writer, activist. Essay, "My Last Talk with Gary Webb," 12/14/2004

Even if I do not see the fruits, the struggle has been worthwhile. If my life has taught me anything, it is that one must fight.

> **Ella Winter**, writer. *And Not to Yield*, 1963

You said that wheat and strife fall upon the land. And that only wheat gives bread. You are right. Here we say that cynicism and rebellion fall upon the land, and that only rebellion brings tomorrows.

> **Subcomandante Marcos**, Mexican Zapatista revolutionary, writer. *Letter to Jóse Saramago*, 12/1/1999

Revolution is a serious thing, the most serious thing about a revolutionary's life. When one commits oneself to the struggle, it must be for a lifetime.

> **Angela Davis**, activist, educator, writer. Attributed.

Chapter 24

"TV Nation"

The Media

Yeah, art may imitate life
But life imitates TV
    Ani DiFranco, singer. From song "Superhero," 1996

The beauty of the democratic systems of thought control, as contrasted with their clumsy totalitarian counterparts, is that they operate by subtly establishing on a voluntary basis...presuppositions that set the limits of debate, rather than by imposing beliefs with a bludgeon. Then let the debate rage; the more lively and vigorous it is, the better the propaganda system is served.
    Noam Chomsky, political analyst, linguist. *After the Cataclysm*, 1979

The media are not *close* to corporate America. They're not *favorable* to corporate America, they *are* corporate America, they're an integral part of corporate America.
    Michael Parenti, historian, writer. Speech, in *The Vinyl Project*, from the Freedom Archives, 2003

Propaganda is to a democracy what violence is to a dictatorship.
    William Blum, writer. *Rogue State*, 2000

Tell me who's got control of your mind, your worldview
Is it the news or the movie you taking your girl to?
    Dead Prez, hip hop group. From song "Propaganda," 2000

Journalists like to think of themselves as a skeptical lot. This is a flawed self-image. The thickest pack of American journalists are all too credulous when dealing with government officials, technical experts, and other official sources. They save their vaunted "skepticism" for ideas that feel unfamiliar to them.
    Jonathan Vankin, writer. *Conspiracies, Cover-ups and Crimes*, 1991

I think that we simply have to be clear about the fact that the media is part of the state's arsenal, they never contradict the state... A guy with a trench coat doesn't meet with all the reporters overnight, to tell them what to write or their editors what to print. These caffeine crazed patriots censor themselves.

> **Kuwasi Balagoon**, former Black Panther and Black Liberation Army member. *A Soldier's Story*, 2001

Correspondents for *The New York Times* like Anthony Lewis or Tom Wicker get very angry when people say look what you're doing, you're subordinate to power. They say no one is telling them what to write. And that's right, nobody is telling them what to write, but if they weren't writing those things they wouldn't have the columns.

> **Noam Chomsky**, political analyst, linguist. Interview, *Guerrilla News Network*, 12/17/2003

By John Jonik

It is not enough for journalists to see themselves as mere messengers without understanding the hidden agendas of the message and myths that surround it.

> **John Pilger**, English filmmaker, writer, 1999

Journalists must seek and speak the truth, for we are the voice of the voiceless millions.

Razia Bhatti, Pakistani journalist, 1994. Attributed.

Commitment need not give rise to propaganda: the writer can make his stand known without advocating it…in two dimensional terms, i.e., in terms of one response to one stimulus.

Ezekiel Mphahlele, South African scholar, writer. *Voices in the Whirlwind and Other Essays*, 1972

My kids used to hate the press, because they felt reporters would come, talk to mama, make mama cry, and then leave. And then life would resume, as before. It didn't do a thing for us, except bring mama some misery.

Elizabeth Eckford, public servant, Pulaski County, AR. Speaking of when she was a desegregation activist for Little Rock's Central High School in 1957. *CNN.com*, 5/17/2004

There is now an increasingly ignored minority in Britain—the intelligent viewer. This minority crosses every possible divide: class, gender, age, race and political affiliations.

Tariq Ali, English historian, writer. Essay, "No Room at the Inn for Mr. Biswas," November 2001

I don't see why people are so upset about cloning sheep. American television networks have been doing that to their audiences for years.

Jello Biafra, singer, poet, activist. Interview, 4/2/1997

I'll never forget CNN saying that 'thousands of people have died today in Rwanda' for 18 seconds. Then they had a one and a half minute feature on the Rwandan gorilla that is becoming extinct.

Saul Williams, hip hop MC, activist. Speech, 1/31/2003

The era of manufacturing consent has given way to the era of manufacturing news. Soon media newsrooms will drop the pretense, and start hiring theatre directors instead of journalists.

Arundhati Roy, Indian writer, activist. Speech, 5/13/2003

By John Jonik

How are we to perceive the world we live in? It is a world described by those who have the microphone. And it is not us in the South who have the microphone.

> **Manfred Max-Neef**, Chilean economist, educator. "Challenging the Notion of 'Underdevelopment,'" 2004

The airwaves belong to the public just like water, just like air, just like the national park system. The airwaves are a national resource, and we have a right as the public to demand that a larger chunk of it be dedicated to our interests.

> **Steve Rendall**, media annalist. Interview, *Guerrilla News Network,* 9/9/2003

Very often there are stories put in the newspapers that I am to be hanged. I don't want that anymore. When a man tries to do right, such stories should

not be put in the newspapers.
>**Geronimo, Apache** medicine man and warrior. From conference with General George Crook of the U.S. Army, 1886

The major media, like its racist projections, is to be rejected, not consumed. For your very patronage gives it life.
>**Mumia Abu-Jamal**, journalist, U.S. political prisoner. Essay, "Media is the Mirage," 1998

Don't hate the media. Become the media.
>**Jello Biafra**, singer, poet, activist. Coined phrase.

Independent media in America is better called "starvation" media: journalists that want to do real reporting don't survive long—Bob Parry, who uncovered the Iran-Contra scandal, lost his job at the AP, Seymour Hersh was pushed off the New York Times—and I'm in exile. Investigative reporting is a quick career path to disemployment.
>**Greg Palast**, writer. Interview, *Truthout.com*, 2003

I know that it is hard to understand why people didn't seem to react to the Japanese internment. A lot of people ask me how could average citizens sit back and let that happen. But a lot of people didn't know the full extent of what was happening. The press didn't report it. I think that is a commentary on the media in 1942 as well as the media today. I still don't think we're getting all the stories.
>**Alba Witkin**, activist who worked with Japanese Americans at the internment camps of the 1940s. *ColorLines RaceWire*, May 2003

Power is very fragile. It can be overthrown. It doesn't take much to overthrow it, even tyrants and surely in more democratic societies. It's very fragile. So as soon as the discipline breaks down, it will be overthrown and they know it. That's why you have such a massive commitment to propaganda, much more so in the free societies than in the tyrannies.
>**Noam Chomsky**, political analyst, linguist. Interview, *Guerrilla News Network*, 12/17/2003

If you allow someone to control the questions surrounding an issue, then you allow them to control the answers, the solutions. The American media has such control.
>**Richard Becker**, activist. Speech, 5/17/2003

TV is a weapon of mass confusion.
    John Parker, activist. Speech, May 2003

Chapter 25

"The Irresistible Revolution"

Art, Music, Expression, Culture

The question is not whether poetry and politics can mix. That question is a luxury for those who can afford it.
> **Martín Espada**, poet, educator. *Poetry Like Bread,* 1994

Art is not a mirror held up to reality, but a hammer with which to shape it.
> **Bertolt Brecht**, German playwright, poet. Attributed.

I was born poor—and colored—and almost all of the prettiest roses I have seen have been in rich people's yards, not in mine. That is why I cannot write exclusively about roses and moonlight—for sometimes in the moonlight my brothers see a fiery cross and a circle of Klansmen's hoods. Sometimes in the moonlight a dark body swings from a lynching tree, but for his funeral there are no roses.
> **Langston Hughes**, writer, poet. Essay, "My Adventures As a Social Poet," 1947

The artist must take sides. He must elect to fight for freedom or slavery. I have made my choice. I had no alternative.
> **Paul Robeson**, activist, scholar, athlete. Speech, 1934

In this climate of anger and fear the question becomes: Where are your allegiances? And can we see those allegiances in your art? If you think that you can avoid having an allegiance, taking a side, then you have done so even in your attempt not to.
> **Ewuare Osayande**, educator, activist, poet. Essay, "Art at War: Revolutionary Art Against Cultural Imperialism," 2004

For me, rap is not a game. It's war. And in this war, rap speaks directly to those who are suffering.
> **Mano Brown**, Brazilian hip hop MC. *Vibe* magazine, November 2002

When the higher forces give you the gift of music, musicianship should be used for the good of humanity.
> **Fela Kuti**, Nigerian singer. Recorded comment.

Hip hop is just something that gets us on the tube, gets us in the media light, something to put the people to sleep. And if you're put in a position that

they think is gonna put people to sleep, it's the responsibility of the athlete or entertainer to say, 'ok, I don't want to put people to sleep, I want to wake them back up.'
>   **Chuck D**, hip hop MC, activist. Comment, circa 1993

What is needed is to return art to the people as a means of expression of their lives. The people have been robbed of this—the power to formulate their own view of the world... To be revolutionary in art today is to act to return the right to culture to the people.
>   **John Weber**, muralist, educator. "Two Letters on Revolutionary Art," 1972

All poets are political. Some just maintain the status quo; some talk about change. Period. So on that level we read some people, and we can see what they are doing. They are out there to maintain the status quo. And there are some who are out there to change.
>   **Sonia Sanchez**, educator, poet, writer. In *Heroism In The New Black Poetry*, 1990

To rebel or revolt against the status quo is in the very nature of an artist.
>   **Uta Hagen**, actress, educator. *Respect for Acting*, 1973

What do you think an artist is? An imbecile who has only eyes, if he is a painter, or ears if he is a musician, or a lyre in every chamber of his heart if he is a poet, or even, if he is a boxer, just his muscles? Far from it: at the same time, he is also a political being, constantly aware of the heartbreaking, passionate, or delightful things that happen in the world, shaping himself completely in their image. How could it be possible to feel no interest in other people, and with a cool indifference to detach yourself from the very life which they bring to you so abundantly? No, painting is not done to decorate apartments. It is an instrument of war.
>   **Pablo Picasso**, Spanish painter, circa 1945

The independence of the artist is one of the great safeguards of the freedom of the human spirit.
>   **Cicely Veronica Wedgwood**, English historian. *Velvet Studies*, 1946

The poet must not put himself in the place of a Christ, a prophet or a politician. The first thing is to express your feelings and your ideas about a given situation, you should not try to write poems to change things, you should write poems to express your ideas... It would appear that I am deliberately sitting to write to oppose the system, but it is my ideas.

>**Mutabaruka**, Jamaican poet, activist. From public internet forum, 2003

At a time when the media were denied the possibility of performing their most basic duty, that of reporting, writers, actors, dancers, musicians, painters, sculptors were forced to assume much of this function—in order to ensure, quite simply, that people were informed about what was happening in the silences surrounding them.

>**Andre Brink**, South African educator. *Reinventions*, 1996

Strike fear and incomprehension in the minds of the powerful. Disrupt the dominant trance. Be calculatedly unpredictable and undermine the spectacle by introducing music of a disorienting or ecstatic nature into the sterile political discourse. Disrupt the stale dichotomy of leftist protest and police cliché. Facilitate the self-actualization of the mob. Be the dope propaganda.

>**Infernal Noise Brigade**, activist marching drum orchestra. From their mission statement for the Seattle, WA protests against the World Trade Organization, 1999

For nearly 300 years we've sung the sorry songs. We shall yet sing the songs of rejoicing and triumph.

>**William Tecumseh Vernon**, minister. Speech, 1905

I write to keep in contact with our ancestors and to spread truth to people.

>**Sonia Sanchez**, educator, poet, writer. In *Black Women Writers at Work*, 1983

I write songs to fan the flames of discontent.

>**Joe Hill**, singer, labor movement martyr. In *Great Labor Quotations*, 2000

Artists are here to disturb the peace.

>**James Baldwin**, writer, educator. *Conversations with James Baldwin*, 1989

Arming You Is Not Harming You
Harming You Is Not Alarming You

Alarming You Is Not Calming You
into submission

> **Tony Medina**, poet, educator. From poem "Ways of Seeing & Saying on Ways of Being," *No Noose is Good Noose*, Harlem River Press, 1998

Poetry of the political imagination is a matter of both vision and language. Any progressive social change must be imagined first, and that vision must find its most eloquent possible expression to move from vision to reality. Any oppressive social condition, before it can change, must be named and condemned in words that persuade by stirring the emotions, awakening the senses. Thus is the need for the political imagination.

> **Martín Espada**, poet, educator. *Poetry Like Bread,* 1994

Even though [Public Enemy] sold millions of albums, nothing much has changed as a result of it. The problem is, there's no institution for liberation the music can reflect. If you have no institution for your people to reinforce your music, then you're really wasting your time. All your songs make no difference.

> **Aaron Brown**, hip hop MC, activist. In *Bomb the Suburbs*, 1994

Progressive and revolutionary art is inconceivable outside the context of political movements for radical change.

> **Angela Davis**, activist, educator, writer. *Women, Culture and Politics*, 1990

The role of the revolutionary artist is to make revolution irresistible.

> **Toni Cade Bambara**, writer, activist. Attributed

There are no revolutions without poets.

> **Rodolfo "Corky" Gonzales**, activist, writer. *I Am Joaquin*, 1972

Revolution is not only won by numbers, but by visionaries, and if artists aren't visionaries, then we have no business doing what we do.

> **Cherríe Moraga**, writer, educator. Essay, "Art in America Con Acento," 1983

Any song that points out something that is wrong, needs fixing, and shows you how to fix it—is the undying song of the working people. If it is made a little jazzy or sexy that ain't wrong—what book could you read to a crowd that would make them dance?

> **Woody Guthrie**, folk singer. *Woody Sez*, 1975

Photo by Hans Bennet

To be a Latino writer and not be political is to be impervious to the needs of your people—and as a Latino writer, you soon learn that all suffering people are your people.

    Gloria Vando, poet. In *Contemporary Hispanic Quotations*, 2003

The values that North America is selling abroad are not the values of its wonderful literature nor its art in general, but the values of McDonald's and Mickey Mouse—in other words, the free market. The free market and literature are not always good allies.

    Yanira Paz, educator, poet. *American Notes and Quiries,* Summer 1997

Art is more powerful when working as an ally of the powerless than it is

when allied to repression. For its essential nature is freedom.
Ngugi Wa Thiong'o, Kenyan playwright, educator. Attributed.

The truth in the hands of artists, even when they are telling a fiction, even when they are inventing something, becomes a very powerful thing. Because what artists do is lend passion and emotion—they lend a kind of spiritual element to reality that enhances the truth, which gives it an intensity that a simple matter of recounting facts will not accomplish.
Howard Zinn, historian, educator. *Resonance Magazine*, November 2003

Art is a lie that makes us realize the truth.
Pablo Picasso, Spanish painter. Attributed.

Everything is changing. People are taking the comedians seriously and the politicians as a joke.
Will Rogers, writer, actor, comedian, 1879-1935

If there are political programs on TV, yet it takes an artist to actually energize political debate, that tells you something really quite frightening about the level of the political debate happening...the political framework itself is so dead and closed that people look to other sources, like artists, because art and music allow people a certain freedom.
Thom Yorke, of rock group Radiohead. *Resonance Magazine*, November 2003

The poet today must be twice-born. She must have begun as a poet, she must have understood the suffering of the world as political...and on the other side of politics she must be reborn again as a poet.
Adrienne Rich, writer, poet. 1974. Attributed.

I have always rejected any special responsibility for the artist... My horizons on humanity are enlarged by reading the writers of poems, seeing a painting, listening to some music, some opera, which has nothing at all to do with a volatile human condition or struggle or whatever. It enriches me as a human being. And so the artists who are lucky to be temperamentally gifted that way should not be tempted to make propaganda of their lives.
Wole Soyinka, Nigerian playwright, educator. Interview, April 1998

I create social images within the work so far as the human condition is social. I create racial identities so far as the subjects are Negro, but I have not created protest images because the world within the collage, if it is authentic, retains the right to speak for itself.

Romare Bearden, painter. Interview, *Art News*, October 1964

When poems stop talking about the moon and begin to mention poverty, trade unions, color, color lines and colonies, somebody tells the police.

Langston Hughes, writer, poet. Essay, "My Adventures As a Social Poet," 1947

The anger that people hear coming from some of the MCs are just these individuals being honest about how they see the world around them. The negative stuff is part of human experience. You can't look down on people for that. They are channeling their anger into rhyming about things instead of acting it out on the physical level. It is a good thing. It's therapy.

Kevin Fitzgerald, filmmaker. Interview, 2003

Now some will say cop killer music might incite
But killer cops wup on niggas each and every night
So tell me who's to blame for the hate that hate produced

Paris, hip hop MC. From song "Bring It To Ya," 1994

The fact that many people of various ages and cultures have some understanding of the joy and pain of the present condition of oppressed people and awareness of Political Prisoners and Prisoners of War is because Tupac and rappers of the hip hop nation have established rap as the revolutionary culture.

Mutulu Shakur, former acupuncturist, activist, now a U.S. political prisoner. Essay, "The FBI and My Son Tupac," *Blu Magazine*, 2000

Hip hop culture speaks directly to our spirit, and that spirit gives birth to our ideas…there are rebels like me out there who are doing more than just writing our name on shit, we are campaigning for revolutionary change. The potential for hip hop to bring about revolutionary change is astronomical.

Refa 1, graffiti artist. *Blu Magazine*, 2000

There is a seed of revolution within the essence of all forms of hip hop culture.

Black August Collective. *Statement of Purpose*, circa 2000

I love hip hop because somebody has to call a muthafucka a muthafucka, and they do that.
> **Nikki Giovanni**, poet. In *The Tables Have Turned,* 2000

Where I come from you can walk up to anyone, and they'll kick the dopest rhyme you've ever heard, but it doesn't matter because people need jobs, and there aren't enough.
> **Ghetto Bastard**, South African hip hop MC. Interview, *Blu Magazine*, 2000

Fear is a prerequisite to bravery and courage...the fearlessness of the MC is probably one of the strongest attractions that people have toward hip hop.
> **Flo Brown**, hip hop MC. Interview, *Blu Magazine*, 2001

[Hip hop] is not just dance music. It's about knowing yourself and knowing who is against you and who is trying to bring you down.
> **Ice Cube**, hip hop MC, actor. *Rap*, 1991

This music is not about rebellion for rebellion's sake. It suggests a revolution within the revolution. The intention, though, is to be constructive and responsible about how we approach the issues that affect Cuba.
> **Pablo Herrera**, Cuban educator, co-founder of Black August, referring to Cuban hip hop. *Oneworld* magazine, January 2004

They say they blame it on a song
when someone kills a cop
what music did they listen to
when they bombed Iraq?
> **Spearhead**, music group. From song "Crime to be Broke in America," 1994

In these deaths the war on graffiti and the war on youth—converging in the ground of race—became all too real. Make no mistake: "quality of life" campaigns have had a body count.
> **Jeff Chang**, writer, on graffiti artists killed by police and vigilantes. *Colorlines Magazine*, Summer 2002

Are you not aware that when you sing, you are leaders telling your people how they should behave? You have responsibilities with the listeners you captivate. Today in Brazil, probably 60 percent of us sing and dance pornography trying to imitate you. It's tragic. Where are the Malcolm Xs, the Martin Luther Kings, the Black Panthers? American hip hop cannot ruin itself this way. It doesn't have this right. It is the only channel and compass of the 'marginalized,' 'excluded,' 'underprivileged' people in the world village, Earth.

> **Marcio VP**, imprisoned kingpin of the Comando Vermelho, Brazil's largest organized gang. *Vibe* magazine, November 2002

Any person, not just a poet, who has anything to do with activism or artistic endeavors that are visible should do it in the spirit of change and advancement. There's a lot of trendy poets out there. It's irksome. Because you sit there and it's like not only do you suck—simply put—but there's no soul in it, just doing it because it's the thing to do.

> **Ursula Rucker**, poet. Interview, *Ammocity.com*, September 2003

The Spoken Word, the new Black poetry, is quickly becoming commercialized. Black poetry is being prostituted in the name of capitalism. It is no longer art for the people; it is now art for the marketplace. It is no longer art as an act of resistance; it is now art as an act of exploitation. And some of us artists are willing participants in this process of cutting the tongue out of the mouth of Black resistance.

> **Ewuare Osayande**, educator, activist, poet. *So The Spoken Word Won't Be Broken*, 1999

Sometimes I believe that some of these MCs sit down and consciously try to figure out how to get more young black men shot.

> **Taalam Acey**, poet. From poem "When the Smoke Clearz," circa 2002

Life imitates bad art.

> **Gary Delgado**, write, activist. *Colorlines Magazine*, Summer 2002

Poetry, like any other "art" form, is meaningless, that is, has no use—beauty or good...unless it be a specific act actual as dance or childbirth, carved bleeding from history, our experience.

> **Keorapetse Kgositsile**, South African poet. In *The Black Aesthetic*, 1972

Our art is a tool that shields us from becoming numb while looking hard at the suffering from the safety of our homes.

> **Peace by Piece**, female artistic collective. From the Painted Bride Art Center schedule, Philadelphia, PA, Spring 2004

Drummers at a march for peace in Washington, DC following the 9/11/2001 World
Trade Center attacks, 2001. Photo by Nick Cooper.

Much of modern art is devoted to lowering the threshold of what is terrible.
By getting us used to what formerly we could not bear to see or hear, because
it was too shocking, painful, or embarrassing, art changes morals.

> **Susan Sontag**, writer. *On Photography*, 1977

Progressive art can assist people to learn not only about the objective forces
at work in the society in which they live, but also about the intensely social
character of their interior lives. Ultimately, it can propel people toward
social emancipation.

> **Angela Davis**, activist, educator, writer. Attributed.

A work of art is good if it has sprung from necessity.

> **Rainer Maria Rilke**, Czechoslovakian poet. *Letters To a Young
> Poet*, re-issued in 1993

Our art can't afford patience.

> **Jerry Quickley**. From essay on the "Mumia 9/11" record jacket,
> 1999

I have a moral commitment to uphold the history that has created hip-hop, I pity the black man who sells our history for a price.
> **MV Bill**, Brazilian hip hop MC, regarding a boycott of certain U.S. hip hop groups in Brazil. *BET.com*, 2/5/2004

You've Taken My Blues and Gone: A Seminar on Black Dance in White America.
> **Title of Conference**, November 1983

Theater is revolutionary when it awakens the individual in the audience, in the black community in this case, who for so long has tended to express his frustrated creativity in certain self-destructive ways, when it opens up to him the very possibility of participating creatively himself in this larger communal process.
> **Wole Soyinka**, Nigerian playwright, educator. Interview, April 1974

Everyone's Imagination is a sovereign nation!...
To reassure us that we need no man's permission to be free
> **Pedro Pietri**, poet, activist. "El Puerto Rican Embassy Manifesto," circa 1994

It's not just any music that threatens the status quo—some music is the status quo. It's one particular kind of song. The song of the outsider. The disenfranchised. The down-and-out. It's the song of those to whom the promise of justice and equality was not kept.
> **Carol Estes**, writer. Essay, "Whose Afraid Of Music?" 2003

[Peter Tosh] didn't necessarily pick up arms, but his arms was his lyrics.
> **Dermott Hussey**, Jamaican journalist. In *"The Red X Tapes,"* 1992

I am here to play the music and to communicate with the Father spiritually so I can be inspired to make music to awaken the slumbering mentality of people.
> **Peter Tosh**, Jamaican reggae artist. In "The Red X Tapes" 1992

There is no simple formula for the relationship of art to justice. But I do know that art—in my own case the art of poetry—means nothing if it simply decorates the dinner table of power which holds it hostage.
> **Adrienne Rich**, writer, poet. From letter refusing to accept the

National Medal for the Arts award, in protest of the policies of the
Bill Clinton administration, 7/3/1997

The white fathers told us: I think, therefore I am. The Black mother within
each of us—the poet—whispers in our dreams: I feel, therefore I can be
free. Poetry coins the language to express and charter this revolutionary
demand, the implementation of that freedom.

Audre Lorde, educator, activist, poet. *Sister Outsider*, 1984

ink and blood are both thicker
than water
We can hold pens and swords
at the same time
in our hands

Giles Li, poet. From untitled poem, circa 2000

Today we should make poems including iron and steel,
And the poet also should know to lead an attack.

Ho Chi Minh, Vietnamese political leader, poet. *The Prison Diary
of Ho Chi Minh,* 1942

Both radical and conservative have to learn that any mode of creative work,
which with true perception portrays social wrongs earnestly and boldly, may
be a greater menace to our social fabric and a more powerful inspiration
than the wildest harangue of the soapbox orator.

Emma Goldman, activist, writer, anarchist. Forward to *The
Social Significance of Modern Drama,* 1914

All truly great art is propaganda.

Ann Petry. *The Writer's Book*, 1950

Poetry is not a shopping list, a casual disquisition on the colors of the sky,
a soporific daydream, or bumpersticker sloganeering. Poetry is a political
action.

June Jordan, poet, educator. *Colorlines*, Winter 1999

Art…cannot be an egotistic activity engulfed in the limits of pure creation,
free of all human contamination.

Nicolás Guillén, Cuban poet. Speech, Cultural and Scientific
Conference for World Peace, New York, 1949

Deliver me from writers who say the way they live doesn't matter. I'm not sure a bad person can write a good book. If art doesn't make us better, then what on earth is it for?

> **Alice Walker**, writer, poet. In *Wit and Wisdom of Famous American Women*, 1986

One good thing about music, when it hits you feel no pain
So hit me with music, hit me with music

> **Bob Marley**, Jamaican reggae singer. From song "Trenchtown Rock," 1973

Free Your Mind...And Your Ass Will Follow

> **Title of album by the group Funkadelic**, 1971

Each day I think about it, it makes me angry; each day I live it, it makes me wanna holla,' it makes me wanna fight. No doubt this has to be reflected in the music, the art, we make. I, personally, can't pretend everything is all right.

> **Not4Prophet**, lyricist for band Ricanstruction. Interview, *Blu Magazine*, 2000

Musicians, all through the ages, when laws and times have changed, have been a part of it somehow or another... You've got to have a song... You've got to have something to build up your courage, or your belief in yourself.

> **Horace Tapscott**, pianist, Pan Afrikan Peoples Arkestra. Attributed.

If they found out you were a dancer, or a singer at the palace, the Khmer Rouge would have killed you. Sometimes you wanted to feel good, to remember the past, but even thinking about the foods of the past—nobody could say anything about that. Some places they would kill you for that... My teacher told us, 'You know who you are. You know how to do the dance. You have to preserve your culture.' My teacher said, 'If you stop dancing, you lose. Then the one cursing you is the one who wins.'

> **Chamroeun Yin**, choreographer, dancer who learned Cambodian dances in Thai refugee camps, 2004

"Woody Guthrie" by Ricardo Levins Morales

I think in general there is a powerful tradition of denying the existence of politics in art. The easiest answer is what Barthes or Brecht says, that the denial of ideology is an ideology—a bourgeois ideology. The way you protect your interests is by pretending you are not speaking from a historically determined or dialectical place, but rather from some position of immutable truth that lies beyond history and critical thinking.

> **Tony Kushner**, playwright, activist. Interview, *Political Affairs*,
> January 2003

To claim that literature on its own is going to change reality would be an act of madness or arrogance. It seems to me no less foolish to deny that it can aid in making change.

> **Eduardo Galeano**, Uruguayan historian, educator. *In Defense of
> the Word*, 1988

It's very frustrating because as artists our role in society is to fantasize, to imagine things. In Palestine you keep on banging against reality and the situation which is the over cloak of everything. It is always there. You can't escape it; you can't fly too high. You start shaking your wings and you bang into a checkpoint.

> **Nizar Zubi**, of Al Kasaba theater company, Palestine. Interview,
> *Revolutionary Worker*, 2002

The poet is both witness and actor in the historical drama, and he is enlisted into this drama with full responsibility. And particularly in our time, his art must be a frontline weapon in the service of the people.

> **Jacques Roumain**, Haitian writer, poet. *The Hammer*, Fall/Winter
> 1998-1999

Listen, punk love reggae and some a dem seh things that Babylon no like. I thought dem was badness first, but now me give dem nine hundred percent right. Dem resist society.

> **Bob Marley**, Jamaican reggae singer, on punk music. *Blu
> Magazine*, 2000

In their sacred hearts, all men and women are always dreaming, are always envisioning things that are not, but should be, and this we must do or perish.

> **Covington Hall**, artist, activist with the Industrial Workers of the
> World. Attributed.

I believe the world is beautiful
and that poetry, like bread, is for everyone.

> **Roque Dalton**, El Salvadorian poet active in the People's Revolutionary Army, murdered in 1975. From poem "Like You," circa 1973

Chapter 26

"Ain't I A Woman"

Women, Women's Liberation, Sexism, Patriarchy, Feminism

Wathint` abafazi, Strijdom!
Wathint` imbokodo uzo kufa!
Now you have touched the women, Strijdom!
You have struck a rock
(You have dislodged a boulder!)
You will be crushed!
> **South African women's protest song**, from a demonstration against apartheid pass laws in front of Prime Minister Johannes Strijdom's building, 1956

Women in this country must become revolutionaries. We must refuse to accept the old, the traditional roles and stereotypes.
> **Shirley Chisholm**, former U.S. Congresswoman. Attributed.

The history of mankind is a history of repeated injuries and usurpations on the part of man toward woman, having in direct object the establishment of an absolute tyranny over her.
> **Elizabeth Cady Stanton**, women's rights activist, slavery abolitionist. "Declaration of Sentiments and Resolutions," 1848

We have known that men would tolerate, even romanticize us as special, as long as our words and actions didn't threaten their privilege of tolerating or rejecting us and our work according to *their* ideas of what a special women ought to be.
> **Adrienne Rich**, writer, poet. *On Lies, Secrets and Silence,* 1980

If the first woman God ever made was strong enough to turn the world upside down all alone, these women together ought to be able to turn it back, and get it right side up again! And now they is asking to do it, the men better let them.
> **Sojourner Truth**, activist, slavery abolitionist, former slave. Speech, Akron OH, 1851

I myself have never been able to find out precisely what feminism is; I only know that people call me a feminist whenever I express sentiments that differentiate me from a doormat or a prostitute.
> **Rebecca West**, Irish writer. *The Clarion*, 1913

Native Youth Movement activists, Philadelphia, PA, 2001. Photo by Hans Bennet

I ask no favors for my sex. All I ask of our brethren is, that they will take their feet from off our necks.

> **Sarah Grimké**, activist, writer. *Letters on the Equality of the Sexes,* 1838

One distressing thing is the way men react to women who assert their equality: their ultimate weapon is to call them un-feminine. They think she is anti-male; they even whisper that she is probably a lesbian.

> **Shirley Chisholm**, former U.S. Congresswoman. *Unbought and Unbossed,* 1970

The stigma of doing, saying, or enjoying anything considered feminine is learned very early and continues to haunt and limit traditional men all their lives.

> **National Organization for Men Against Sexism**, Tenets, circa 1992

Women workers from the National O-Ring maquiladora demonstrate for women's rights during the May Day parade. Their factory was closed, and the women laid off and blacklisted after they filed charges of sexual harrassment against their employer. Tijuana, Mexico. Photo by David Bacon

Change comes from within, from emancipation of the mind. Only if you want change you can achieve it. And who, in third world countries would most like to see their world changed for the better most? Who do you immediately think of when we start running our mouths on the topic of emancipation, change and reform? Indeed, women.
    Minke-An Ligeon, writer. Essay, "Third Wave," 2004

Without revolution, the destruction of imperialism and the building of socialism, there will be no freedom for women. Without the full participation of women, there will be no revolution.

> **Bernardine Dohrn**, activist, former Weather Underground member, circa 1968. In *The Roots of Resistance*, from the Freedom Archives, 2002

Woman beating is part of everyday life on the reservation. The white man oppresses the half-blood, the half-blood oppresses the full-blood, and everybody takes out their anger, despair, and feeling of helplessness on the women.

> **Mary Brave Bird**, writer. *Ohitika Woman*, 1993

Imperialism and militarism do not further women's liberation in western countries either. Women have to be brought into line to support racist imperialist goals and practices, and they have to live with the men who have been brutalized in the waging of war when these men come back. Men who kill women and children abroad are hardly likely to come back cured of the effects of this brutalization.

> **Sunera Thobani**, Canadian educator. Essay, "War Frenzy," 10/17/2001

Centuries of being rendered helpless while racism, crime, drugs, poverty, depression, and violence robbed us of our men has left us misguidedly over-protective, hopelessly male-identified, and all too often self-sacrificing.

> **Joan Morgan**, writer. *When Chickenheads Come Home to Roost,* 1999

The first problem for all of us, men and women, is not to learn, but to unlearn.

> **Gloria Steinem**, activist, writer. *New York Times*, 1971

No passing of legal enactments can set free a woman with a slave mind.

> **Teresa Billington-Greig**, English activist. *The Militant Suffrage Movement*, 1911

I didn't fight to get women out from behind the vacuum cleaner to get them on the board of Hoover.

> **Germaine Greer**, Australian-born activist, educator. In *One Hundred Red Hot Years*, 2004

The ceiling isn't glass; it's a very dense layer of men.

> **Ann Jardim**. *The New Yorker*, 1996

Women of today are still being called upon to stretch across the gap of male ignorance, and to educate men as to our existence and our needs. This is an old and primary tool of all oppressors to keep the oppressed occupied with the master's concerns.

> **Audre Lorde**, educator, activist, poet. Speech, Second Sex Conference, September 1979

The history of men's opposition to women's emancipation is more interesting perhaps than the story of that emancipation itself.

> **Virginia Woolf**, writer. *A Room of One's Own*, 1929

The central argument of the backlash [is] that women's equality is responsible for women's unhappiness.

> **Susan Faludi**, writer. *Backlash,* 1991

Foolish men, who accuse woman without reason, without seeing that you are yourselves the cause of the very thing that you blame!… What humor can be more extraordinary than that, lacking good counsel, the same person should tarnish the mirror and regret that it is not clear?

> **Sor Juana Inés de la Cruz**, Mexican poet. Essay, "Roundels," circa 1670

[Man] has done all he could to debase and enslave her mind; and now he looks triumphantly on the ruin he has wrought, and says, the being he has thus deeply injured is his inferior.

> **Sarah Grimké**, activist, writer. *Letters on the Equality of the Sexes*, 1838

Feminism remains a pretty simple concept, despite repeated—and enormously effective—efforts to dress it up in greasepaint and turn its proponents into gargoyles.

> **Susan Faludi**, writer. *Backlash*, 1991

We, all the women, we are the pillar of any nation. We carry, we deliver, we nurture, we educate.

> **Mariam Makeba**, South African singer. Interview, Africa Festival, Würzburg, Germany, May 2001

Man without woman is only 180 degrees of revolution.

> **Marinieves Alba**, educator, journalist, on gender equality in social justice work. *Oneworld* magazine, January 2004

A leading woman is one who works for a meaningful cause, speaks out in the face of oppression, fear, and opposition, takes on a challenge, represents her community in government, raises her children to be active global citizens, writes, sings, paints, dances with abandon, believes in equality, and inspires others to action.

    World Birth Magazine web site, July 2003

Remember all our women in the jails
Remember all our women in campaigns
Remember all our women over many fighting years
Remember all our women for their triumphs, and for their tears

    From "Women's Day Song," from the anti-apartheid movement
    of South Africa, 1980s

If God is male, then the male is God. The devine patriarch castrates women as long as he is allowed to live on in the human imagination.

    Mary Daly, theologian, educator. *Beyond God the Father,* 1973

There are times when a woman reading *Playboy* feels a little like a Jew reading a Nazi manual.

    Gloria Steinem, activist, writer. Essay, "What 'Playboy' Doesn't
    Know About Women Could Fill a Book," 1970

Rape is not aggressive sexuality, it is sexualized aggression.

    Audre Lord, writer, educator. *Sister Outsider*, 1984

'The bones of Bruce Lee are alive!!'
Just to beat the shit out of 'em [those who exoticize Asian women]
I ain't allowing 'em
That's right, I never gave 'em permission
To put our women in submission

    Taiyo, hip hop MC. From song "Vendetta," on exotification and
    sexual exploitation of Asian women, circa 1999

Rape is a culturally fostered means of suppressing women. Legally we say we deplore it, but mythically we romanticize and perpetuate it, and privately we excuse and overlook it.

    Victoria Billings, writer. *The Womensbook*, 1974

The negative images of Black women had always made them vulnerable to sexual assault.

    Paula Giddings, writer, educator. *When and Where I Enter*, 1984

It is obvious that the suppression of sexual agency and exploration, from within or from without, is often used as a method of social control and domination. Witness widespread genital mutilation and the homophobia that dictatorially mandates heterosexualality; imagine the stolen power of the millions affected by just these two global murderers of self-authorization and determination.
> **Rebecca Walker**, writer. Essay, "Lusting for Freedom," 1995

The sad truth is that hip hop artists' verbal and visual renderings of black women are now virtually indistinguishable from those of 19th century white slave owners. ...[It is] a truth so basic that I wish I did not have to state it: anything that harms black women harms black people.
> **William Jelani Cobb**, historian. Essay, "Past Imperfect: The Hoodrat Theory," April 2004

Your revolution will not happen between these thighs.
> **Sarah Jones**, poet. From poem, "Your Revolution," 1999. The Federal Communications Commission attempted to ban the poem for obscenity.

Any feminism that fails to acknowledge that black folks in nineties America are living and trying to love in a war zone is useless to our struggle against sexism. Though it's often portrayed as part of the problem, rap music is essential to that struggle because it takes us straight to the battlefield.
> **Joan Morgan**, writer. *When Chickenheads Come Home to Roost,* 1999

[There is the idea that] you don't go to a man's room at 2 o'clock in the morning.
Yes, that one always gets me, how the time of day somehow makes rape less a crime.
Or as if rape doesn't occur at 3 in the afternoon or 9 in the morning.
> **Trula Breckenridge**, writer, and Aishah Shahidah Simmons, filmmaker, in conversation. *Afro Mama* web site, circa 2003

There is no difference between being raped and being hit by a truck, except that after rape men ask you if you liked it.
> **Anonymous Mexican woman**. In *Upside Down,* 1998

It is insane...to suggest that sexual contact taking place during war between occupiers and the occupied of any gender, but particularly women, could be anything but rape. Most know that a rape culture pervades in times of war.

> **Tiffany King**, writer, educator. Essay, "Sexist and Racist Sexual Politics Censors and Suppresses the Rape and Torture of Iraqi Women in Abu Ghraib Prison," Spring 2004

I have a question...[for] those men who raped me. Why did you not kill me? It was a mistake to spare my life. I will not "shut up," I will not stop my work or travel to Chiapas or my work in the United States as a representative of the Zapatistas.

> **Cecilia Rodriguez**, activist, representative of the Zapatista National Liberation Army. *Current Biography,* May 1999

Bad judgement and carelessness are not punishable by rape.

> **Pearl Cleage**, playwright, activist, writer. *Deals With the Devil,* 1993

One tool of the Great-American-Double-Think is to blame the victim for victimization: Black people are said to invite lynching by not knowing our place; Black women are said to invite rape and murder and abuse by not being submissive enough, or by being too seductive, or too...

> **Audre Lorde**, educator, activist, poet. *Sister Outsider,* 1984

she was begging for it
the singer'll claim
we're all just mammals/born for fucking
the record company'll hide
voyeurs peeking from behind bar-graphs
the consumers were begging for it
they'll say of the product
the cash register's practically singing.

> **John Paul Davis**, poet. From spoken poem, "the cash register's practically singing," on the sexual exotification and exploitation of Asian women in popular culture, circa 1999

Women who have children can start by educating their sons about rape and abuse. But really, men have to stop it. I really don't think women can stop rape...it is up to men.

> **Aishah Shahidah Simmons**, filmmaker. Interview, *Afro Mama* web site, 2003

Men have the power collectively to end rape. Unfortunately, so far, this male collectively appears to be composed mainly of men who rape, men who hold attitudes similar to rapists, and men who undoubtedly do care in our own personal lives yet remain quiet in the community where rape takes place.

> **Charlie Jones**. "Male Responsibility For Rape And Rape Awareness," circa 2000

The pitting of anti-racist and anti-sexist struggles against one another allows some vocal fighters to dismiss blatantly the existence of either racism or sexism within their lines of action, as if oppression comes in separate, monolithic forms.

> **Trinh T. Minh-ha**, filmmaker, educator. *Woman, Native, Other*, 1989

Feminism is a struggle to end sexist oppression. Therefore, it is necessarily a struggle to eradicate the ideology of domination that permeates Western culture on various levels.

> **bell hooks**, writer, educator, activist. Attributed.

Historically, too, African American women never had the luxury of being simply *a woman*. It had to always be so much more: the keeper of secrets, the provider, the nurturer, all of this. We just couldn't be a woman. You're more than that. You're a beast of burden. Someone to breed, this and that. There were always these preconceived assignments that were put on you. You couldn't just be sitting on a veranda sipping a mint julep.

> **Julie Dash**, filmmaker. *Daughters of the Dust,* 1992

I have seen feminism that is not ecological become a new oppressor. I have seen environmentalism that is not feminist enough also become a new elitism. Ecofeminism prevents those two new forms of elitism by saying, No, it's about society and nature. It's about other ways of thinking. You can't just have a few women get into power. Carla Hills and Madeleine Albright do not symbolize a new equality for women.

> **Vandana Shiva**, Indian scientist, activist. Interview, *Z Magazine*, December 2002

[Feminism] is the political theory and practice that struggles to free *all* women... Anything less than this vision of total freedom is not feminism, but merely female self-aggrandizement.

> **Barbara Smith**, educator, activist, scholar. *The Truth that Never Hurts*, 1998

Womanist is to feminist as purple is to lavender.
> **Alice Walker**, writer, poet. *In Search of Our Mothers' Gardens*, 1983

Knee-jerk feminists who want to act like it's a struggle against men... [are] the strand of feminism that people most hear about, not the kind of revolutionary feminism that says, patriarchy is life threatening to Black men. When we look at the Black men who are killing each other—who think that their dick is a gun, and a gun is a dick—those men need a critique of that notion of patriarchal masculinity to save their lives.
> **bell hooks**, writer, educator, activist. Interview, *Z Magazine*, December 1995

And she had nothing to fall back on; not maleness, not whiteness, not ladyhood, not anything. And out of the profound desolation of her reality she may well have invented herself.
> **Toni Morrison**, writer, educator. Essay, "What the Black Women Think About Women's Lib," 1971

[W]e might ask then, who are we as ourselves? What would we say to Anita Hill outside the earshot of whites or men or our mothers and fathers? What do we feel about a Million Man March, notwithstanding the participation of our sons and brothers and husbands? Who are we when no one yearns for us, or when we are in full possession of our sexuality? Who are we when we are not someone's mother, or daughter, or sister, or aunt, or church elder, or the first black women to be this or that?
> **Paula Giddings**, writer, educator. *When and Where I Enter*, 1984

A nation is not conquered until the hearts of its women are on the ground. Then it is done, no matter how brave its warriors nor how strong their weapons.
> **Cheyenne proverb**, circa 1700s

What would happen if one woman told the truth about her life?
The world would split open.
> **Muriel Rukeyser**. "Kathe Köllwitz," 1968

Who is the more at fault in an erring passion, she who falls through entreaty, or he who entreats her to fall? Or which is the more to blame, although both do ill, she who sins for pay or he who pays for sinning?
     Sor Juana Inés de la Cruz, Mexican poet. Essay, "Roundels," circa 1670

We know now that women are the ones who are essential to support. This isn't just a touchy-feely idea; the research has been done. If you educate women, even just a little bit, and the infant mortality rate goes down, particularly with access to clean water, women will have less children and that benefits the whole family, the whole community, the planet.
     Melody Ermachild Chavis, private investigator, journalist. Interview, *Guerrilla News Network*, 8/25/2003

The battle lines are not drawn between women and men. They are drawn between particular world views.
     Arundhati Roy, Indian writer, activist. Interview, 8/16/2004

There are no such things as women's issues. All issues are women's issues.
     Aileen Clarke Hernandez, National Organization of Women. Speech, 1971

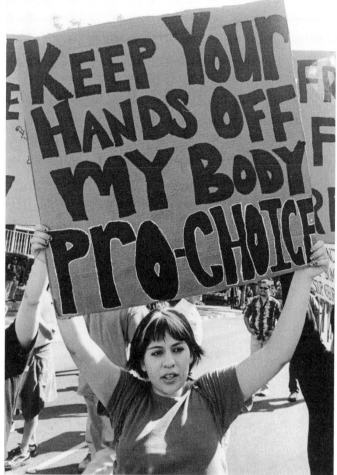

Protesters greet George W. Bush at a fundraiser, Stockton, CA, 2002.
Photo by Bill Hackwell

Too many women in too many countries
speak the same language of silence.

> **Anasuya Sengupta**, Indian activist, poet. From poem, "Silence,"
> 1995

An indigenous feminism has been present in every culture in the world and
in every period of history since the suppression of women began.

> **Robin Morgan**, writer. *Sisterhood is Global*, 1984

Sexism goes so deep that at first it's hard to see; you think it's just reality.

> **Alix Shulman**, writer. *Burning Questions*, 1978

People keep asking me about women's rights and I always find it a little difficult to answer because the men in Burma have no rights either. I feel that first of all we have to get basic rights for everybody and then we have to attack this area.

> **Aung San Suu Kyi**, Burmese human rights activist, Nobel Peace Laureate. *The New Internationalist*, June 1996

In the theory of gender I began from zero. There is no masculine power or privilege I did not covet. But slowly, step by step, decade by decade, I was forced to acknowledge that even a woman of abnormal will cannot escape her hormonal indentity.

> **Camille Paglia**, educator, writer. *Sex, Art, and American Culture*, 1992

Male chauvinism is an *attitude*—male supremacy is the objective *reality, the fact.*

> **Robin Morgan**, writer. *Subterranean News*, February 1970

The man of today did not establish this patriarchal regime, but he profits by it, even when he criticizes it. And he has made it very much a part of his own thinking.

> **Simone de Beauvoir**, French writer, philosopher. *Ms.* magazine, 1972

That man over there says that women need to be helped into carriages, and lifted over ditches, and to have the best place everywhere. Nobody ever helps me into carriages, or over mud-puddles, or gives me any best place! And ain't I a woman? Look at me! Look at my arm! I have ploughed and planted, and gathered into barns, and no man could head me! And ain't I a woman? I could work as much and eat as much as a man—when I could get it—and bear the lash as well! And ain't I a woman? I have borne thirteen children, and seen most all sold off to slavery, and when I cried out with my mother's grief, none but Jesus heard me! And ain't I a woman?

> **Sojourner Truth**, activist, slavery abolitionist, former slave. Speech, Akron OH, 1851

Anybody who knows anything of history knows that great social changes are impossible without feminine ferment.

> **Karl Marx**, German political theorist. Attributed. In *The Worker* socialist newspaper, Nepal, 2001

Benevolent patriarchy is still patriarchy.

> **Elizabeth A. Johnson**, theologian. *She Who Is*, 1993

It had been decreed long ago by man-made laws that living things were not equal. It had been decreed that women should be possessions, slaves, pawns in the hands of men with ways of beasts. It had been decreed that women were to be walloped effigies to burn upon the alters of men.

> **Estela Portillo Trambley**, playwright. *Rain of Scorpians and Other Writings*, 1976

China doll. Meek, submissive, mysterious and sultry. White man's geisha. She shrieks at the sight of a mouse. She takes insults as a reminder to improve upon her flawed self. She is the survivor of abuse by Asian men from her past, just as she watched her mother abused by the hands of her father. She endures. She sits quietly alone, waiting for her white knight to come untie her from generations of misery. Who is she?... She is a creation. She is a fantasy Asian woman crafted by the minds of white men.

> **Julia Oh**, writer. Essay, "Why 'Joy Luck' Brings Me Misery," 2001

If the men won't fight for the liberation of Puerto Rico then we women will.

> **Lolita Lebrón**, Puerto Rican independence activist, former U.S. political prisoner. *Blu Magazine*, 2000

When men of any culture and background say we intimidate them, that is sweet. Because the most beautiful words to any woman's ears should be that she is strong.

> **Michelle Myers**, poet, educator. Essay, "Yellow Rage: Asian American Women Invincible," 2002

Usually, when people talk about the strength of black women they are referring to the way in which they perceive black women coping with oppression. They ignore the reality that to be strong in the face of oppression is not the same as overcoming oppression, that endurance is not to be confused with transformation... The tendency to romanticize the black female experience that began in the feminist movement was reflected in the culture as a whole.

> **bell hooks**, writer, educator, activist. *Ain't I a Woman?*, 1981

Zap Mama is a women band and men follow us. But we don't have to push up our breasts for men—The breast is there to feed babies!

> **Zap Mama**, Belgian music group. Interview, *Blu Magazine*,
> 2001

No march, movement or agenda that defines manhood in the narrowest terms and seeks to make women lesser partners in this quest for equality can be considered a positive step.

> **Angela Davis**, activist, educator, writer, on the Million Man
> March, Washington, DC 1995. *CNN.com*, 1995

WITCH lives and laughs in every woman. She is the free part of each of us, beneath the shy smiles, the acquiescence to absurd male domination, the make-up or flesh-suffocating clothes our sick society demands. There is no "joining" WITCH. If you are a woman and dare to look within yourself, you are a WITCH. You make your own rules.

> **Women's International Terrorist Conspiracy from Hell**
> (WITCH), from leaflet by the activist group, New York, NY,
> 1969

Chapter 27

Pride

Lesbian, Gay, Bi-Sexual, Trans-Gendered, Two Spirit and Queer Liberation, Homophobia

during the day
maybe she is really a he
trapped by the limitations of our
imagination
>**Staceyann Chin**, poet. From poem "Cross-fire," 2002

Make no mistake about it, gay and lesbian people are hated. Homophobia kills, and testament to this is the number of young gay and lesbian people who attempt to take their own lives because this society rejects them.
>**Jack**, at anti-war meeting, Philadelphia, PA, June 2003

If you are free, you are not predictable and you are not controllable. To my mind, that is the keenly positive, politicizing significance of bisexual affirmation...to insist upon the equal validity of all of the components of social/sexual complexity.
>**June Jordan**, poet, educator. Attributed.

EVERY REAL revolutionary has ALWAYS supported homosexual struggles for justice!!! They are all aware that oppression is universal. NONE OF US ARE FREE UNTIL ALL OF US ARE FREE!!!
>**Alicia Banks**, radio talk show host, writer. "Eloquent Fury: Revolutionary African Truth." circa 2000

And as for the alleged "laws of nature," what about those lesbian seagulls on Catalina Island, off the coast of California? Or the fact that homosexuality and lesbianism existed among cats, dogs, primates, and other creatures?
>**Paula Christian**, writer. *The Cruise*, 1982

If homosexuality is a disease, let's all call in queer to work. "Hello, can't work today, still queer."
>**Robin Tyler**, activist, comedian. Speech, 1993

Homophobia is a social disease.
>**Tee shirt**, 2001

I have been told, even by other queer Indian women, that my lesbianism is a private matter and not the stuff of political struggle. But lesbianism can never be a private matter until it is publicly protected. Still, I draw the greatest hope from the Native notion of Two Spirit. I dream a world where truly Two Spirit folks—I speak here especially of my younger transgendered brothers and sisters—can fully inhabit the gender they experience.

> **Cherríe Moraga**, writer, educator. In *The Vinyl Project*, from the Freedom Archives, 2003

Well, well, well. President George was in one hell of bind this week when it turned out that Saudi Arabia funded Al Qaeda, not Iraq. Realizing we'd invaded the wrong country, Bush did the honorable thing: he's come out against gay marriages.

> **Greg Palast**, writer. Satirical essay, "Bush and the Saudis Sitting in a Tree...," 8/1/2003

Everybody says it was me that threw the first bottle. No, it was somebody behind me that threw it. But when that first bottle went by me, I said, "Oh lord, the revolution is finally here! Hallelujah, it's time to go do your thing!" The movement was born that night, and we knew that we had done something that everybody in the whole world would know about. They would know that gay people stood up and fought, and that would make everybody else stand up and fight.

> **Sylvia Rivera**, activist, recounting her experiences in the Stonewall Rebellion, 1969

My darling, it means sweet motherfucking nothing at all. You can rape me, rob me, what am I going to do if you attack me? Wave the Constitution in your face? I'm just a nobody black queen...but you know what? Ever since I heard about that Constitution, I feel free inside.

> **South African drag queen**, on having a clause banning dis- crimination on the basis of sexual orientation included in the nation's Constitution. In *Different Rainbows*, 2000

For many folks, it's easier to think that one partner is "the woman," while the other is trying to be a man, than to expand their definitions of manhood and womanhood.

> **Samiya Bashir**, writer, poet. Essay, "Double Take."

Male and female represent the two sides of the great radical dualism. But, in fact, they are perpetually passing into one another. Fluid hardens to solid, solid rushes to fluid. There is no wholly masculine man, no purely feminine woman.

> **Margaret Fuller**, activist, writer. *Woman in the Nineteenth Century*, 1845

I do believe deeply that all human beings, male and female, are sexual beings, most likely bisexual beings channeled this way and that by cultures terrified of boundary crossings without passports stamped GAY or STRAIGHT.

Robin Morgan, writer. *The Anatomy of Freedom*, 1982

We are all androgynous, not only because we are all born of a woman impregnated by the seed of a man but because each of us, helplessly and forever, contains the other—male in female, female in male, white in black and black in white.

James Baldwin, writer, educator. *The Price of the Ticket*, 1985

Even people who would call themselves open-minded give off the impression that [my butch partner] can't really help being a lesbian. But since I polish my nails and wear skirts the logic is that I could get a man if I tried. For me that's not even part of the equation.

Sheryl, last name not given. *BET*.com, 2004

There is something compelling about being both male and female, about having an entry into both worlds. I, like other queer people, am two in one body, both male and female. I am the embodiment of *hieros gamos*: the coming together of opposite qualities within.

Gloria Anzaldúa, writer, poet. *Borderlands/La Frontera*, 1989

The woman who defies her role as subservient to her husband, father, brother, or son by taking control of her own sexual destiny is purported to be a "traitor to her race" by contributing to the "genocide" of her people—whether or not she has children. In short, even if the defiant woman is *not* a lesbian, she is purported to be one; for, like the lesbian in the Chicano imagination, she is una *Malinchista*. Like the Malinche of Mexican history, she is corrupted by foreign influences which threaten to destroy her people.

Cherríe Moraga, writer, educator. *Loving In the War Years*, 1983

To the racist, Black people are so powerful that the presence of one can contaminate a whole lineage; to the heterosexist, lesbians are so powerful that the presence of one can contaminate the whole sex. This position supposes that if we do not eradicate lesbianism in the Black community, all Black women will become lesbians. It also supposes that lesbians do not

have children. Both suppositions are patently false.
>   **Audre Lorde**, educator, activist, poet. *Sister Outsider,* 1984

Few words are as guaranteed to set off an explosion of fear in her belly as the word *bulldike* when it is used on a woman like a whip.
>   **Judy Grahn**, writer. *Another Mother Tongue*, 1984

Closets stand for prisons, not privacy.
>   **Robin Tyler**, activist, comedian, 1979

The walls of the closet are guarded by the gods of terror, and the inside of the closet is a house of mirrors.
>   **Judy Grahn**, writer. *Another Mother Tongue*, 1984

Too many people see homosexuality as a sin that cannot be expiated, an indelible and contagious stigma or an invitation to ruin that tempts the innocent.
>   **Eduardo Galeano**, Uruguayan historian, educator. *Upside Down*, 1998

True African scholars do not blame the white man for biology or that which is documented before his invasion of our motherland. And, they do not fictionalize Africa as a selective and macho utopia... Do not believe the hype!!! I am no less African because I am a lesbian. I am no less revolutionary because I am not an incubator, a maid, or a babysitter. I am no less afrocentric because my reality is absent from gay media.
>   **Alicia Banks**, radio talk show host, writer. Essay, "Gay Racism: White Lies/Black Slander," 1997

The male party line concerning Lesbians is that women become Lesbians out of reaction to men. This is a pathetic illustration of the male ego's inflated proportions. I became a Lesbian because of women, because women are beautiful, strong and compassionate.
>   **Rita Mae Brown**, writer. *A Plain Brown Rapper*, 1976

I had a chance to read a copy of *The Well of Lonliness* that had been translated into Polish before I was taken into the camps. I was a young girl at the time, around twelve or thirteen, and one of the ways I survived in the camp was by remembering that book. I wanted to live long enough to kiss a woman.
>   **Jewish woman who survived a Nazi concentration camp**, anonymous. In *The Lesbian Herstory Archives Newsletter*, June 1992

For many well-off white women, there is a justifiable fear that fighting for acceptance of all lesbians by challenging racial or class barriers may rock the tidy boat they've built for themselves in the past few decades, and send them all back into the abyss of "otherness."

> **Samiya Bashir**, writer, poet. *Curve* magazine, 2000

We should be willing to discuss the insecurities that many people have about homosexuality. When I say "insecurities," I mean the fear that they are some kind of threat to our manhood. I can understand this fear. Because of the long conditioning process that builds insecurity in the American male, homosexuality might produce certain hang-ups in us.

> **Huey Newton**, co-founder, Black Panther Party. *Revolutionary Suicide*, 1973

This is a celebration of individual freedom, not of homosexuality. No government has the right to tell its citizens when or whom to love. The only queer people are those who don't love anybody.

> **Rita Mae Brown**, writer. Speech, Gay Olympics, San Francisco, 1982

We have heard the moralists argue that our love, our lives, and our families are an abomination. To them we can only say, govern your lives according to your god's wishes—and grant to everyone else the same privilege, the same choice.

> **Douglass and Stephen Drozdow-St.Christian**, husbands-to-be, Canada. From statement regarding their wedding, *CBC News Sunday*, 2/15/2004

A Community Problem With Deep Roots

CELEBRATE DIVERSITY

Protestors against racial discrimination in the Castro District, San Francisco, CA, 2004. By Bill Hackwell

We should be careful about using those terms that might turn our friends off. The terms "faggot" and "punk" should be deleted from our vocabulary, and especially we should not attach names normally designed for homosexuals to men who are enemies of the people, such as Nixon or Mitchell. Homosexuals are not enemies of the people.

> **Huey Newton**, co-founder, Black Panther Party. *Revolutionary Suicide*, 1973

As long as we are distracted by sexuality, we will never focus upon our real enemies. Our REAL ENEMIES are NOT consenting adults who love each other. They are racist elitists who hate everyone who is not rich, neocon, and white.

> **Alicia Banks**, radio talk show host, writer. "Eloquent Fury: Revolutionary African Truth." circa 2000

In this country, lesbianism is a poverty—as is being brown, as is being a woman, as is being just plain poor. The danger lies in ranking the oppressions.

> **Cherríe Moraga**, writer, educator. *La Guera*, 1983

One feature of lesbian oppression consists precisely of making women out of reach for us, since women belong to men. Thus a lesbian *has* to be something else, a not-woman, a not-man, a product of society, not a product of nature, for their is no nature in society.

      Monique Wittig. Essay, "One is Not Born a Woman," 1992

The Lesbian [in male pornography] is colonized, reduced to a variant of woman-as-sex-object, used to demonstrate and prove that male power pervades and invades even the private sanctuary of women with each other...the women still sexually service the male, for whose pleasure they are called into existence.

      Andrea Dworkin, writer. *Sinister Wisdom*, Fall 1980

I feel like a minority within a minority in the gay community. You're in a subculture. In the Indian community you feel like you're in a sub-subculture. And the paths of the gay community and the Indian community don't even cross. I don't want that separation, I want all of it together.

      Leota Lone Dog. In *Lesbians at Midlife*, 1991

I pounded on my car and screamed, "They misspelled it! They misspelled it!" For some reason, that offended me more than anything else.

      Elaine Noble, after finding "Lesbean" scratched on her car. *The Advocate*, October 1992

Of course it is extremely difficult to like oneself in a culture which thinks you are a disease.

      Chrystos, writer. Essay, "I Don't Understand Those Who Have Turned Away From Me," 1983

There are probably all of three lesbian killers in the entire country, and they're all in *Basic Instinct*. America's 12 million lesbians are not pathetic creatures. We have wonderful, diverse lives. It's Hollywood's responsibility to show what's really going on in this country.

      Ellen Carton. *Glamour* magazine, May 1992

Apparently, in many minds the leap from the butch to the butcher knife is but a tiny one.

      Lindsy Van Gelder, writer. *Ms.* magazine, January/February 1992

Chapter 28

"Life and Debt"

Money, Economics, Capitalism, Corporations, the Wealthy

O weapon of mass
destruction, we've inspected
you all our lives
and find you everywhere
capitalism…
> **Jack Hirschman**, poet, activist. From poem "Weapon of Mass Destruction," 2003

The money king is only an illusion. Capitalism is blind and barbaric. It poisons the water and the air. It destroys everything. And to the U'wa, it says that we are crazy, but we want to continue being crazy if it means we can continue to exist on our dear mother earth.
> **U'wa indigenous activists in Colombia**, in statement after an oil company was forced to withdraw from their land, 2002

All systems of political administration or governmental machinery are but the reflex of the economic forms which underlie them.
> **James Connolly**, Irish socialist. Essay, "Socialism and Nationalism," 1897

The laws of the market are not natural laws. The market cannot be regulated and geared to making people happy. We can't use it like the law of gravity and say that those who stumble should fall, that those who aren't competitive should die. That's economic Darwinism. What's missing really is a moral revolution. The problem is ethical, profoundly ethical and cultural. We've had a technological revolution, but we haven't had an ethical revolution.
> **Oswaldo de Rivero**, Peruvian writer, activist, former diplomat. Interview, *UNESCO Courier*, circa 2004

If humanity is going to come out of this mess, it must base its strategy on equity. All our local communities should be organized so as to look after each individual person's welfare. We now have a global community that calculates how to maximize the benefits for some at the expense of the majority.
> **Tewolde Berhan Gebre Egziabher**, Ethiopian educator, activist, writer. Essay, "How (Not) To Feed Africa," 2003

The main point is that the US economy has been converted into a credit and debt scam aimed against the rest of the world, and backed up by military force. But the scheme is falling apart as the rest of the world is losing the ability and willingness to pay.

> **Stan Goff**, writer, former U.S. Army sergeant. Interview, *Truthout*, 7/16/2003

We're given the idea that if we didn't have these people to exploit, that American wouldn't be rich enough to let us have these little petty material things in our lives and basic standards of living. No, that's wrong. It's the business giants and the government officials who make all the real money. We have whatever they kick down to us.

> **Immortal Technique**, hip hop MC. From song, "Poverty of Philosophy," Viper Records, 2001

Today Americans believe as part of our political understanding of the world that we are the most generous nation on earth in terms of foreign aid, overlooking the fact that the net dollar flow from almost every Third World nation runs *toward* the United States.

> **James Loewen**, historian. *Lies My Teacher Told Me,* 1995

"Developing countries" is the name that experts use to designate countries trampled by someone else's development.

> **Eduardo Galeano**, Uruguayan historian, educator. *Upside Down,* 1998

In my lifetime the United States has force fed to Native, Asian, African and Spanish speaking America a poisoned alphabet economic soup—WTO, the IMF, NAFTA, FTAA,—where development has meant little more than la Finka being replaced by the Maquiladora.

> **Cherríe Moraga**, writer, educator. In *The Vinyl Project*, The Freedom Archives, 2003

Is freedom, freedom, when it's not distributed equally?
Can any one country truly prosper over all others peacefully?

> **Khalil Crisis**, hip hop MC. From song "Centurion," 2002

Economically, colonialism programmed African countries to consume what they do not produce and to produce what they do not consume.

> **Bade Onimode**, Nigerian political economist, educator. *A future for Africa,* 1992

I am 56 years old, a farmer from South Korea who has strived to solve our problems with the great hope in the ways to organize farmers' unions. But I have mostly failed, as many other farm leaders elsewhere have failed.

> **Lee Kyung Hae**, Korean farmer and activist. From statement he read minutes before committing suicide at a mass protest against the World Trade Organization in Cancun, Mexico, 9/10/03

It is said that our indigenous ancestors, Mayas and Aztecs, made human sacrifices to their gods. It occurs to me to ask: How many humans have been sacrificed to the gods of Capital in the last five hundred years?

> **Rigoberta Menchú Tum**, Guatemalan Mayan human rights activist. Interview, 1992

From the point of view of the economy, the sale of weapons is indistinguishable from the sale of food.

> **Eduardo Galeano**, Uruguayan historian, educator. *Upside Down*, 1998

Participant at the World Social Forum, Porto Allegre, Brazil, 2003. Photo by Nick Cooper

I could persuade a millionaire on a Friday to subsidize a revolution for Saturday out of which he would make a huge profit on Sunday even though

he was certain to be executed on Monday.
> **Saul Alinsky**, community organizer, writer. *Rules for Radicals*, 1971

Our factories are all overseas. All we produce here are rich executives.
> **Bumper sticker**, 2004

Piracy—Hostile Takeover Without the Paperwork.
> **Union tee shirt**, 2004

You show me a capitalist, I'll show you a bloodsucker.
> **Malcolm X**, Black nationalist leader. Speech, New York, NY 1964

All riches come from inequity, and unless one has lost, another cannot gain. Hence, that common opinion seems to be very true, 'the rich man is unjust, or heir to an unjust one.' Opulence is always the result of theft, if not committed by the actual possessor, then by his predecessor.
> **Saint Jerome**, scholar, circa 347-420. Attributed.

Your motto is Service. Back on the farm, when I heard that the bull was "servicing" the cows, I looked behind the barn. And gentlemen, what that bull was doing to the cow is exactly what you people have been doing to the public all these years.
> **Will Rogers**, writer, actor, comedian, speaking to board of directors of Standard Oil Company. *Too Funny to be President*, 1988

Pickpockets lurking on street corners practice a low-tech version of the art of speculators who fleece the multitudes by computer.
> **Eduardo Galeano**, Uruguayan historian, educator. *Upside Down*, 1998

What's breaking into a bank compared with founding a bank?
> **Bertolt Brecht**, German playwright, poet. From play, *The Threepenny Opera*, 1928

Thievin' in a suit and tie, gentlemen
You murder, think you civilized
> **Meshell Ndegeocello**, singer. From song, "Gentleman," 2002

By John Jonik

We do not want riches, but we want to train our children right. Riches would do us no good. We could not take them with us to the other world. We do not want riches, we want peace and love.

Red Cloud, Lakota leader, warrior. Speech, New York, NY, June 1870

You report of the anarchists that 'most are autonomous, unaccountable, small in numbers, and unwilling to divulge tactics. Prepared to attack people and property.' That just about sums up the global economy.

John Lodge, in letter to *The Guardian*, July 2001

When our fears have all been serialized, our creativity censored, our ideas "marketplaced," our rights sold, our intelligence sloganized, our strength downsized, our privacy auctioned; when the theatricality, the entertainment value, the marketing of life is complete, we will find ourselves living not in a nation but in a consortium of industries, and wholly unintelligible to ourselves except for what we see a through a screen darkly.

Toni Morrison, writer, educator. Essay, "Racism and Fascism," circa 1996

You sell your soul like you sell a piece of ass
Slave to the dead white leaders on paper

Meshell Ndegeocello, singer. From song "Dead Nigga Blvd," 2002

The relationship between those with power and those under their command lies at the foundation of capitalism. Our capacity to create and to produce is separated from that which is produced—the 'product,' so instead of deciding together the best ways we can meet our own needs, while respecting the needs of others and the planet, our energies are appropriated to produce for the profit of others.

Notes from Nowhere, editorial collective. *We Are Everywhere*, 2003

Planner A: "One often hears the argument that public land ownership is communistic."
Planner B: "But there are societies which believed that God said land should be held in a common trust for the people."
Planner C: "God was a communist."

Anonymous, at Public Land Ownership Conference, York University, Toronto, 1975

When it comes to trade, we are totally forgotten. It is a Muslim tradition that if you are rich you should give zachat (a quarter of what you earn) to the poor. If George Bush walked in here now I would ask him to come to my village to see how we really live and ask him to give the Malian farmers a zachat. They talk about eliminating poverty, but why then must they subsidize their farmers?

Soloba Mady Keita, Malian farmer. Interview, *Baobabconnections. org*, 2003

Their motto seems to be "Money, money, get money, get rich, and be a

gentleman." With this sentiment, they fly about in every direction, like a swarm of bees, in search of the treasure that lies so near their hearts.
    Peter Jones/Kahkewaquonaby, Ojibwe Methodist minister, 1802-1856

We are not a market—first and foremost, we are a people.
    Declaration of the South American Chemical and Paper Workers. In *We Are Everywhere*, 2003

What is definite at this time is that there can be no compromise between neoliberal globalization and lives of the workers and people. They have already started to aim their guns and proclaim war against the peoples around the world.
    Mi-Kyeong Ryu, Secretary of KoPA, a Korean union association. Speech, Genoa, Italy, at protests against the G8 Summit, July 2001

It should not be overlooked that the WTO [World Trade Organization] itself is a kind of cop, or rather a kind of tyrants' watchdog—a symbolic hyper-watchdog at the portals of the new, improved, post-colonial, multicultural, genetically modified, low-fat imperialism.
    Author unknown. Essay, "Who Needs The WTO?" *Baobabconnections.org*, 2003

From the same prolific womb of governmental injustice we breed the two great classes—tramps and millionaires.
    Populist Party, from Omaha Platform of the People's Party of America, July 1892

The basic law of capitalism is you or I, not both you and I.
    Karl Liebknecht, German attorney, activist. Speech, 1907

Humans must breath, but corporations must make money.
    Alice Embree, activist. In *Sisterhood is Powerful*, 1970

A small business may survive on profits, but at least its basic purpose is to provide sustenance for the owners, who are human beings with a sense of place in their communities. But a corporation has no purpose for its existence, nor any moral guide to its behavior, other than to make profits. And today's global corporations are beyond the control of any nation or government.
    Judi Bari, environmental activist. Speech, June, 1996

By John Jonik

Nothing exists outside the dominant logic of capitalism.
>   ***Adbusters Magazine,*** January-February 2003

If everything that was yours has to be bought from someone else, quite clearly everyone's life becomes indebted.
>   **Vandana Shiva**, Indian scientist, activist, regarding Indian farmers
>   who have committed suicide because of debts incurred to biotech
>   seed companies. Interview, *Rabble.com*, May 2004

In a society that judges self-worth on productivity, it's no wonder we fall prey to the misconception that the more we do, the more we're worth.
>   **Ellen Sue Stern**, writer. *The Indispensable Woman,* 1988

Capitalism robs you and makes a wage slave of you. The law upholds and protects that robbery. The government fools you into believing that you are independent and free. In this way you are fooled and duped every day of your life.
>   **Alexander Berkman**, activist. *What is Communist Anarchism,*
>   1920

Chapter 29

"Solidarity Forever"

Work, Labor, Unions

When people ask me, 'Why can't labor organize the way it did in the thirties?' the answer is simple: everything we did then is now legal.
> **Thomas Geoghegan**, attorney, writer. *Which Side Are You On?* 1991

All the martyrs of the working class, those in Lausanne like those in Paris, those in Le Havre like those in Martinique, are victims of the same murderer: international capitalism. And it is always in belief in the liberation of their oppressed brothers, without discrimination as to race or country, that the souls of these martyrs will find supreme consolation.
> **Ho Chi Minh**, Vietnamese political leader, poet. Essay, "Oppression Hits All Races," 1923

The story of coal is always the same. It is a dark story. For a second more sunlight, men must fight like tigers. For the privilege of seeing the color of their children's eyes by the light of the sun, fathers must fight as beasts in the jungle. That life may have something of decency, something of beauty—a picture, a new dress...for this, men who work down in the mines must struggle and lose, struggle and win.
> **Mother Jones**, union organizer, activist. *The Autobiography of Mother Jones*, 1925

In the past, some people used to suggest that there was one struggle of the union movement for economic progress...and a separate struggle of the people with disabilities, people of color, women, immigrants, and lesbians and gays for dignity. But the truth is they are not separate. They are one struggle and one dream.
> **Linda Chavez-Thompson**, labor organizer. *Current Biography*, March 2000

Work itself isn't humiliating if it gives you financial independence. There is dignity in that. The indignity comes when management perceives you as so many worker bees, not as contributing individuals.
> **Brian Kremer**, artist. In *Great Labor Quotations*, 2000

There is an enormous mass of labour which is just merely wasted; many thousands of men and women making nothing with terrible and inhuman

toil which deadens the soul and shortens mere animal life itself.
> **William Morris**, Canadian socialist, poet. "Art and Socialism," 1884

The key issue is jobs. You can't get away from it: jobs. Having a buck or two in your pocket and feeling like somebody.
> **Studs Terkel**, radio journalist. *Great Labor Quotations*, 2000

When blacks are unemployed, they are considered lazy and apathetic. When whites are unemployed, it's considered a depression.
> **Jesse Jackson**, civil rights activist, reverend. *Time* magazine, 4/6/1970

In spite of oppressors, in spite of false leaders, in spite of labor's own lack of understanding of its needs, the cause of the worker continues onward. Slowly his hours are shortened, giving him leisure to read and to think. Slowly his standard of living rises to include some of the good and beautiful things of the world.
> **Mother Jones**, labor organizer, activist. *The Autobiography of Mother Jones*, 1925

I am the people—the mob—the crowd—the mass. Do you know that all the great work of the world is done through me?
I am the workingman, the inventor, the maker of the world's food and clothes.
> **Carl August Sandburg**, journalist, poet, 1878-1967. Attributed.

Arise ye workers from your slumbers
Arise ye prisoners of want
For reason in revolt now thunders
And at last ends the age of cant.
Away with all your superstitions
Servile masses arise, arise
We'll change henceforth the old tradition
And spurn the dust to win the prize.
> **Eugene Pottier**, French singer, activist. From song "The International," 1871

Members of organized labor protest at the Republican National Convention, New York, NY, 2004. Photo by Bill Hackwell

You can never retire from the working class. If you want to eat, live decently, have a nice house and help your children and grandchildren, the struggle has to go on.

>**Albert Fitzgerald**, United Electrical, Radio and Machine Workers
>of America. in *Great Labor Quotations*, 2000

Conditions they are bad,
And some of you are sad;
You cannot see your enemy,
The class that lives in luxury.
You workingmen are poor,—
Will be forevermore,—
As long as you permit the few
To guide your destiny.

>**E.S. Nelson**, singer. From song, "Workingmen, Unite!" circa
>1908

They used to say, "Once you pass the gates of General Motors, forget about the United States Constitution."

> **Genora Dollinger**, labor organizer. From her recollection of the General Motors sit down strike of 1936-1937. *Striking Flint*, 1995

If you think that by hanging us, you can stamp out the labor movement—the movement from which the downtrodden millions, the millions who toil and live in want and misery—the wage slaves—expect salvation—if this is your opinion, then hang us! Here you will tread upon a spark, but there, and there, and behind you and in front of you, and everywhere, flames will blaze up. It is a subterranean fire. You cannot put it out.

> **August Spies**, labor organizer and one of eight anarchists tried and executed after being accused of involvent in the Haymarket bombing in Chicago, IL. From court statement, 10/7/1886

Hell, everyone says unions like the Teamsters are too powerful. Well, you show me a union that's more powerful than GM or Standard Oil.

> **Al Barkett**, Teamster member. In *The Teamsters*, 1978

Management is the art of getting other people to do all the work.

> **Bumper sticker**

Black people, brown people, they're all part of the union. If you don't like it, then get out, but we're not going to change it.

> **César Chávez**, union and labor organizer. *César Chávez,* 1975

United We Bargain, Divided We Beg.

> **Button**, 2002

When labor speaks of free medical care, it is saying we need it for blacks who do not have it and whites who are concerned that they will have to pay for giving it to them. When labor calls for full employment, it is talking about blacks who are without jobs and whites who want to protect the ones they have. When labor says we must build more homes, it is seeking to create a society where the black brother need not be enraged because he does not have a home and the white need not fear for the home he has.

> **Bayard Rustin**, Congress of Racial Equality. In *Overcoming Middle Class Rage*, 1971

THE QUOTABLE REBEL

I don't blame that white trade unionist for not wanting a black man to get his job, and I don't blame the black man for wanting to get that job; I want to see a policy under which they can both have jobs!

Jesse Jackson, civil rights activist, reverend. In *Great Labor Quotations*, 2000

A union movement in America will always be a scandal... The subversive thing about labor is not the strike, but the idea of solidarity.

Thomas Geoghegan, attorney, writer. *Which Side Are You On?*, 1991

Any executive who thinks the ultimate in busyness consists of having two important phone calls on hold and a major deadline in 20 minutes, should try facing six tables full of clients simultaneously demanding that you give them their check, fresh coffee, a baby seat, and a warm, spontaneous smile.

Barbara Ehrenreich, activist, writer. *The Worst Years of Our Lives*, 1990

The working class, the dirty, uneducated, uncouth class, is actually responsible for every gain that the world has. Responsible yes, but you don't get the credit for it. The bosses, the professionals, the moneymen, they get the credit. They're considered to be the real world shakers; dynamos. But they know without you, they would have nothing.

Ron Hively, steelworker. In *Overtime*, 1990

The Labor Movement: The Folks Who Brought You the Weekend.

Bumper sticker, 2004

Management: The folks who brought you the Labor Movement.

Bumper sticker, 2004

The working class and the employing class have nothing in common. There can be no peace so long as hunger and want are found among millions of working people and the few, who make up the employing class, have all the good things of life.

Industrial Workers of the World, Constitution preamble, 1908

O' I like my boss—
He's a good friend of mine;
That's why I am starving

Out in the bread-line.
From folk song "Hallelujah on the Bum," circa 1897

Keep my slacks creased to go work for the beast
As my rent don't cease, his pockets get obese
The Coup, hip hop group. From song "20,000 Gun Salute,"
1998

For every dollar the boss has and didn't work for, one of us worked for a
dollar and didn't get it.
William "Big Bill" Haywood, labor leader and co-founder,
Industrial Workers of the World. In *Great Labor Quotations*,
2000

What freedom? To be wage-slaves, hired and fired at the will of a soulless
corporation?
Elizabeth Gurley Flynn, labor organizer. *The Rebel Girl*, 1955

A red is any son of a bitch who wants thirty cents when we're paying twenty-
five.
John Steinbeck, writer. *The Grapes of Wrath*, 1939

Our lives shall not be sweated from birth until life closes;
Hearts starve as well as bodies; give us bread but give us roses!
James Oppenheimer, singer. From song "Bread and Roses,
inspired by striking women textile workers, 1912

Chapter 30

"Dem Belly Full But We Hungry"

Poverty, Class Struggle

We should be careful about how we castigate the poor, the hopeless, the uneducated. The God of Plenty, who has not yet visited them, except with children that they cannot feed, might be tempted to take our goods to feed them.
> **Linda E. Edwards**, writer. "A Letter to Bill Cosby, Mr. Joseph and Mr. Mootoo of Canada," 2004

The curse of poverty has no justification in our age. It is socially as cruel and blind as the practice of cannibalism at the dawn of civilization, when men ate each other because they had not yet learned to take food from the soil or to consume the abundant animal life around them. The time has come for us to civilize ourselves by the total, direct and immediate abolition of poverty.
> **Martin Luther King, Jr.,** civil rights leader. *Where Do We Go From Here: Chaos or Community?*, 1967

Glaring poverty is the negation of human rights: the right to nutrition, the right to housing, the right to health care, and education.
> **Shirin Ebadi**, Iranian human rights activist. Speech, 5/14/2004

The Depression affected people in two ways. The great majority reacted by thinking money is the most important thing in the world. Get yours. And get it for your children. Nothing else matters. And there was a small number of people who felt that the whole system was lousy. You have to change it.
> **Virginia Durr**. In *When and Where I Enter*, 1984

Poor man fought all the battles, poor man would fight again today
He would do anything you ask him in the name of the U.S.A.
> **Bessie Smith**, singer. From song "Poor Man's Blues," 1930

In most of the traditional cultures of the world, homelessness would be impossible; first because of large protective kin systems, and second because homes were easily constructed from materials at hand. In America today we consider homelessness as a lack of shelter, not as a breakdown of community.
> **Lynn Maria Laitala**, writer. "In the Aftermath of Empire," 1992

A ghetto can be improved in only one way: out of existence.
>   **James Baldwin**, writer, educator. *Nobody Knows My Name*, 1961

The ghettos are the Sowetos of the world. They're of earth. And we as human beings should not think of ourselves just so much as geographic locations, but rather we should think of ourselves as earthlings, born of earth and universe.
>   **Piri Thomas**, writer. *Blu Magazine*, 1999

Anyone who has ever struggled with poverty knows how extremely expensive it is to be poor.
>   **James Baldwin**, writer, educator. *Nobody Knows My Name*, 1961

We can't offer young blacks a job at Wendy's or McDonalds as an alternative to selling crack.
>   **Louis Farrakhan**, leader of the Nation of Islam. Interview, *Washington Post*, February 1990

The only things you get for free are misery and poverty. The only thing you cannot buy is dignity.
>   **Felix Maendel**, singer. From song "From the Mountains of Chiapas," circa 1999

Privatization is a new kind of apartheid. Apartheid separated whites from blacks. Privatization separates the rich from the poor.
>   **Richard Makolo**, South African water rights activist. *New York Times,* 5/29/2003

Once a person who once penniless, hopeless, insecure, and degraded has used drug dealing as his tool to overcome that multiple psychological oppression, he will go to all extremes to prevent his return to it. Any type of freedom is a hard thing to willingly surrender. My ancestors died fighting for freedom. Prisoners have been gunned down attempting to scale razor wire fences, trying to return to freedom. Wealthy businessmen have cheated their partners, and have sometimes killed to preserve their financial freedom. So, then, although illegal and moralistically wrong, it becomes clearer why many of my people, including myself, resorted to drug dealing as a means to prosperity and maintaining it.
>   **Reginald Alexander**, writer, U.S. prisoner. Essay, "Inner-City Mayhem," 1998

As children, we're taught to despise bullies, yet we watch our country pulling on its boots, winking and smiling in open acknowledgement that it's okay to have a double standard for Poland and PATCO; that it's okay, to have two Americas, one impoverished and below the water line, struggling for the breath of life, and the other waxing fat and gluttonous.
> **Ed Asner**, actor, activist. Speech, 1984

Poverty makes a free man become a slave.
> **Proverb**, Ghana and Ivory Coast

To be a poor man is hard, but to be a poor race in a land of dollars is the very bottom of hardships.
> **W.E.B. Du Bois**, scholar, educator. *The Souls of Black Folk*, 1903

The first of the month falls every month, too, North or South. And them white folks who sends bills never forgets to send them.
> **Langston Hughes**, writer, poet. *Simple Speaks His Mind*, 1950

You cannot pull yourselves up by your bootstraps if you have no shoes. You cannot get out of poverty if you have no education. Your brain does not absorb learning when it is protein starved.
> **Linda E. Edwards**, writer. "A letter to Bill Cosby, Mr. Joseph and Mr. Mootoo of Canada," 2004

The rich rob the poor and the poor rob one another.
> **Sojourner Truth**, activist, slavery abolitionist, former slave. Attributed.

When the rich concern themselves with the poor, that's called charity. When the poor concern themselves with the rich, that's called revolution.
> **William Winpisinger**, union leader, writer. In *Great Labor Quotations*, 2000

Chapter 31

"The System"

Government, Democracy, the State, Patriotism

Our democracy is but a name. We vote? What does that mean? It means that we choose between two bodies of real, though not avowed, autocrats. We choose between Tweedledum and Tweedledee.

> **Helen Keller**, educator, socialist activist. Letter, 1911

For Americans, 'democracy' is a cover for business dominance. It is the same all over the world where the Americans claim to want to 'spread democracy.' The Holy Grail of this modern-day Crusade is wealth—the same as for all other empires before it, no matter what the justifications.

> **Mumia Abu-Jamal**, journalist, U.S. political prisoner. Essay, "The Rule of the Market," April 2004

Democracy has become Empire's euphemism for neo-liberal capitalism.

> **Arundhati Roy**, Indian writer, activist. Speech, 5/13/2003

Democracy is supposed to give you the feeling of choice, like Painkiller X and Painkiller Y. But they're both just aspirin.

> **Gore Vidal**, writer. *The Observer*, February 1982

We don't have democracy, we have an auction.

> **Bumper sticker**, 2004

Democracy is not a gift delivered on a golden tray. Democracy is a historical growth that has to go through its evolutionary process... Let's not forget, you cannot export democracy with weapons. You cannot pour human rights on people's heads with cluster bombs. Democracy and human rights can only be achieved with the understanding of the people.

> **Shirin Ebadi**, Iranian human rights activist. Speech, 5/14/2004

Verily, poor as we are in democracy, how can we give of it to the world?

> **Emma Goldman**, activist, writer, anarchist. From statement to jury during her trial for opposing the World War I draft, 1917

Is there not something worthy of perpetuation in our Indian spirit of democracy, where Earth, our mother, was free to all, and no one sought to impoverish or enslave his neighbor?

> **Ohiyesa, a.k.a. Charles Eastman**, Lakota physician, writer, 1858-1939

A democratic state is not proven by the welfare of the strong but by the welfare of the weak.

> **June Jordan**, poet, educator. "For the Sake of a People's Poetry," 1980

There is a profound contradiction at the heart of American political life: the claim to a democracy, and the bitter struggle to deny it to almost everyone else in the world.

> **Mumia Abu-Jamal**, journalist, U.S. political prisoner. Essay, "Democracy, Dictatorships & Empire," 2003

Of all tyrannies, a tyranny exercised for the good of its victims may be the most oppressive. It may be better to live under robber barons than under omnipotent moral busybodies. The robber baron's cruelty may sometimes sleep, his cupidity may at some point be satiated; but those who torment us for our own good will torment us without end, for they do so with the approval of their own conscience.

> **C.S. Lewis**, Irish-English writer. Attributed.

Beware the Land of Oz. For it is only in the Land of Oz that a handful of vainglorious men could send hundreds of thousands of young soldiers off to fight in an illegal war. And only in the Land of Oz can The Grand Wizard erode basic civil rights and call it enhanced security. And where but in Oz could a felon, convicted of lying in public, be put in charge of Total Information Awareness? 75 million Americans had no health insurance in 2001 or 2002. Unemployment is at an 8-year high. Meanwhile, at the Wizard's court, men of dubious reputation gorge themselves at the people's expense. Expose the Grand Wizard; this is our America, not Oz.

> **Cynthia McKinney**, former U.S. Congresswoman. From text of newspaper ads picturing George W. Bush as a wizard controlling the media from behind a curtain, 2003

People say they don't care about politics, they're not involved or they don't want to get involved, but they are. Their involvement just masquerades as indifference or inattention. It is the silent acquiescence of the millions that supports the system. When you don't oppose a system, your silence becomes approval, for it does nothing to interrupt the system. People use all sorts of excuses for their indifference. They even appeal to God as a shorthand route for supporting the status quo. They talk about law and order. But look at the system, look at the present social "order" of society. Do you see God? Do you see law and order? There is nothing but disorder, and instead of law there is only the illusion of security. It is an illusion because it is built on a long history of injustices: racism, criminality, and the enslavement and genocide of millions. Many people say it is insane to resist the system, but actually, it is insane not to

Mumia Abu-Jamal, journalist, U.S. political prisoner. "Politics," 1997

I believe that no government can exist for a single moment without the cooperation of the people, willing or forced, and, if people suddenly withdraw their cooperation in every detail, the government will come to a standstill.

Mohatma Gandhi, Indian activist, political leader. Attributed.

A people does not marry its government for an eternity, as in a church wedding. They are tied together in a modern way that allows a change of relationship when things do not work.

Octavio Paz, Mexican writer. *New York Times*, 4/2/1989

Man is a social rather than a political animal; he can exist without a government.

José Ortega y Gasset, Spanish philosopher. *Obiter Scripta*, 1936

It is lamentable, that to be a good patriot one must become the enemy of the rest of mankind.

Voltaire, French writer, philosopher, 1694-1778

People broken down from years of oppression
Become patriots when they way of life is threatened

Talib Kweli, hip hop MC. From song "The Proud," 2002

Patriotism is the last refuge of a scoundrel.

Samuel Johnson, English writer, lexicographer, 1709-1784

It is not flag-burners who are "un-American," it is those who try to define Americanism who are, in fact, un-American... Patriotism, to me, means for someone to do as much as they can to improve their country, even when it means opposing one's government, or the actions or beliefs of a majority of its citizens.

Mike M, a writer on *TeenInk.com*, 2003

May Day rally, San Francisco, CA, 2000. Photo by Hans Bennet

The real question is, "Who is the Real Patriot?" The one that speaks honestly about the American experience or the one that keeps silent as those with the power and control misuse and abuse the authority invested in them by the American people?

> **Ewuare Osayande**, educator, activist, poet. *Black Anti-Ballistic Missives*, 2003

One of the great attractions of patriotism—it fulfills our worst wishes. In the person of our nation we are able, vicariously, to bully and cheat. Bully and cheat, what's more, with a feeling that we are profoundly virtuous.

> **Aldous Huxley**, English writer, 1894-1963. Attributed.

I'm going to tell you a number of things, but you really only have to remember two words: *governments lie.*

> **Howard Zinn**, historian, educator. In *The Vinyl Project*, from the Freedom Archives, 2003

A democracy cannot long endure with the head of a God and the tail of a demon.

> **Josephine Yates**, writer, educator. Essay, "The Voice of the Negro," 1904

The state is no more than a machine for oppression of one class by another. This is as true of democracy as it is of monarchy.

> **Friedrich Engels**, German political theorist. *The Civil War in France*, 1871

There is a difference between holding government accountable and cooperating with government.

> **Ewuare Osayande**, educator, activist, poet. Speech, December 2002

Every day what becomes clearer and clearer is the desperation of this system. The United States bourgeoisie reminds me of a man running away from a lion, who keeps throwing out pieces of meat until finally his little bag is empty and the only piece of meat left is himself.

> **Amiri Baraka**, poet, educator. *Conversations with Amiri Baraka*, 1994

I don't make jokes. I just watch the government and report the facts.

> **Will Rogers**, writer, actor, comedian. 1879-1935. Attributed.

What, to the American slave, is your Fourth of July? I answer: A day that reveals to him, more than all other days in the year, the gross injustice and cruelty to which he is the constant victim. To him your celebration is a sham.

> **Frederick Douglass**, slavery abolitionist, political theorist. Speech, 7/5/1852, Rochester, NY

May the Great Spirit shed light on your path, so that you may never experience the humility that the power of the American government has reduced me to.

> **Black Hawk**, Sauk leader, warrior, circa 1835

"Vetoed Dreams," collage by Theodore Harris

The way I see it, serikali (government) means a cruel secret (siri kali). It is a cruel secret because they are people who take things that are not true, and make them true. They take things that are wrong and make them right, but only as long as they are the ones doing them. If ordinary people do them, we can be imprisoned, tortured and killed.

> **Lesikar Ole Ngila**, Tanzanian Maasai activist. Serikali, a Swahili word for government, can be directly translated as "cruel secret." Essay, "Reflections of a Maasai Warrior," March 2004

To believe in external government is to believe that the force that put you here on this earth would give the wisdom, the coordinating power for your life to someone else. Why wouldn't that force give you the coordinating power for your own life? That don't make sense, do it? Everybody is equipped to coordinate their own lives.

> **Ramona Africa**, activist, MOVE Organization member. *Blu Magazine*, 2001

The same people who maintain the status quo in America where over 2 million people are locked in prison, are the same people who have propped up dictators like Saddam Hussein only so they can put him out of power when they no longer need him. This is the kind of "freedom" they will bring to you, and take it from those in the belly of the beast—this system has no freedom nor justice nor peace to provide for us in America.

> **Kevin Ramirez**, activist. Interview, *Africasgateway,* South Africa, September 2003

Government is an association of men who do violence to the rest of us.

> **Leo Tolstoy**, Russian writer. *The Kingdom of God is Within You,* 1893

War is Peace. Freedom is Slavery. Ignorance is Strength.

> **George Orwell**, English writer. *1984,* 1949

Fascism is not synonymous with repressive government. All governments are repressive to a greater or lesser degree, in some cases very much so, as with police states or military dictatorships. But fascism elevates terror to a universal.

> **William Mandel**, activist, writer. *Comment,* 5/20/2003

When fascism comes to the U.S., it won't be wearing swastikas—it will be waving red, white and blue and whistling Yankee Doodle Dandy.

> **Elridge Cleaver**, writer, former black power actvist. Attributed.

What government is best? That which teaches us to govern ourselves.

> **Johann Wolfgang von Goethe**, German writer. Attributed.

Freedom consists in converting the state from an organ superimposed upon society into one completely subordinate to it.

> **Karl Marx**, German political theorist. Essay, "Critique of the Gotha Program," 1875

I don't want a piece of the American pie. I want to burn it to the crust.

> **Kwame Toure, a.k.a Stokeley Carmichael**, civil rights/Black power activist. Attributed.

Fear Flag by Colin Matthes

The society that will organize production on the basis of a free and equal association of the producers will put the whole machinery of state where it will then belong: into the museum of antiquities, by the side of the spinning wheel and the bronze axe.

Friedrich Engels, German political theorist. Essay, "Origin of the Family, Private Property and the State," 1884

Chapter 32

"The United Snakes"

America

America is the greatest of opportunities and the worst of influences.
>   **George Santayana**, Spanish educator, poet. *The Last Puritan*, 1935

The United States: what is it? A nation built on the soil of conquest, battened on the theft of human beings. Yet it is not only this. The United States was also created out of the doctrine of natural rights, whose restrictive application was continually eroded by the struggles of the excluded.
>   **Howard Winant**, sociologist. In *The House that Race Built*, 1997

Americans are clearly faced with a choice. On the one hand, they can continue in their collective pretense that "the opposite of everything is true," prattling on about "innocent Americans" being "the most peaceful people on earth" while endorsing the continuous U.S. disposition of death, destruction, and domination in every quarter of the globe. On the other, they must at last commence the process of facing up both to the realities of their national history and to the responsibilities that history has bequeathed. In effect, Americans will either become active parts of the solution to what they and their country have wrought, or they will remain equally active parts of the problem. There is no third option.
>   **Ward Churchill**, educator, activist. *On the Justice of Roosting Chickens*, 2003

Americans are not critical thinkers by and large. We suffer from a collective sociogenic learning disability based on the complete commodification of our consciousness by consumerism and electronic media. So we are not only bitterly unhappy and alienated, we are intensely stupid and attached to denial.
>   **Stan Goff**, writer, former Sergeant with U.S. Special Forces. Interview, *Truthout*, 7/16/2003

The white man, who possesses this whole vast country from sea to sea, who roams over it at pleasure and lives where he likes, cannot know the cramp we feel in this little spot [the reservation] with the undying remembrance of the fact…that every foot of what you proudly call America not very long ago belonged to the Red man.
>   **Washakie**, Shoshoni leader. Speech to Wyoming Governor's Conference, 1878

The blood of my ancestors soaks this soil and their blood has been shed on every foreign battlefield for the preservation of this nation. Therefore, we as a people feel a deep sense of ownership of America as much as any American.

  Louis Farrakhan, Minister, Nation of Islam. From letter to George W. Bush, 12/1/2001

The true history of the conquest and colonization of America is a story of unceasing dignity. There was not a day without rebellion.

  Eduardo Galeano, Uruguayan historian, educator. *Upside Down*, 1998

"In Defense of Thomas Jones," collage by Theodore Harris

For four hundred years America has been nothing but a wolves den for twenty million so-called Negroes.

  Malcolm X, Black nationalist leader. Speech, June 1963

I have lived inside the monster and know its entrails—and my weapon is only that of David.

> **José Martí**, Cuban political theorist, poet, referring to his time in the U.S. From letter to Manuel Mercado, 1895

I wanna hear an American poem, an American poem about sharecroppers on the side of the road or families in cardboard boxes, not about kings or majestic lands or how beautiful ugly can be. I wanna hear some American poetry about projects and lead poison, poverty and children in jail...

> **Ras Baraka**, poet, Deputy Mayor of Newark, NJ. From poem "American Poem," circa 1999

The brand "America" is like Clorox corporation: it sells both toxic bleach (Clorox) and salad dressing (Hidden Valley Ranch). If the salad dressing came with the Clorox label, we wouldn't buy it. If "America" came with images of poverty and of military domination, it would fail as fantasy.

> **Vijay Prashad**, writer. *Keeping Up With the Dow Joneses*, 2003

I love America deeply. But, I will never love Amerikkka unconditionally. Blind patriots are fools. Though the soil of this country is rich with the blood of my people, its grounds are increasingly cruel places upon which to walk.

> **Alicia Banks**, radio talk show host, writer. Essay, "On Amerikkka: 2000," 1999

America: love it enough to change it.

> **Grace Lee Boggs**, activist. *The Boggs Center* web site, 2004

In this country, American means white. Everybody else has to hyphenate.

> **Toni Morrison**, writer, educator. Attributed.

As the African-Americans "awaken" today, we find ourselves in a strange land that has rejected us.

> **Malcolm X**, Black nationalist leader. Speech, "Appeal to African Heads of State," Cairo, Egypt, July 1964

Many folk involved in the anti-war movement from the white community have this nostalgic notion of America. See, they don't want to give up this false notion that America is a fair and just country... There are no "good ol' days" in this country for Black folks with some level of consciousness.

There is nothing redeemable about America.
>   **Ewuare Osayande**, educator, activist, poet. Speech, 4/3/2003

There is the America of the American dream, and there is the America of the American nightmare.
>   **Eldridge Cleaver**, writer, former black power activist.
>   "Conversation with Eldridge Cleaver," 1970

Some have been foolish enough to call it the "cradle of liberty." If it is the "cradle of liberty," they have rocked the child to death.
>   **William Wells Brown**, writer, former slave. Speech, Salem, MA
>   1847

No, I'm not an American. I'm one of the 22 million black people who are the victims of Americanism. One of the 22 million black people who are the victims of democracy, nothing but disguised hypocrisy. So, I'm not standing here speaking to you as an American, or a patriot, or a flag-salutor, or a flag-waver—no, not I.
>   **Malcolm X**, Black nationalist leader. Speech, "The Ballot or the
>   Bullet," April 1964

I defy any part of an insolent, dominating America, however powerful; I defy any errand boys, Uncle Toms of the Negro people to challenge my Americanism, because by word and deed I challenge this vicious system to death.
>   **Paul Robeson**, activist, scholar, athlete. Speech, "Welcome Home
>   Rally," New York, NY, June 1949

In this world of religious flag waving you hear it said "you reap what you sow," "everything that goes around comes around," and "there's karma to pay," etc. If any of this is true, America has a terrible day of reckoning coming for its mistreatment of my people and the earth.
>   **Leonard Peltier**, writer, U.S. political prisoner. From statement
>   to supporters, 12/07/2003

Our every action is a call for war against imperialism and a cry for the unity of the peoples against the great enemy of the human species: the United States of North America.
>   **Ernesto "Che" Guevara**, Argentinean-Cuban revolutionary and
>   military leader. Essay, "Two, Three, Many Vietnams," 1967

How does it become a man to behave toward the American government today? I answer, that he cannot without disgrace be associated with it.

> **Henry David Thoreau**, writer, philosopher. *Civil Disobedience*, 1849

I hunger for freedom. If I die, I do not want this tragic country [the U.S.] to swallow my bones. They need the warmth of Borinquén. At least let them strengthen the worms there and not here.

> **Julia de Burgos**, Puerto Rican poet, 1914-1953. In *Notable Latino Americans*, 1997

The United States seems destined to plague and torment the [Latin American] continent in the name of freedom.

> **Simón Bolívar**, Venezuelan revolutionary leader, military general, 1783-1830. In *One Hundred Red Hot Years*, 2004

One ever feels his two-ness,—an American, a Negro; two souls, two thoughts, two unreconciled strivings; two warring ideals in one dark body, whose dogged strength alone keeps it from being torn asunder.

> **W.E.B. Du Bois**, scholar, educator. *The Souls of Black Folk*, 1903

Sitting at the table doesn't make you a diner. You must be eating some of what's on that plate. Being here in America doesn't make you an American. Being born here in America doesn't make you an American.

> **Malcolm X**, Black nationalist leader. Speech, "The Ballot or the Bullet," April 1964

America's great, I love America. But if you're black, you gotta look at America a little bit different. You gotta look at America like the uncle who paid for you to go to college...but molested you.

> **Chris Rock**, comedian. "Never Scared," *HBO*, 2004

The land of the free and the home of the brave, the nation that was born as the vehicle for a new freedom, rests on the denial not only of freedom, but of life itself, to a whole group of people—for the crime of getting in the way of what the European invaders wanted for themselves, the land and its resources.

> **Robert Jensen**. Essay, "What the 'Fighting Sioux' Tells Us About Whites," 2003

I see America through the eyes of the victim. I don't see any American dream; I see an American nightmare.

> **Malcolm X**, Black nationalist leader. Speech, "The Ballot or the Bullet," April 1964

When you live in the United States, with the roar of the free market, the roar of this huge military power, the roar of being at the heart of empire, it's hard to hear the whispering of the rest of the world. And I think many U.S. citizens want to.

> **Arundhati Roy**, Indian writer, activist. *The Checkbook and the Cruise Missile*, 2004

I live in the United States, but I do not know exactly where. My address is wherever there is a fight against oppression. My address is like my shoes; it travels with me. I abide where there is a fight against wrong.

> **Mother Jones**, union organizer, activist. In *Great Labor Quotations*, 2000

They should get down on their hands and knees every morning and thank God that 22 million black people have not become anti-American. You've given us every right to. The whole world would side with us, if we became anti-American. You know, that's something to think about.

> **Malcolm X**, Black nationalist leader. Speech, "Prospects for Freedom in 1965," January 1965

While envisaging the destruction of imperialism, it is necessary to identify its head, which is no other than the United States of America.

> **Ernesto "Che" Guevara**, Argentinean-Cuban revolutionary and military leader. From "Message to the Tricontinental," April 1967

What a laugh! America the beautiful. Home of the brave. Friend of the underdog. You once had a beautiful dream—but even then, while you dreamed that dream, you were foul and corrupt and rotten in your heart, but you were a minor league brigand then and when you compared yourself to the other tyrannies of the world, you looked innocent by contrast to their greater evil. The innocent blood they had shed was a vast and ancient ocean, and yours was a fresh new stream. But now your little stream has become vaster than the sky and your evil dwarfs everything that has gone before. Now you stand naked before the world, before yourself, a predatory,

genocidal Dorian Grey, stripped of all egalitarian democratic makeup.
> **Eldridge Cleaver**, writer, former Black power activist. Essay, "Credo for Rioters and Looters," circa 1969

We have met the enemy and he is U.S.
> **Bumper sticker**, 2003

The red, white and blue flag stands for the annihilation of my nation, the annihilation of my relatives.
> **Without Rezervation**, hip hop group. From song "Red, White and Blue," 1994

Flags are bits of colored cloth that governments use first to shrink-wrap people's minds and then as ceremonial shrouds to bury the dead.
> **Arundhati Roy**, Indian writer, activist. *War Talk*, 2003

Hip-hop represents people fighting for freedom and justice. The American flag does not. No one will be admitted to a Coup show wearing red white and blue. They represent violent gang colors.
> **The Coup**, hip hop group. From statement regarding 9/11 World Trade Center attacks, 2001

The United States is in many ways the biggest ghetto in the world, and the biggest administrator in the world, and that gets complicated.
> **Selma James**, English activist, founder, Global Women's Strike. Anti-war meeting, Philadelphia, PA June 2003

Americans exist beneath a one-way magnifying glass that forces everyone else to acquire insight into American culture whether they want it or not, while Americans seem to learn about everyone else by force of will.
> **Jeremy Tavares**, Jamaican writer. Essay, "Caribbean Karma," 2003

American history is longer, larger, more beautiful, and more terrible than anything anyone has ever said about it.
> **James Baldwin**, writer, educator. *Saturday Review*, December 1963

Chapter 33

"Corrupting Absolutely"

Power, Authority, Privilege

The only thing the privileged can do is divest themselves of their privilege. The only thing a racist can do is become a race traitor. The only thing the slave master can do is stop being a slave master. But the slave has still gotta break his own chains.

> **Not4Prophet**, lyricist for band Ricanstruction. Interview, *Clamor* magazine, Spring 2001

In our world, many of us who live in the U.S. are perched, quite by accident, amidst inordinately luxurious surroundings, relative to the rest of the world. We're the luckiest. We're the most blest. And we have the greatest responsibility to build a better world.

> **Kathy Kelly**, peace activist. *Guerrilla News Network*, 2004

Recognizing your many positions of marginalization, privilege and power is one of the most important steps in engaging in activism that uses an anti-oppression framework at its core. However, it should not be a debilitating step. I believe that guilt is a useless emotion. To me, recognizing where you have power over others means that you recognize that you have a responsibility to work towards changing things.

> **Helen Luu**, activist. Interview, *Clamor* magazine, 2003

The only justification for repressive institutions is material and cultural deficit.

> **Noam Chomsky**, political analyst, linguist. *For Reasons of State*, 1973

I am driven by many things. I know what some of them are. The misery that people suffer and the misery for which I share responsibility. That is agonizing. We live in a free society, and privilege confers responsibility.

> **Noam Chomsky**, political analyst, linguist. *New York Times magazine*, 11/2/2003

Bodies in power tend to stay in power, unless external forces disturb them.

> **Catharine Stimpson**, writer. *The Power to Name,* 1979

Nobody is as powerful as we make them out to be.

> **Alice Walker**, writer, poet. *In Search of Our Mothers' Gardens*, 1983

We strike the pose of self-sufficiency while ignoring the advantages we have been afforded in every realm of activity... We ignore the fact that at almost every turn, our hard work has been met with access to an opportunity structure denied to millions of others. Privilege, to us, is like water to the fish: invisible precisely because we cannot imagine life without it.

> **Tim Wise**, activist, educator. Essay, "Whites Swim in Racial Preference," 2003

It is only in folk tales, children's stories, and the journals of intellectual opinion that power is used wisely and well to destroy evil. The real world teaches very different lessons, and it takes willful and dedicated ignorance to fail to perceive them.

> **Noam Chomsky**, political analyst, linguist. Speech, 12/8/2001

Power concedes nothing without a demand. It never did and it never will.

> **Frederick Douglass**, slavery abolitionist, political theorist. Speech, Canandaigua, NY, 8/4/1857

Chapter 34

"Rules of the Game"

Law and Legality

Written laws are like spider's webs and will, like them, only entangle and hold the poor and weak, while the rich and powerful easily break through them.
> **Anacharsis**, Scythian philosopher, circa 600 B.C.

Law never made men a whit more just; and, by means of their respect for it, even the well-disposed are daily made the agents of injustice.
> **Henry David Thoreau**, writer, philosopher. *Civil Disobedience*, 1849

Laws are made for lawless people. This is a nation of laws, and lawless people, and that's why the white man lies to you all the time. That's why this is a society of liars, and they pass more laws every year and build more jails. You can always tell how civilized the reservation is becoming by the amount of jails. The older Diné remember when there were no jails on this reservation. You're civilized now, a part of this great country of freedom and democracy: pick up a gun, let me train you to be a murderer of human beings. Then let me train you to be proud to be a trained murderer of human beings, and to fight for this piece of cloth. That's what I want you to do, and if you don't do it, I'll put you in jail because there are laws.
> **Russell Means**, activist, actor, former leader in the American Indian Movement. Speech, Navajo Community College, Arizona, 1995

There is no crueler tyranny than that which is exercised under cover of law, and with the colors of justice.
> **Legal case**, *U.S. v. Jannotti*, 1982

With Congress, every time they make a joke it's a law, and every time they make a law it's a joke.
> **Will Rogers**, writer, actor, comedian. 1879-1935. Attributed.

I submit that an individual who breaks a law that conscience tells him is unjust, and willingly accepts the penalty by staying in jail to arouse the conscience of the community over its injustice, is in reality expressing the very highest respect for law.
> **Martin Luther King, Jr.,** civil rights leader. "Letter from Birmingham City Jail," 4/16/1963

No great idea in its beginning can ever be within the law.
>   **Emma Goldman**, activist, writer, anarchist. *Mother Earth*, 1917

No man can point to any law in the U.S. by which slavery was originally established. Men first make slaves and then make laws.
>   **Frederick Douglass**, slavery abolitionist, political theorist. Speech, 1889

If the Nuremberg laws were applied, than every post-war American President would have been hanged.
>   **Noam Chomsky**, political analyst, linguist. Speech, circa 1990

Condemn me. It does not matter. History will absolve me.
>   **Fidel Castro**, Cuban revolutionary, political leader. Speech during his trial after attack on the Moncada army barracks, 1953

I have no power to describe the feeling of horror that possessed every member of the race in Memphis when the truth dawned upon us that protection of the law was no longer ours.
>   **Ida B. Wells**, journalist, activist, after mass lynchings of Black people in Tulsa, OK, circa 1892

It is not inevitable, nor is it wise, that natural objects should have no rights to seek redress in their own behalf. It is no answer to say that streams and forests cannot have standing because streams and forests cannot speak. Corporations cannot speaks either; nor can states, estates, infants, incompetents, municipalities or universities. Lawyers speak for them, as they customarily do for the ordinary citizen with legal problems.
>   **Christopher D. Stone**, educator, attorney. *Southern California Law Review*, Spring, 1972

In the old days all you needed was a handshake. Nowadays you need forty lawyers.
>   **Jimmy Hoffa**, union leader. In *Hoffa, The Real Story,* 1975

Egypt had its locusts, Asiatic countries their cholera, France its Jacobins, England its black plague, Memphis had the yellow fever…but it was left for unfortunate Indian Territory to be afflicted with the worst scourage of the 19th century, the Dawes Commission.
>   **Anonymous**. In *Native American Testimony,* 1991. The Dawes Commission was established by the U.S. government in 1893 to

end self-governance among five American Indian nations.

Exactly at that moment when we have begun to suspect that law is congealed injustice, that the existing order hides an everyday violence against body and spirit, that our political structure is fossilized, and that the noise of change—however scary—may be necessary, a cry rises for 'law and order.' Such a moment becomes a crucial test of whether the society will sink back to a spurious safety or leap forward to its own freshening. We seem to have reached such a moment in the United States.

Howard Zinn, historian, educator. "Disobedience and Democracy," 1968

Chapter 35

"Pimps, Pirates and Parasites"

Politics, Politicians, Elected Officials, Elections

Look around, ya see so many social hypocrites
Like to make rules for others while they do just the opposite.
>   **Bob Dylan**, singer. From song, "Ain't No Man Righteous (No Not
>   One)," 1981

If we got one-tenth of what was promised to us in these acceptance speeches
[of politicians] there wouldn't be any inducement to go to heaven.
>   **Will Rogers**, writer, actor, comedian. 1879-1935. Attributed.

Our 500 plus year colonial condition is someone else's politics in our face.
Our imperialization is their politics. Our enslavement is their emancipation.
Our color is their capitalism. The genocide we survived, the poverty and
homelessness we endure, the racism we face, the ghettoization and starvation
and sterilization, the drugs we sell or the food we steal, and the bombs they
drop, are all someone else's politics.
>   **Not4Prophet**, lyricist for band Ricanstruction. *Clamor* magazine,
>   Spring 2001

Any politics we pick up and follow, they are not our politics. They are alien
politics, but we've been put in the position of having to use those alien
politics to try to accomplish....if we are going to use a political structure, then
let's recognize that's what we are doing. It's a tool. It's not an identity.
>   **John Trudell**, poet, activist, former chairman of the American
>   Indian Movement. Interview, 1998

Especially for people of color, our lives are so tied together with our politics.
Everything we do is political in this nation and especially for women of Color.
A lot of times the outlets we are left to express our politics is through our lives,
so how we raise our children, how we laugh, how we engage in relationships
becomes extremely political in a sexist white supremacist society.
>   **Walidah Imarisha**, activist, poet. Interview, *GeoClan.com*, May
>   2004

Political power, properly so called, is merely the organized power of one
class for suppressing another.
>   **Karl Marx and Friedrich Engels**, German political theorists.
>   *The Communist Manifesto*, 1848

The criminals that run this society can give us nothing. They cannot give us our freedom because they are not free themselves. They cannot give us our respect because they have no respectful ways. They cannot give us our dignity because they have no dignity.

> **John Trudelll**, poet, activist, former chairman of the American Indian Movement.

Whatever is good for the People is bad for their Governors; and what is good for the Governors is pernicious for the People.

> **Thomas Gordan**, English writer. *Cato's Letters*, 1748

Everyone knows that politicians routinely exaggerate, distort, and make promises that they know full well they can never fulfill. They are selling illusions of themselves; they are coached and packaged by professional public relations teams who have made a science out of the marketing of politics.

> **John Stockwell**, activist, writer, former CIA agent. *The Praetorian Guard*, 1990

It's true you can humiliate and you can hound and you can smash and burn and terrify and smirk and boast and defame and demonize and dismiss and incinerate and starve, and yes, you can force somebody—force a people to surrender…But all of us who are weak, we watch you. And we learn from your hatred, and we do not forget. And we are ready, Mr. President. We are most of the people on this god-forsaken planet.

> **June Jordan**, poet, educator. Speech opposing the Gulf War, Hayward, CA 2/21/1991

The people that run this government are a foul group of pimps, pirates and parasites! That's what they are. They feed off us, don't give nothing back, and they get rich and powerful by finding ways to get other people to do their work for them.

> **Abdul Jon**, activist. Political prisoners supporter's meeting, Philadelphia, PA, 2002

There's nothing more dangerous than a brilliant strategic mind with no heart.

> **Adrienne Maree Brown**, activist. *How to Get Stupid White Men Out of Office*, 2004

By John Jonik

Who make money from war
Who make dough from fear and lies
Who want the world like it is
Who want the world to be ruled by
imperialism and national
oppression and terror violence, and hunger
and poverty.

> **Amiri Baraka**, poet, educator. From poem "Somebody Blew Up America," 2001

There's a sort of Peter Principle at work here. Laurence Peter wrote that in a hierarchy every employee tends to rise to his level of incompetence. Perhaps we can postulate that in a foreign policy establishment committed to imperialist domination by any means necessary, employees tend to rise to

the level of cruelty they can live with.
> **William Blum**, writer. *Rogue State,* 2000

This country has come to feel the same when Congress is in session as when a baby gets hold of a hammer.
> **Will Rogers**, writer, actor, comedian. 1879-1935. Attributed.

The two old parties have combined against us to nullify our power by a 'gentlemen's agreement' of non-recognition, no matter how we vote... May God write us down as asses if ever again we are found putting our trust in either the Republican or the Democratic parties.
> **W.E.B. Du Bois**, scholar, educator. *An ABC of Color*, 1963

We hang the petty thieves and appoint the great ones to public office.
> **Aesop**, ancient fabulist, storyteller, ex-slave of Northern African or Greek birth, circa 620 to 560 B.C. Attributed.

Maybe the reason the majority of Americans don't vote is that they're tired of having to choose between tweedledum and tweedledumber. The choices are always so pathetic, aren't they? If you went to a restaurant and the waiter told you, "We're sorry, but the only choices we have left on the menu are cottage cheese and fried breadsticks," you'd leave. Nobody would think you were crazy, lazy, apathetic, or not hungry.
> **Michael Moore**, filmmaker, writer. *Downsize This!*, 1996

If we consider ourselves anti-militarists, why are we trying to pick the commander-in chief of the US armed forces? It's like me voting for Grand Wizard of the Ku Klux Klan, in the hopes that I can elect a kinder, gentler, and more benevolent Grand Wizard.
> **Mario Hardy Ramirez**, activist, on voting. Interview, *Insubordination* magazine, September 2003

Fuck the president
I voted for assassination
> **Immortal Technique**, hip hop MC. From song "Revolutionary," Viper Records, 2001

Don't vote. It only encourages them.
> **Bumper sticker**, 2002

Elections are designed to legitimize the rule of the dominant class. After each election, political pundits and think-tank spokespersons all get together and puff up on TV to congratulate America for another peaceful transition, even as 2,000,000 people rot in prison, crappy factory jobs that pay $13 an hour become crappier fast-food jobs that pay $6 an hour, cops turn Miami into a paramilitary zone, thousands of women are beaten half to death by controlling spouses, and whole neighborhoods look more and more like the Third World.

> **Stan Goff**, writer, former U.S. Army sergeant. Essay, "War, Race, and Elections," 2003

We know we can't win anything with Republicans, but our people are not celebrating about these Democrats either. The Democrats have become Republican and the Republicans have become extremists. We're voting for these people but then we still have to fight everything they do.

> **Brian Drapeaux**, community activist, Democratic campaigner on the Pine Ridge reservation, South Dakota. In *How to Get Stupid White Men Out of Office*, 2004

If we're trying to vote against genocide and mass murder, it won't work, because there's no one out there to elect, and the playing field is rigged.

> **Mario Hardy Ramirez**, activist. Interview, *Insubordination* magazine, September 2003

If you want systemic change and all you do is vote, you are wasting your time. If you want systemic change and you fail to vote for candidates calling for change, you are wasting an opportunity. If you want systemic change and you vote for candidates opposed to change, you are working against your own goals.

> **David Cobb**, Green Party candidate for U.S. president, 2004. Interview, *Z Magazine*, September 2004

Rousseau thought that representative government was an absolute farce. He says the moment you vote and give up your power to some other people, they begin to represent themselves or other interests, not the interests of the people.

> **C.L.R. James**, Trinidad journalist, playwright. "Modern Politics," 1960

What this country needs is more unemployed politicians.

> **Angela Davis**, activist, educator, writer. Speech, 1967

By John Jonik

You can't complain if you don't participate. Even if you don't feel the candidates in the major races, at least familiarize yourself with and vote on local measures in your area. While it is not the only solution, voting is part of the solution.

    Paris, hip hop MC. *Guerrilla Funk Newsletter*, May 2004

We are not interested in your elections. We are interested in freedom.

    Desmond Tutu, South African archbishop and activist. *CBS News*, 9/1/1989

I'd rather vote for something I want and not get it than vote for something I don't want, and get it.

    Eugene Debs, activist, labor organizer, socialist. 1855-1926. Attributed.

A ballot is like a bullet. You don't throw your ballots until you see a target, and if that target is not within your reach, keep your ballot in your pocket.

    Malcolm X, Black nationalist leader. Speech, "The Ballot or the Bullet," April 1964

The power of the ballot we need in sheer self-defence,—else what shall save us from a second slavery?

W.E.B. Du Bois, scholar, educator. *The Souls of Black Folk*, 1903

Activist movements, if at all serious, pay virtually no attention to which faction of the business party is in office, but continue with their daily work, from which elections are a diversion—which we cannot ignore, any more than we can ignore the sun rising; they exist.

Noam Chomsky, political analyst, linguist. In *Ralph's Revolt*, 2004

By John Jonik

The trouble with practical jokes is that very often they get elected.

Will Rogers, writer, actor, comedian. 1879-1935. Attributed.

We never asked the government for the right to vote—we were forced to become citizens of this country and then *told* we had to vote. Many people on this rez believe we are our own sovereign Lakota Nation, so why the hell should we vote for any state or national race? We have our own traditional way of doing things.

> **Nick Tilsen**, activist for a 2002 U.S. Senate election, Pine Ridge Reservation, SD, 2004

Politicians, modern day magicians
Physicians of death

> **Outkast**, hip hop group. From song "War," 2003

But I wanted to come here today to let you know that some of us are not afraid, that even though we may be elected, we'll say what's on our mind, but we must understand that we are freedom fighters first and all the other things come next. That I am a Black man first and then a State Representative. I don't confuse the two and I think it's time for us to wake up and understand that you got a lot of us that are willing to go to battle because of freedom. We ain't goin' never be free unless we take it. There's too many of us sitting around thinking that it's gonna come to us on some damn silver plate.

> **David P. Richardson**, Pennsylvania State Representative. Speech demanding a fair trial for Mumia Abu-Jamal, Philadelphia, PA 8/12/1995

I'm an old lady, all white and all scared but there's no escape, even on the edge of death. I thought we had done what we could to make things right, back then when I was young, but we raised these kids and we put these monsters in office—again. And frankly, it's that much harder because we should have known better.

> **Ms. Daisy Lynn C**. From e-mail intended for Mumia Abu-Jamal, May 2004

i was not alive during the rise of fascism in the 1930s, but i am sure for many people, Hitler and Mussolini must have seemed invincible. Today's fascists are even more dangerous and they are present at the highest levels of the U.S. Government... In this turbulent political climate many people feel confused, powerless and overwhelmed. The imperialist powers that rule this planet are vicious, evil, and powerful, but they can, and they will be defeated.

> **Assata Shakur**, former Black Panther, in exile in Cuba. From her greeting to U.S. political prisoner Mumia Abu-Jamal on the occasion of his 50th birthday, 4/24/2004

Chapter 36

"Republicrats"

Reform, Reaction, Liberalism, Conservatism

Today, "liberal" is just another word for "not nuts." Don't go around invading countries that do not pose a threat and lie to the world to justify it; don't destroy the nation's fiscal health in order to give trillion-dollar gifts to the wealthy; don't gratuitously insult countries whose help we need to maintain world peace and security; don't shred the Constitution at every opportunity.

> **Eric Alterman**, writer. *The Nation*, June 2003

The more you read and observe about this Politics thing, you got to admit that each party is worse than the other. The one that's out always looks the best.

> **Will Rogers**, writer, actor, comedian. 1879-1935. Attributed.

I should say that I am not a liberal. I find most liberals to be conservatives who want to be forgiven.

> **Stan Goff**, writer, former U.S. Army sergeant. Interview, *Truthout*, 7/16/2003

A liberal is an aesthete, much preoccupied with form and means and techniques. He looks out on a raging battlefield and sees error everywhere, and he thinks he can find the truth by avoiding error.

> **Lerone Bennett**, writer, historian. "Tea and Sympathy: Liberals and Other White Hopes," 1964

The white liberal differs from the white conservative only in one way: The liberal is more deceitful than the conservative. The liberal is more hypocritical than the conservative. Both want power, but the white liberal is the one who has perfected the art of posing as the Negro's friend and benefactor; and by winning the friendship, allegiance, and support of the Negro, the white liberal is able to use the Negro as a pawn or tool in this political "football game" that is constantly raging between the white liberals and white conservatives.

> **Malcolm X**, Black nationalist leader. Speech, "God's Judgment of White America," 12/4/1963

A moderate is a cat who will hang you from a low tree.

> **Dick Gregory**, activist, nutritionist, comedian, circa 1964

All reactionaries are paper tigers... From a long-term point of view, it is not the reactionaries but the people who are really powerful.

Mao Tse-Tung, Chinese revolutionary, political theorist. "Talk with the American correspondent Anna Louise Strong," 1946

I always say to interviewers, "This is not a conspiracy." There's no secret badge or anything. It's much looser. This is how the vast right-wing conspiracy works, by being associates, friends.

Jeffrey Sharlet. Interview, *Guerrilla News Network*, 2002

At the core of political conservatism is the resistance to change and a tolerance for inequality.

Kathleen Maclay, writer. *UC Berkeley News*, 7/22/2003

"Neo-liberalism" is essentially conservatism with a sweet smile. For, as the conservatives serve the business interests of capital, and are thus tied to them for resources, in truth, so too are the liberals. They both serve a system that protects capital above all else.

Mumia Abu-Jamal, journalist, U.S. political prisoner. Essay, "When Liberals Attack," 2002

Chapter 37

"No Justice, No Peace"

Police, Prisons, Crime, the Criminal Justice System, Capital Punishment

I have seen criminals and whores
And spoken with them. Now I inquire
If you believe them, made as now they are
To drag their rags in blood and mire
Preordained, an evil race?
You to whom all men are prey
Have made them what they are today.

> **Louise Michel**, French anarchist rebel leader in the 1871 Paris Commune. Poem, in *Louise Michel*, 2004

There is something wrong in this country; the judicial nets are so adjusted as to catch the minnows and let the whales slip through and the federal judge is as far removed from the common people as if he inhabited another planet.

> **Eugene Debs**, activist, labor organizer, socialist, 11/23/1895

Poor people have access to American courts in the same sense that the Christians had access to the lions when they were dragged into a Roman arena.

> **Earl Johnson, Jr.**, judge. Attributed.

The courts have become a universal device for re-enslaving blacks.

> **W.E.B. Du Bois**, scholar, educator. *The Souls of Black Folk*, 1903

If you don't get a fair trial, you have a lynching.

> **Rick Hart and the Blue Horse Band**. Album cover, 2002

Perhaps we can shrug off and shred some of the dangerous myths laid on our minds like a second skin—such as…the "right" to a fair trial even. They're not rights—they're privileges of the powerful and rich. Don't expect the media networks to tell you, for they can't. Because of their incestuousness… with government and big business.
I can.
Even if I must do so from the valley of the shadow of death, I will.

> **Mumia Abu-Jamal**, journalist, U.S. political prisoner. *Live from*

Death Row, 1995

The more lawless our government becomes, the more it stresses and prosecutes law-breaking on the part of its citizens, and the more it builds jails and prisons, and the more it imprisons and for longer and longer periods of time.
> **Elizabeth McAlister**. In *Global Uprising*, 2001

A busy courtroom is a sign of a bankrupt culture.
> **Nidal Sakr**, human rights activist.

The D.A.'s Office is filled with some low down, sinister son-of-a-guns who don't give a damn about your innocence or guilt.
> **Pam Africa**, activist, MOVE Organization member. Comment at political prisoners conference, 3/16/2003

Where justice is denied, where poverty is enforced, where ignorance prevails, and where any one class is made to feel that society is in an organized conspiracy to oppress, rob, and degrade them, neither persons nor property will be safe.
> **Frederick Douglass**, slavery abolitionist, political theorist. Speech, Washington, DC, April 1886

Who is a thug anyway? A boy-made-man by violent urban divestment? A boy whose image-world became a temple of saccharine Eurocentric consumerism? A boy who saw no intelligent visions of himself? An exile whose neighborhood was run-down, torn-down, rebuilt, and gentrified without him inside?
> **Adam Bahner**. Essay, "If I Get Shot by the Police," 2004

It seems the only gang colors allowed are Red, White, and Blue together.
> **Fernando Reals**, activist. Essay, "The War is On and the Youth are Rising Up," 2000

There's this perception that people in urban communities are hardened killers and it's not true. They're bright and intelligent individuals, but they're wounded deeply and carrying that around, which is basically a trigger. They're only emulating what they see taking place in the world.
> **Aqeela Sherrills**, youth gang peace organizer. Interview, *Satya* magazine, November 2002

Every crime that I did was petty
Every criminal is rich already
> **The Coup**, hip hop group. From song "Everything," 2001

There exists among the intolerably degraded the perverse and powerful desire to force into the arena of the actual those fantastic crimes of which they have been accused, achieving their vengeance and their own destruction through making the nightmare real.
> **James Baldwin**, writer, educator. *Notes of a Native Son,* 1955

While there is a lower class, I am in it, and while there is a criminal element I am of it, and while there is a soul in prison, I am not free.
> **Eugene Debs**, activist, labor organizer, socialist. Speech to court upon conviction for violation of the U.S. Espionage Act for speaking publicly against World War I, September 1918

Crime is naught but misdirected energy.
> **Emma Goldman**, activist, writer, anarchist. *Anarchism,* 1910

You can't imprison all the blacks, you can't imprison all the poor whites, and you can't imprison all the brown people. You gotta do something different. Be tough on crime. That means being tough in your neighborhood, working with the youth, not imprisoning them. Trying to give them a chance, give them a second chance, a third chance, give them a vision of hope.
> **Magdaleno Rose-Avila**, gang nonviolence organizer, Los Angeles, CA. *Blu Magazine,* 2000

And these Crackers say we get a jury of our own peers. Know that if we really got a jury of our own peers we'll put the system on trial.
> **Hedrush, Dead Prez, People's Army**, hip hop MCs, activists. From song "Murda Box," circa 1999

Only in a country as morally corrupt as America in 2003 can three nuns who took part in a largely symbolic protest at a Colorado missile base get prison sentences of 30 to 41 months the same week the Massachusetts Attorney General announces that he can't find anything to charge the Catholic Church with even as it's revealed the organization covered up something like 1,000 sex abuse cases in the Boston area over the last six decades.
> **"Anthony, NYC,"** alias of writer on *Guerrilla News Network* internet forum, 2003

By John Jonik

There's no crime that you're going to get caught for as long as you're doing it as a part of the fascism, 'cause fascism doesn't punish its own. And if they do, it's a smack on the wrist and a million dollar book contract. Look at what happened with Richard Nixon. We should all have such hardships of being thrown out of office!

> **Gary Null**, physician, health educator. Speech, "Fascism in Medicine," May 1994

There can never really be justice on stolen land.

> **KRS One**, hip hop MC. From song "Sound of Da Police," 1993

Innocence is the weakest defense. Innocence has a single voice that can only say over and over again, "I didn't do it." Guilt has a thousand voices, all of them lies.

> **Leonard Peltier**, writer, U.S. political prisoner. *Prison Writings,* 1999

I have been locked by the lawless.
Handcuffed by the haters.
Gagged by the greedy.
And, if I know any thing at all,
it's that a wall is just a wall
and nothing more at all.
It can be broken down.

> **Assata Shakur**, former Black Panther, in exile in Cuba. From poem "Affirmation," circa 1987

Jails and prisons are designed to break human beings, to convert the population into specimens in a zoo—obedient to our keepers, but dangerous to each other.

> **Angela Davis**, activist, educator, writer. In *The Black Scholar*, 1971

Prisoners are repositories of rage, islands of socially acceptable hatreds, where worlds collide like subatomic particles seeking psychic release.

> **Mumia Abu-Jamal**, journalist, U.S. political prisoner. *Live from Death Row*, 1995

Because there's nothing valuable in prison. Prison is the lowest level that a human being can exist on without being dead. There is nothing rehabilitative about prison. Nothing. Prison is there for one of two reasons, which are: to keep you there for as long as the system has sentenced you there, or if you don't wish to stay there, to kill you. And all of the other stuff about philosophy and about repentance has no point in reality.

> **Rubin "Hurricane" Carter**, activist, former champion boxer framed for murder. Interview, *Blu Magazine*, 2000

The degree of civilization in a society can be judged by entering its prisons.

> **Fyodor Dostoyevsky**, Russian writer. Attributed.

I know far too much about prisons. More than I ever wished to know. From every category of male relative I can name—grandfather, father, son, brother, uncle, nephew, cousin, in-laws—at least one member of my family has been incarcerated.

> **John Edgar Wideman**, writer. Essay, "Doing Time, Marking Race," circa 1996

Those of us on the outside do not like to think of wardens and guards as our surrogates. Yet they are, and they are intimately locked in a deadly embrace with their human captives behind the prison walls. By extension so are we.
> **Jessica Mitford**, writer, activist. *Kind and Usual Punishment*, 1973

We are men! We are not beasts and we do not intend to be beaten or driven as such.
> **L.D. Barkley**, a prisoner who participated in the Attica Prison Uprising and was killed by police and the National Guard. From statement written by prisoners and read by Barkley during the rebellion, 9/9/1971

Society eliminates by sending to prison people whom prison breaks up, crushes, physically eliminates; the prison eliminates them by "freeing" them and sending them back to society; ...the state in which they come out insures that society will eliminate them once again, sending them to prison.
> **Michel Foucault**, French philosopher who traveled to the U.S. to study its jails in 1972, speaking of the Attica and Philadelphia County prisons. Interview, *Social Justice*, Fall 1991

Men copied the realities of their hearts when they build prisons.
> **Richard Wright**, writer. *The Outsider*, 1953

The character and mentality of the keepers may be of more importance in understanding prisons than the character and mentality of the kept.
> **Jessica Mitford**, writer, activist. *Kind and Usual Punishment*, 1973

Prison is a very cruel reality. But unusual? Imprisonment has become a common experience.
> **Leonard Peltier**, writer, U.S. political prisoner. Essay, "Cruel and Unusual Punishment," August 2004

A reservation Indian is already well-prepared to go to the penitentiary. Before he gets there he has already practiced being in prison. And even on the reservation, many Indians are still having a barbed-wire attitude—I try to teach my children and my people to get rid of the barbed-wire mind.
> **Leonard Crow Dog**, Lakota medicine man. In *In the Spirit of Crazy Horse*, 1983

Why is it that our society continues to pour investment into punishing

humans for crimes, instead of investing in educating to prevent crimes and/ or pinpoint what causes these crimes in the first place?
> **Floyd Peterson**, activist. *Infoshop.org*, 2001

Trying to solve the crime problem by building more prison cells is like trying to solve the problem of AIDS by building more hospitals.
> **James Austin**, writer. *The Washington Post*, 1988

The cruelty of prison rests in locking up people who are often already feeling remorse and low self-esteem because of past actions and then heaping upon them more reasons to feel badly about themselves and allowing almost no means to improve their situation.
> **Kathy Kelly**, peace activist. From her prison diary, 3/29/2004

You who enjoy mid-autumn in the midst of your families,
Remember those in prison, who drink the dregs of misery.
> **Ho Chi Minh**, Vietnamese political leader, poet. *The Prison Diary of Ho Chi Minh*, 1942

You can never imagine the heartfelt comfort it brings to know you're not forgotten in prison.
> **Leonard Peltier**, writer, U.S. political prisoner. Statement to supporters, 1/23/2004

They lockin' brothers in the poorhouse
who can't afford Moorhouse [college]
politicians nervous
it's the only free service they provide
> **Spearhead**. From song "Crime to be Broke in America," 1994

You quickly learn within the walls that you're at the mercy of anyone with a sadistic streak; and there's seldom any shortage of those.
> **Leonard Peltier**, writer, U.S. political prisoner. *Prison Writings*, 1999

The most profound horror of prison lives in the day-to-day banal occurrences. Prison is a second-by-second assault on the soul, a day-to-day degradation of the self, an oppressive steel and brick umbrella that transforms seconds into hours and hours into days.
> **Mumia Abu-Jamal**, journalist, U.S. political prisoner. *Live from Death Row*, 1995

Soul in Prison by Mac McGill

For one to go to Con Son was never to be seen again.
>   **Adage**, Vietnam, circa 1970, referring to an infamous prison.
>   *Covert Action Quarterly*, Fall 2002

It's so hard to believe that one moment I can touch, feel and love my children and the next minute it is all taken away so fast for no reason. When I sit in my cell I will wonder, 'was I ever really out,' and the heartache of my children will be there with me. I am lost for words.
>   **Theresa Cruz**, imprisoned for conspiracy to commit murder after
>   her friend shot a domestic abuser in the legs. From statement
>   before being returned to a California prison. *Sparks Fly*, 1998

She bursts into the tiny visiting room, her brown eyes aglitter with happiness; stopped, stunned, staring at the glass barrier between us; and burst into tears at this arrogant attempt at state separation. In milliseconds, sadness and shock shifted into fury as her petite fingers curled into tight fists, which banged and pummeled the Plexiglas barrier, which shuddered and shimmied but didn't shatter. Why can't I hug him? Why can't we kiss? Why can't I sit in his lap? Why can't we touch? Why not?

> **Mumia Abu-Jamal**, journalist, U.S. political prisoner, describing his young daughter's first visit to him in prison. *Live from Death Row,* 1995

Everytime we spend the green written in God We Trust
We helping our oppressors to build more iron and steal resorts for us

> **Apani B-Fly Emcee**, featuring L.I.F.E., hip hop MCs. From song "Outa Site," circa 1999

'Cause the prison door slam locks
It don't open when your fam knocks
'Less you rich and have stocks

> **The Coup**, hip hop group. From song "Get Up," circa 2001

I spent years in prison down South, so when people ask me where I went to school, I'm very proud to say 'Mississippi State.'

> **Kwasi Sietu**, former U.S. political prisoner. Comment at political prisoners conference, 3/16/2003

They put kids in jail for a life they ain't even get to start.

> **Talib Kweli**, hip hop MC. From song "Joy," 2002

We have to prove that that thing won't work here, and the only way to prove it is resistance, once inside, and then that resistance has to be supported of course from the street, as we understand that the function of prison, within the prison state, within the police state, has to be explained, has to be elucidated, has to be gotten across to the people on the street, because we can't fight alone.

> **George Jackson**, writer, Black Panther member, killed by prison guards in 1971. From taped statement, circa 1970

When the prison-doors are opened, the real dragon will fly out.

> **Ho Chi Minh**, Vietnamese political leader, poet. *The Prison Diary of Ho Chi Minh,* 1942

There are two possibilities: first, police violence is a deviation from the rules governing police procedures in general. Second, these various forms of violence (e.g., racial profiling, street murders, terrorism) are the rule itself as standard operation procedure... Even those who take seriously the second possibility (violence as a rule) find that the language of alternatives and the terms of relevance are constantly dragged into the political discourse they seek to oppose, namely, that the system works and is capable of reform.

> **Steve Martinot & Jared Sexton**. Essay, "The Avant-garde of White Supremacy," 2002

We have to remember the original mindset of policing in this country: to protect the haves from the have-nots.

> **Ron Hampton**, National Black Police Association. Attributed.

Cop Holding Him Back by Rodney Camarce

The police become necessary in human society only at that juncture in human society where there's a split between those who have and those who ain't got.

> **Omali Yeshitela**, activist, writer. From Speech, circa 1998

I go through Watts, I go through Chicago, I go through Harlem, and I see that the people in what's called the ghetto—the Black communities, or the colonies or whatever you want to call them—were treated almost exactly the way we just got done treating Vietcong, or Vietnamese people in Vietnam. So I begin to draw parallels that the police departments in these various situations, in these cities, were actually the same thing we were in Vietnam—occupying forces.

> **Geronimo "Ji Jagga" Pratt**, activist, former Black Panther and political prisoner. Interview, circa 1990

If we're going to talk about police brutality, it's because police brutality exists. Why does it exist? Because our people in this particular society live in a police state.

> **Malcolm X**, Black nationalist leader. Speech, Militant Labor Forum Hall, New York, NY, 5/29/1964

They point their guns in your face
The guns which they have taken your taxes to buy

> **Fela Kuti**, Nigerian singer. From song, "Alagbon Close," 1974

[The police] learned something from them Harlem riots. They used to beat your head right in public, but now they only beat it after they get you down to the station house.

> **Langston Hughes**, writer, poet. *Simple Speaks His Mind*, 1950

Virtually every riot has begun from some police action. If you try to tell the people in most Negro communities that the police are their friends, they just laugh at you.

> **Martin Luther King, Jr.**, civil rights leader. *A Testament of Hope*, 1986

Let me add that Amadou Diallo's death was a classic example of the police not feeling any pressure from a united black people. When black people are united, cops don't go off like that because they know they are going to receive some retribution, they know there is going to be something coming their way.

> **Abiodun Oyewole**, poet. Interview, *Blu Magazine,* 2000

He may be a very nice man. But I haven't got the time to figure that out. All I know is, he's got a uniform and a gun and I have to relate to him that way. That's the only way to relate to him because one of us may have to die.

> **James Baldwin**, writer, educator. *A Dialogue*, 1973

You have the right to remain oppressed
What you say doesn't matter when you're under arrest
You'll be found guilty in the court of law anyway
It doesn't matter what you do, don't matter what you say
> **Trends**, hip hop group. From song "Assume the Position," circa 2002

I would like to suggest that what's going on in our heads and our attitudes also can have deadly consequences for every person in this country unless we start copping to it that we all do it. It's not just the police.
> **June Jordan**, poet, educator, on racial profiling. Interview, *Z Magazine*, March 2001

The police killed 187 people in NYC alone from 1992 to 1996. Yet when they shoot us in the back, choke us to death or push us off a roof, they want us to believe that this is not based on a conscious, well thought out, premeditated policy of oppression, hatred and fear.
> **Refuse & Resist! Artist's Network**, text from poster, 2003

Research has shown Socialism to be a universal failure wherever practiced by secret police.
> **Allen Ginsberg**, poet. From poem "Research," 1994

Could not recognize the faces standing over me
They were all dressed in uniforms of brutality
> **Bob Marley**, Jamaican reggae singer. From song "Burnin' and Lootin'," 1973

The police force and the ranks of prison officers attract many aberrant characters because they afford legal channels for pain-inflicting, power-wielding behavior, and because these very positions confer upon their holders a large degree of immunity.
> **Hans von Hentig**, educator, writer. *The Criminal and His Victim*, 1948

REASONABLE FORCE, n. A police term which refers to a vicious beating or unwitnessed murder. The exact meaning, however, will vary considerably depending upon the victim's race and economic status.
> **Robert Tefton**, writer. Attributed.

Blessed so swift with the nightstick, the Devil's fork
> **Will Villainova**, hip hop MC. From song "Devils in a Blue Dress,"
> circa 2000

You never seen a police break up a strike
By hittin' the boss wit his baton pipe
> **The Coup**, hip hop group. From song "U.C.P.A.S." 1998

In Czechoslovakia the police ate the feet of a generation that can't walk
and you don't know it, you don't know it
> **Allen Ginsberg**, poet. From poem "You Don't Know It," 1994

Fuck the police, comin' straight from the undaground
A young nigga got it bad 'cause I'm brown
> **NWA**, hip hop group. From song "Fuck Tha Police," 1989

Black cop, Black cop Black cop Black cop
Stop shooting Black people, we all gonna drop
> **KRS One**, hip hop MC. From song "Black Cop," 1993

I believe that white sheets have now been replaced by blue uniforms
Nooses have been replaced with nines
> **Kirk Nugent**, poet. From poem "I believe," circa 1999

Murder and capital punishment are not opposites that cancel one another,
but similars that breed their kind.
> **George Bernard Shaw**, Irish playwright, writer. *Maxims for Revolutionists*, 1903

The big thieves hang the little ones.
> **Proverb**, Czechoslovakia

Whole system stink like a loaded bowel
'Cause ain't no billionaires on the murder trial
> **The Coup**, hip hop group. From song "Gunsmoke," 1994

If Jesus had been killed twenty years ago, Catholic school children would
be wearing little electric chairs around their necks instead of crosses.
> **Lenny Bruce**, comedian. 1925-1966

Hell is not the Dantean creation of eternal cacophony, marked by the fevered
screams of the tortured.
No.
Hell is quiet, still and chilled.

I know.
I live there.

> **Mumia Abu-Jamal**, journalist, U.S. political prisoner, describing death row. Essay, "Walking in the Shadow of Death," 1995

The executioner's face is always well hidden.

> **Bob Dylan**, singer. From song, "A Hard Rain's A-Gonna Fall," 1963

I would like to say that I did not kill Bobby Lambert. That I'm an innocent Black man that is being murdered. This is a lynching that is happening in America tonight. There's overwhelming and compelling evidence of my defense that has never been heard in any court of America. What is happening here is an outrage for any civilized country to anybody anywhere to look at what's happening here is wrong. We will prevail. We may lose this battle, but we will win the war... I died fighting for what I believe in.

> **Shaka Sankofa**, U.S. prisoner. From last words before execution by State of Texas, June 22, 2000

Stupid men—you would believe in laws which punish murder by murder.

> **George Sand**, French writer. *Intimate Journal*, 1837

Many of us do not believe in capital punishment, because thus society takes from a man what society cannot give.

> **Katharine Fullerton Gerould**, writer. *Modes and Morals*, 1920

Consider for a second how, if at all, you justify the death penalty. Now take out all the "buts," "howevers," and "ifs" and you'll find that either you're for killing people or you're against killing people.

> **Toby Oshiro**, student at Occidental College, CA. From introduction to broadcast of taped address by Mumia Abu-Jamal at graduation ceremony for Occidental's class of 2001, 5/20/2001

While it is my life that will be taken, and my body filled with poison, I will not say that this is my execution! That's because it is not, it is just a continuation of the historic system of capital punishment that all poor people all over this world have been and are subjected to. To personalize this crime against humanity as "my execution" would be to ignore the universal plight, struggle and murder of poor people all over this planet we call Earth. This I cannot and will not do! If I must be murdered by the state, then I will do so with my dignity intact.

> **Kevin Cooper**, California death row prisoner. 1/22/2004

We must continue to move forward and do everything we can to outlaw legal lynching in America. We must continue to stay strong all around the world, and people must come together to stop the systematic killing of poor and innocent Black people. We must continue to stand together in unity and to demand a moratorium on all executions.

> **Shaka Sankofa**, U.S. prisoner. From last words before execution by State of Texas, 6/22/2000

It was a lynching case in old Alabam'
That caused the Feds to first intervene.
Now federal law gives every state a rope
And man don't their hands look clean

> **Rick Hart and the Blue Horse Band**. From song "The Ballad of Mumia Abu-Jamal," 2002

Do you think you can cure the hatreds and maladjustments of the world by hanging them?

> **Clarence S. Darrow**, attorney. Leopold and Loeb Murder trial, 1924

I speak from Pennsylvania's death row, a bright, shining, highly mechanized hell. In this place, a dark temple to fear, an alter of political ambition, death is a campaign poster, a stepping stone to public office. In this space and time, in this dark hour, how many of us are not on death row?

> **Mumia Abu-Jamal**, journalist, U.S. political prisoner. *All Things Censored,* 2000

I come from a country where we have had, in northern Ireland, many people who are imprisoned for political reasons and whose voices are silenced... So I feel a certain sisterhood with this particular cause. I'm against the death penalty because it shames me. I think that we only stand at the door of the cave as far as civilization goes but I would like to think that I could move out into the light without shame and I can't do that until the death penalty is erased.

> **Fionulla Flanagan**, actress. Speech for "Mumia 911" event, Los Angeles, CA September 1999

Those who ain't got the capital, get the punishment.

> **Adage regarding capital punishment**

No civilized society would insist upon maintaining the anachronism of the death penalty. An imperfect system cannot ask for a perfect punishment, which is death. Therefore any country that maintains the anachronism of the death penalty by that very fact is an uncivilized society.

Rubin "Hurricane" Carter, activist, former champion boxer framed for murder. *Blu Magazine*, 2000

Chapter 38

"Behind Enemy Lines"

Political Prisoners, Prisoners of War, Political Detainees

To the oppressed I am the angel of deliverance
To the oppressor I am the angel of destruction
So who I am
Depends on who you are...

> **Albert Nuh Washington**, activist, U.S. political prisoner. From poem, August 1975

The political prisoner is the most abused victim of an order that nurses a callous contempt for human suffering. But he is also the beleaguered revolutionary, fighting on his own battleground.

> **Ruth First**, South African activist, writer, referring to Nelson Mandela, circa 1980

As I travel through my country, people often ask me how it feels to have been imprisoned in my home... I say, that in an authoritarian state it is only the prisoner of conscience who is genuinely free. Yes, we have given up our right to a normal life. But we have stayed true to that most precious part of our humanity—our conscience.

> **Aung San Suu Kyi**, Burmese human rights activist, imprisoned by military regime. *Parade Magazine*, 3/9/2003

I'll go back to death row for my belief. I spent nine years fighting capital punishment from behind the walls. I'm free today as a human being, but my soul is not free, because my brothers and sisters are still behind bars.

> **Shujaa Graham**, former U.S. political prisoner. Speech, political prisoners conference 3/16/2003

For political prisoners, the act of breaking through the walls of gray silence and attempting a symbolic link with the outside world is an act of resistance. And resistance, even at the level of asserting one's rights, of maintaining one's ideological beliefs in the face of any systematic onslaught, is in fact the only way a political prisoner can maintain his or her sanity and humanity.

> **Jafar Saidi**, U.S. political prisoner. From message to supporters, 3/30/2003

It is the accumulated indignation against organized wrong, organized crime, organized injustice which drives the political offender to his act. To condemn him means to be blind to the causes which make him.

> **Emma Goldman**. Statement to jury after being tried under the Espionage Act, with co-defendant Alexander Berkman, for organizing against the draft for World War I. They were sent to prison, and deported from the country upon release. 7/9/1917

Jails were made for men who fight for their rights. My spirit was never in jail. They can jail us, but they can never jail the cause.

> **César Chávez**, union and labor organizer. Attributed.

I would not wish to a dog or to a snake, to the most low and misfortunate creature of the earth—I would not wish to any of them what I have had to suffer for things that I am not guilty of. I am suffering because I am a radical and indeed I am a radical; I have suffered because I was an Italian, and indeed I am an Italian; I have suffered more for my family and for my beloved than for myself; but I am so convinced to be right that you can only kill me once but if you could execute me two times, and if I could be reborn two other times, I would live again to do what I have done already.

> **Bartolomeo Vanzetti**, Italian immigrant and anarchist, sentenced to death with Nicola Sacco on fraudulent charges and executed. From statement to court upon being sentenced to death, April 1927

If you take a look back in our history, there were many people like you who felt this was not their battle until they woke up in chains. This is definitely your battle. Never let anyone tell you otherwise... I say to you that we as political prisoners will not stop resisting within these hells and you, the people, must not stop exposing, challenging and resisting this system. To all political prisoners, we will prevail!

> **Jamal Hart**, U.S. political prisoner, son of U.S. political prisoner Mumia Abu-Jamal. From statement presented to rally supporting his father, April 24, 2004

Every time I was transferred to a new jail, I was treated like a venereal disease, because they did not like my politics, and branded me a trouble maker.

> **Kwasi Sietu**, former U.S. political prisoner. Speech, political prisoners conference, 3/16/2003

As long as we are alive, we will never abandon our innocent brothers and sisters in jail, and they know we will never abandon them, and this city gonna always have a problem until every last one of our brothers and sisters is home.

> **MOVE Organization**, on their nine members who are U.S. political prisoners. *20 Years On The MOVE,* 1991

If we're serious, then we have to overcome our fears of imprisonment. After all, it is little compared to the price paid by freedom fighters in other countries who are tortured or given ridiculously long sentences for the least degree of resistance. And it is nothing compared to the animals in zoos and aquariums who are sentenced to solitary confinement without hope of parole, or the animals sitting in labs, factories and fur farms whose only escape is death.

> **Rod Coronado**, animal rights activist, serving a four year sentence for arson of an animal testing laboratory at the time of interview. *Satya* magazine, May 1997

Prison...provides insight into the state of conditions for all the animals imprisoned on farms, ranches, zoos, laboratories, game parks, and aquariums. Most of the world's citizens spend their entire life in captivity; and the death penalty is the most common sentence given to non-humans after serving their time.

> **Paul Watson**, environmental activist, "pirate" who has attacked and sank illegal whaling ships, on facing possible prison time. Interview, *Satya* magazine, March 2004

I would like to take a walk at night and hug my baby. I'd like to do all the things that people take for granted in their so-called freedom... I tell myself I am all right. But who can be all right after all these years under these conditions? Still I am in command of my politics. I can laugh and love, so the damage is not that bad. Whatever strength I have comes from the knowledge that I am a political prisoner and the things we stand for were/ are correct.

> **Albert Nuh Washington**, activist, U.S. political prisoner. *Can't Jail the Spirit*, 1992

The government that dropped napalm on Vietnam, that provides the cluster bombs used against civilians in Lebanon, and that trains the torturers in El Salvador calls us "terrorists." The rulers who have grown rich on generations of slave labor and slave wages violently imposed on Black people label us "criminals." The police forces of Amerika who have murdered 2,000 Third World people in the last five years and who flood the communities with drugs say that we "have no respect for human life." We are neither terrorists nor criminals. It is precisely because of our love of life, because we revel in the human spirit, that we became freedom fighters against this racist and deadly imperialist system.

> **Kuwasi Balagoon, Judy Clark and David Gilbert**, black liberation and white anti-imperialist activists captured during one of their clandestine armed actions. From court statement during pre-trial proceedings, September 1982

Political prisoners: they are inside for us, we are outside for them.

> **Slogan on political prisoners**

The ruling circles are refusing to recognize that my freedom was won in the streets of this country and in the streets of the whole world.

> **Angela Davis**, activist, educator, writer. Speech, in celebration of her court acquittal, 1972

We all stand on trial, my lord, for by our actions we have denigrated our Country and jeopardized the future of our children... I predict that the scene here will be played and replayed by generations yet unborn. Some have already cast themselves in the role of villains, some are tragic victims, some still have a chance to redeem themselves. The choice is for each individual.

> **Ken Saro-Wiwa**, Nigerian Ogoni writer, human rights/ environmental activist. From his closing statement at Nigerian military tribunal prior to execution, 1995

As we in Cape Town look out across the bay at Robben Island where Nelson Mandela was incarcerated for 27 years, our thoughts and hearts are with Leonard Peltier and his family and loved ones, and the many people around the globe who shout from the rooftops...Free Peltier !!! And today we shall sit above the clouds on Table Mountain and shout Free Peltier !!! And Mother Earth shall hear us...and as South Africans shouted in the struggle against oppression, Amandla !!! The struggle will be won !!!

> **Dion Futerman**, South African human rights activist. From message to U.S. political prisoner Leonard Peltier, June 2004

We must all act like mothers, to protect all life. Even the worst days in jails and prison were a blessing because of my commitment to this role.

> **Donna Hastings Howard**, former anti-militarism U.S. political prisoner, sentenced to prison for disabling a trigger mechanism for nuclear missiles. *Sparks Fly*, 1998

When you get out of jail you will see where the jail is thinly concealed in the shopping mall, the school, the television program. You will know that at every moment you do truly have a choice: to acquiesce, to resist, to create something new.

> **Starhawk**, activist, writer. "Making it Real: Initiation Instructions—Seattle, 1999," to activists protesting the World Trade Organization, 1999

The Chicago Eight, the group that was prosecuted for conspiring to get clubbed by police at the Democratic National Convention in August 1968.

> **Satire on Hippy.com**, 2004, referring to activists charged for conspiracy to commit violence.

Only a handful of you in this vast country are aware that the fate intended for us political prisoners and for the numberless prisoners in this country's concentration camps is a fate, which is about to engulf you, too... And we know that, for the perpetuation of this system, we have all been mercilessly brutalized, and we have been told nothing but lies, lies about each other, and ourselves and about life, death, and love and war.

> **Jafar Saidi**, U.S. political prisoner. From message to supporters, 3/30/2003

Don't waste any time mourning. Organize!

> **Joe Hill**, labor leader. Telegraph sent just before his execution, 1915

A people who are not free cannot free their political prisoners.

> **Huey P. Newton**, co-founder, Black Panther Party. Attributed.

They may imprison my body, but they will never imprison the truth I know in my soul. I will continue to fight for justice and truth in Haiti until I draw my last breath.

> **Annette Auguste "Sò Anne,"** Haitian folk singer, activist, arrested by U.S. marines and held as a political prisoner in Haiti. Statement, 5/23/2004

Chapter 39

"New World Border"

Immigration, Migration, Deportation

Borders crumble; they won't hold together on their own; we have to shore them up constantly. They are fortified and patrolled by armed guards, these fences that divide a party of elegant diners on one side from the children on the other whose thin legs curve like wishbones, whose large eyes peer through the barbed wire at so much food—there is no wall high enough to make good in such a neighborhood.

> **Barbara Kingsolver**, writer. *Small Wonder*, 2002

We came here looking for freedom, safety, and justice. Instead we found nothing but traps, built of steel bars, bad laws, and dishonest politics. Inside these cages, children have grown into adults. Young men's hair has turned white. Babies have been born, taken their first steps, spoken their first words. Most of us, separated from our families, have become like ghosts to our mothers, our wives, our children.

> **Asylum seekers in Australia**, in letter to a refugee advocate, January 2003. In *We Are Everywhere*, 2003

I have been asked by my detractors that if I, as a woman, I am so critical of western domination, why do I live here? It could just as readily be asked of them that if they are so contemptuous of the non-western world, why do they so fervently desire the oil, trade, cheap labour and other resources of that world? Challenges to our presence in the West have long been answered by people of colour who say, 'We are here because you were (are?) there!'

> **Sunera Thobani**, Canadian educator. Essay, "War Frenzy," 10/17/2001

The U.S.-Mexican border *es una herida abierta* where the Third World grates against the first and bleeds. And before a scab forms it hemorrhages again, the lifeblood of two worlds merging to form a third country—a border culture.

> **Gloria Anzaldúa**, writer, poet. *Borderlands/La Frontera*, 1987

There are things that are very hard in exile—let alone practicing your own rituals, your own language. Once you stop practicing your own language, when you stop speaking your own language, it kills a man's pride. It kills you.

> **Mogauwane Mahloele**, South African musician, in exile in the U.S., 2004

A lot of the same things that are being said about Latin and Asian immigrants today were said about Italian and Russian Jewish immigrants at the turn of the 19th century. It's the same kind of phobia—the immigrants are dirty, more criminal, less intelligent. It's a script that's been written and performed many times. We can't seem to have any sort of intelligent discussion informed by our past. We seem to have to learn everything all over again every 20 years or so.

> **Steve Rendall**, media analyst. Interview, *Guerrilla News Network*, 9/9/2003

Segregation serves not simply as the institutional and ideological buttress of the white monopoly of power at a time of rapid social change; it is the central mechanism for the reproduction of cheap and coercible migrant labor.

> **Shula Marks**, South African historian. In *Penguin Dictionary of South African Quotations,* 1994

XENOPHOBIA: An illness which disappears with the appearance of profit.

> **Rolando Hinojosa-Smith**, writer. "The Mexican American Devil's Dictionary," Fall 1976

There were no border guards at Bering Strait when the first men, women, and children crossed over from Asia fifteen to thirty thousand years ago. There were no green cards demanded of the Spanish conquerors, settlers, and missionaries who came into the Southwest and Florida in the sixteenth century.

> **Carlos Fuentes**, Mexican writer, playwright. *Americanos*, 1999

Chapter 40

"Or Does it Explode?"

Oppression, Prejudice, Injustice, Political Repression, Bigotry

Find out just what people will submit to, and you have found out the exact measure of injustice and wrong which will be imposed upon them; and these will continue until they are resisted with either words or blows, or both. The limits of tyrants are proscribed by the endurance of those whom they oppress.

> **Frederick Douglass**, slavery abolitionist, political theorist. Speech, Canandaigua, NY, 8/4/1857

In order to perpetuate itself, every oppression must corrupt or distort those various sources of power within the culture of the oppressed that can provide energy for change.

> **Audre Lorde**, educator, activist, poet. "Uses of the Erotic," 1978

Though they may have no basis in reality, stereotypes are real in their social consequences, notably with regard to the allocation of roles. They tend to function as self-fulfilling prophecies. The targets of stereotyping are maneuvered into certain roles, so that a vicious cycle develops, in which social reality seems to endorse the stereotype.

> **Jan Nederveen Pieterse**, educator, writer. *White on Black,* 1992

Those who can make you believe absurdities can make you commit atrocities.

> **Voltaire**, French writer, philosopher, 1694-1778

The apologist for oppression becomes himself the oppressor. To palliate crime is to be guilty of its perpetuation.

> **William Lloyd Garrison**, slavery abolitionist. *The Liberator,* 1/1/1831

When the bigots came it was time to fight, and fight we did. Fought hard—femme and butch, women and men together.

> **Leslie Feinberg**, activist, writer. *Stone Butch Blues,* 1993

If you're going to hold someone down you're going to have to hold onto the other end of the chain. You are confined by your own system of repression.

> **Toni Morrison**, writer, educator. In *I Dream a World,* 1989

That a Jew is despised or persecuted is bad for him, of course—but far worse for the Christian who does it—for although persecuted he can remain a good Jew—whereas no Christian who persecutes can possibly remain—if he ever was one—a good Christian.
Phyllis Bottome, writer. *The Mortal Storm*, 1938

Do not ask what the Jews are, but what we have made of the Jews.
Jean-Paul Sartre, French writer, 1946. In *White on Black,* 1992

The only way that we can stand in fact
Is when you get your foot off our back
Nina Simone, singer. From song "Revolution (Part I)," 1969

The bones of injustice have a peculiar way of rising from the tombs to plague and mock the iniquitous.
Marcus Garvey, Jamaican Black nationalist leader. *Philosophy and Opinions*, 1923

If given a choice, I would have certainly selected to be what I am: one of the oppressed instead of one of the oppressors.
Miriam Makeba, South African singer. *Makeba*, 1987

Chapter 41

"Burnin' and Lootin'"

Riots and Insurrections

Every broke muthafucka fin ta form a gang,
and when we come we takin' everythang
> **The Coup**, hip hop group. From song "Everything," 2001

A riot is at bottom the language of the unheard.
> **Martin Luther King, Jr.**, civil rights leader. *Where Do We Go From Here—Chaos or Community?*, 1967

How much injustice can any community absorb before an eruption of extraordinary proportions occurs?
> **Cynthia McKinney**, former U.S. Congresswoman. Speech, 8/6/2003

I don't know if the riots is wrong
but whitey's been kicking my ass for too damn long
> **Gil Scott Heron**, poet, musician. From poem "Small Talk at 125th and Lenox," 1970

Black people don't own Harlem, so why should Black people care whether it burns down or not?
> **Floyd B. McKissick**, Congress of Racial Equality. PBS, 1991

The first excuse given to the civilized world for the murder of unoffending Negroes was the necessity of the white man to repress and stamp out "race riots." …It was always a remarkable feature of these insurrections and riots that only Negroes were killed during the rioting, and that all the white men escaped unharmed.
> **Ida B. Wells**, journalist, activist. *A Red Record*, 1895

What these white people do not realize is that Negroes who riot have given up on America. When nothing is done to alleviate their plight, this merely confirms the Negroes conviction that America is a hopelessly decadent society.
> **Martin Luther King, Jr.**, civil rights leader. Essay, "A Testament of Hope," 1968

How are you going to incite people who are living in slums and ghettos? It's the city structure that incites… Don't ever accuse a black man for voicing

his resentment and dissatisfaction over the criminal condition of his people as being responsible for inciting the situation.
Malcolm X, Black nationalist leader, in his last radio appearance. *WINS* radio, New York, NY February 1965

"Seize the Time," collage by Theodore Harris

No one wants someone who hates them to be anywhere in the periphery. Their mere presence poses a threat. All the years before the riots white people could ignore the history and the crimes. That was a long time ago, we were taught in school. But then Lincoln freed the slaves. But now the grandchildren and the great-grandchildren of those slaves were cutting up, acting out hatred that went all the way back through centuries of abuse.
Walter Mosley, writer. *What Next*, 2003

A single spark can start a prairie fire.
Proverb, China, made famous by Mao Tse-Tung

Chapter 42

"Power to the People"

Society, the People

You gotta have faith. One thing you can't lose is faith in the masses. What humbles me is we are only as strong as our weakest link no matter what. I don't care how strong the rest of this whole shit is. And the people have all the answers. They will pull it out on you and show you what you been doing wrong the whole time but you gotta have faith.

> **M-1**, of hip hop group Dead Prez. Interview, *Allhiphop.com*, 2003

The people have a deep sense of justice above and beyond the hairsplitting of jurisprudence. The people wield simple but implacable logic, in conflict with all that is absurd and contradictory.

> **Fidel Castro**, Cuban revolutionary, political leader. Speech during trial after attack on the Moncada army barracks, 1953

What societies really, ideally, want is a citizenry which will simply obey the rule of society. If a society succeeds in this, that society is about to perish. The obligation of anyone who thinks of himself as responsible is to examine society and try to change it and to fight it—at no matter what risk.

> **James Baldwin**, writer, educator. Essay, "A Talk to Teachers," 1963

But how can you believe in a future if you don't believe in people who are going to make it? How can you believe in human rights unless you believe in human beings? How can you say you believe in justice, without believing in social justice, political justice and economic justice for all people?

> **Assata Shakur**, former Black Panther member, in exile in Cuba. Essay, "The Prison Industrial Complex," circa 2002

The rebel army is the people in uniform.

> **Camilo Cienfuegos**, Cuban revolutionary, military commander. Attributed.

Try to do something for your people—something difficult. Have pity on your people and love them. If a man is poor, help him. Give him and his family food, give them whatever they ask for. If there is discord among your people, intercede.

> **From a Winnebago lesson**, 1700s. In *The Wisdom of Native Americans*, 1999

People say, "That's nonsense, Gary, the average person doesn't support fascism." I say, "Yes they do." At the height of the Vietnam war you had 625,000 people in Washington D.C. challenging the war for its immorality. That was one half of one percent of the American population.

> **Gary Null**, physician, health educator. Speech, "Fascism in Medicine," May 1994

Humankind is only as humane as its most inhumane soul.

> **Omékongo Dibinga**, poet, musician. Attributed.

I have the audacity to believe that peoples everywhere can have three meals a day for their bodies, education and culture for their minds, and dignity, equality, and freedom for their spirits. I believe that what self-centered men have torn down, other-centered men can build up.

> **Martin Luther King, Jr.**, civil rights leader. In *The Words of Martin Luther King, Jr.*, 1983

From time immemorial men have followed with blind loyalty the strong men who had the power of money and of armies. Even while battlefields were piled high with their own dead they have tilled the lands of the rulers and have been robbed of the fruits of their labor. They have built palaces and pyramids, temples and cathedrals that held no real shrine of liberty.

> **Helen Keller**, educator, socialist activist. Speech opposing U.S. entry into World War I, 1/5/1916

An alert, intelligent and vigilant citizenry needs to make sure its leaders do not get away with murder.

> **Tariq Ali**, English historian, writer. Essay, "This is Not Sovereignty," July 2004

Chapter 43

"Seeds of the Future"

Children, Youth, Generations

What do we tell young
people? How do we say, "your
voice means nothing to those
who think life is about power
over others and greed?"

> **Suheir Hammad**, poet. From poem "On the brink of...," circa
> 2002

There's nothing wrong with the youth, unless you look at NBC and CBS
and ABC. All we got to do is go and give the youth the truth, and they will
respond.

> **Dick Gregory**, activist, nutritionist, comedian. Attributed.

At this point in history, the bottom line is that young people dominate the
expression of rebellion and resistance in their struggle against the pain and
towards mental, physical, and spiritual liberation.

> **Mutulu Shakur**, former acupuncturist, activist, now a U.S.
> political prisoner. Essay, "The FBI and My Son Tupac," *Blu
> Magazine*, 2000

This system's greatest fear has been that folks like you, young people, people
who have begun to critically examine the world around them, some perhaps
for the first time, people who have yet to have the spark of life snuffed out,
will do just that: learn from [the lives of past radicals], be inspired, and then
live lives of opposition to the deadening status quo.

> **Mumia Abu-Jamal**, journalist, U.S. political prisoner. Graduation
> speech to students at Evergreen State College, taped in prison,
> 6/11/1999

But in our society, "youthful rebellion" has become a ritual: every generation
is expected to revolt against the social order for a few years, before "growing
up" and "accepting reality." This negates any power for real change that the
fresh perspective of youth could have.

> **CrimethInc. Worker's Collective**. *Days of War, Nights of Love*,
> 2000

Just as we say that Prison is but a "microcosm" of society in general, so too is the Home. Home is that part of society which is first entrusted with the mission, or responsibility of molding us into what the Ruling Order has defined and instituted as acceptable. Those cultural forces converge upon each human being at the youngest of age.

> **Ashanti Alston**, former Black Panther member, anarchist activist. Essay, "Childhood & The Psychological Dimension of Revolution," 1983

When I am grappling with ideas which are radical enough to upset grown-ups, then I am likely to put these ideas into a story which will be marketed for children, because children understand what their parents have rejected and forgotten.

> **Madeleine L'Engle**, writer. *Walking on Water*, 1980

Everyone is someone's child, even when they are grown. Even when they take paths we don't approve of. Even when they become soldiers, and are sent to pay for lies with their bodies and hearts and the blood of others.

> **Stan Goff**, writer, former U.S. Army sergeant. Essay, "Don't Extend Them & Don't Replace Them—Just Bring 'Em on Home Now!," 7/26/2003

I have come to recognize that true relatives aren't always related by the blood that flows in your veins, but by the blood, sweat and tears that is given for the common good of all.

> **Leonard Peltier**, writer, U.S. political prisoner. From message to supporters, 5/6/2004

It's been said that the hip-hop generation is a "sleeping giant." Shit, you'd be tired too if the Man always had his foot in your ass. We are criminalized like no other generation in American history. Our educational system is fucked up. Our employment options are few, and the problems go on and on.

> **Cherryl Aldave**, activist. In *How to Get Stupid White Men Out of Office*, 2004

Tired of you saying,
That my generation doesn't care
What have you left for us,
Besides a lot of despair?

> **Mwalim**, griot, educator. From song "The Storm," 2001, Burgundy Streak Music, (ASCAP)

We dropped the torch—the 60's generation had it, we were going with it and then we dropped it and ran off to play money games and drive the corporate slave ship.

> **Colia Lafayette Clark**, activist. Interview, *Blu Magazine*, 2000

Every generation must, out of relative obscurity, discover its mission, fulfill it, or betray it.

> **Franz Fanon**, Martiniquen psychiatrist, writer. *The Wretched of the Earth,* 1963

Most people don't think of revolutionaries as family men. All you see is him in is his image on the battle line. But when you see him with his children and with his wife and that atmosphere at home, you realize that revolutionaries are human beings too.

> **Malcolm X**, Black nationalist leader, referring to Abdul Rahman Muhammad Babu, Tanzanian political leader. Speech, New York, NY, 12/13/1964

So what is it you guys want from the Elders? Secrets? Mystery?… I can tell you right now there are no secrets. There's no mystery. There's only common sense.

> **Oren Lyons**, educator, Chief of the Turtle Clan of the Onondaga Nation, speaking to two journalists. *Wisdom Keepers*, 1990

The old Lakota was wise. He knew that man's heart, away from nature, becomes hard; he knew that lack of respect for growing, living things soon led to lack of respect for humans, too. So he kept his children close to nature's softening influence.

> **Chief Joseph**, Nez Perce leader, 1840-1904

We speak for the no longer and the not yet.

> **Subcomandante Marcos**, Mexican Zapatista revolutionary, writer. Mexico, circa 1997. Attributed.

Only mothers can think of the future, because they give birth to it in their children.

> **Maxim Gorky**, Russian writer. *Guerrilla News Network*, 8/25/2003

The glorification of truth needs to be pushed in our generation. For far too long the youth have been considered "gullible." If it takes the youth of South

Africa to show that the youth need truth, then so be it.

> **Kes i Waa**, South African activist. *Baobabconnections.org,* 2003

We strongly believe that our future is in the hands of the young folks.

> **Mutulu Shakur**, former acupuncturist, now a U.S. political prisoner. Essay, "The FBI and My Son Tupac," *Blu Magazine,* 2000

There are many reasons why babies cry when they are born, and one of them is the sudden separation from the world of pure dreams, where all things are made of enchantment, and where there is no suffering.

> **Ben Okri**, Nigerian writer, poet. *The Famished Road*, 1991

By Rodney Camarce

We have not inherited the world from our forefathers—we have borrowed it from our children.

Proverb, Kashmir

Look and listen for the welfare of the whole people and have always in view not only the present but also the coming generations, even those whose faces are yet beneath the surface of the earth—the unborn of the future Nation.

From Constitution of the Five Nations, made up of the Cayuga, Mohawk, Oneida, Onondaga and Seneca nations, circa 1400s

Do we hate our enemies more than we love our kids?

Sheila Buell, activist, on disparity between military and education spending. From e-mail, 2003

Can't imagine how these young people make a life, make a living. How can they stand it, going out in the world with only $10 and a hydrogen bomb?

Allen Ginsberg, poet. From poem "Yiddishe Kopf," 1994

Let us put our minds together and see what kind of life we can make for our children.

Sitting Bull, American Indian leader. Attributed.

Young people say, "What good can one person do? What is the sense of our small effort?" They cannot see that we must lay one brick at a time, take one step at a time; we can be responsible only for the one action of the present moment.

Dorothy Day, activist, co-founder, Catholic Worker Movement, 1933. Interview, *Blu Magazine*, 2000

Chapter 44

"True Wealth"

Health

My goal in life is not to be rich or wealthy
True wealth comes from good health and wise ways
> **Dead Prez**, hip hop group. From song "Be Healthy," 2000

Natural selection over millions of years shaped our ancestors in ways that suited earlier environments. We do not know how well we are now suited biologically and behaviorally to the world our species has so rapidly made.
> **David A. Hamburg and Sarah Spaght Brown**. *Science*, May 1978

What is the nature of wellness? And unless you ask that, then all of the health-care in the world is not going to make a whole lot of difference. All it will do is make certain individuals wealthier than what they already are. Is the idea that if we had more doctors, more hospitals, and more medicine we would have more healthy people?
> **Gary Null**, physician, health educator. Speech, "Fascism in Medicine," May 1994

For one to be a revolutionary doctor or to be a revolutionary at all, there must first be a revolution... Today one finally has the right and even the duty to be, above all things, a revolutionary doctor, that is to say a man who utilizes the technical knowledge of his profession in the service of the revolution and the people.
> **Ernesto "Che" Guevara**, Argentinean-Cuban revolutionary and military leader. Speech, to Cuban militia, 1960

Well, health is important. Your vitality is important because it helps your brain, which helps your spirit, which helps your consciousness, which connects you back to all of us, and we need you. So of course health is very, very important. That vitality will get you everywhere. Just feeling good will help you to make the right choices. If you feel like shit, you do fucked up shit.
> **Erykah Badu**, singer. Interview, *San Francisco Bay View*, 2003

In other words, for a prudent toxicological policy, a chemical should be considered guilty until proven innocent.
> **Umberto Saffiotti**, physician. Comment at 11th Canadian Research Conference, 1976

By John Jonik

The poor shall inherit the earth...and all the toxic waste thereof.
> **Greenpeace**, slogan in support of the Waste Trade Project, 1991

But neither tonics, nor pills, nor exercise, nor a healthy diet will suffice if the source of those things—the earth, the air, the water—is full of sickness. We live in a world where thousands of lakes are pools of stagnant death; where oceans spawn red tides... In such a world, how can we speak of health? What can it mean?
> **Mumia Abu-Jamal**, journalist, U.S. political prisoner. Essay, "A Matter of Health," September 2004

The instinctive human fear of radioactivity is not irrational, as the nuclear advocates assert; it is also so universal and so enduring that it is a political fact of life.
> **Peter Pringle and James Spigelman**. *The Nuclear Barons*, 1981

Capitalist isotopes and Marxist isotopes visit each other amicably in the

skeletons of our children.
>   **Jean Rostand**, on radiation fallout from U.S/Soviet arms race.
>   *Inquietudes d'un Biologiste,* 1967

Hell no, we won't glow.
>   **Anti-nuclear slogan**, circa 1982

'Tis a sordid profit that's accompanied by the destruction of health.
>   **Bernardino Ramazzini**, Italian physician. *Treatise on the Diseases of Tradesmen*, 1705

The nation's largest cancer research laboratory is the American workplace.
>   **Susan Q. Stranahan**, writer. *Philadelphia Inquirer*, March 1976

Almost everything we know now about occupational cancer comes from counting dead bodies.
>   **J. William Lloyd**. *Cancer and the Worker,* 1977

[The United States has become] thoroughly persuaded of the teachings of Genesis—carcinogenesis, teratogenesis, and mutagenesis.
>   **Anonymous English scientist**, Royal Society of Medicine, 1985

The sulfur oxides, hydrocarbons, carbon monoxide, oxides of nitrogen, particulates, and many more contaminants amounts to compulsory consumption of violence by most Americans.
>   **Ralph Nader**, activist, U.S. Presidential candidate. *Vanishing Air*, 1970

Cancer in the last quarter of the 20th century can be considered a social disease, a disease whose causation and control are rooted in the technology and economy of our society.
>   **Umberto Saffiotti**, physician. *Time*, 1975

If we are to live so intimately with these chemicals—eating and drinking them, taking them into the very marrow of our bones—we had better know something about their nature and their power.
>   **Rachel Carson**, biologist, writer. *Silent Spring*, 1962

The AIDS epidemic has rolled back a big rotting log and revealed all the squirming life underneath it, since it involves, all at once, the main themes of our existence: sex, death, power, money, love, hate, disease and panic.
>   **Edmund White**, writer. *States of Desire*, 1986 ed.

I think the Reagan and Bush administrations will be remembered one hundred years hence as the people who could have stopped the plague but chose not to because the right people were dying.
> **Rita Mae Brown**, writer. *Venus Envy*, 1993

Living with AIDS is like living through a war which is happening only for those people who happen to be in the trenches. Every time a shell explodes, you look around and you discover that you've lost more of your friends, but nobody else notices.
> **Vito Russo**, activist, writer. "Why We Fight," 1988

Health is a human right, not a privilege to be purchased.
> **Shirley Chisholm**, U.S. Congresswoman. From the Congressional Record, 1970

[If] you ain't got insurance that be costin' G's
They be actin' hands off like you got a disease
> **The Coup**, hip hop group. From song "Breathing Apparatus," on being hospitalized without insurance, 1998

Every organ of sense is injured in an equal degree by artificial elevation of the temperature, by the dust-laden atmosphere, by the deafening noise, not to mention danger to life and limb among the thickly crowded machinery, which, with the regularity of the seasons, issues its list of the killed and wounded in the industrial battle.
> **Karl Marx**, German political theorist. *Das Kapital*, 1867

The same people who tell us that smoking doesn't cause cancer are now telling us that advertising cigarettes doesn't cause smoking.
> **Ellen Goodman**, writer. *The Boston Globe*, 7/16/1986

Ecstasy, coke, you say it's love but it's poison
Schools without learning, they should be burned, it's poison
> **Nas**, hip hop MC. From track "What Goes Around," 2001

Indians and animals know better how to live than white man; nobody can be in good health if he does not have all the time fresh air, sunshine, and good water.
> **Flying Hawk**, Lakota leader, 1852-1931. Attributed.

Chapter 45

"The Angels of Bread"

Food and Hunger

Our movement in India seeks to defend our seed freedom (Bija Swaraj) and food freedom (Anna Swaraj) by defending our rights, and refusing to cooperate with immoral and unjust laws (Bija Satyagraha)... Our bread is our freedom. Our freedom will ensure our bread.

> **Vandana Shiva**, Indian scientist, activist. From essay, "Biotech Wars: Food Freedom vs. Food Slavery," 2003

Ethiopia reminds us that there are still people for whom food is primarily a means to biological survival. Here...food has come to mean much more: status, authority, entertainment, style, possibly religion.

> **Barbara Ehrenreich**, writer. *The Worst Years of Our Lives*, 1990

When I give food to the poor, they call me a Saint. When I ask why the poor have no food, they call me a Communist.

> **Dom Helder Camara**, Brazilian Catholic priest, liberation theologist, 1909-1999

To understand the source of one's next meal is to understand one's own political vulnerability.

> **Michael Kramer**, writer. *Three Farms*, 1981

Your nation supposes that we, like the white people, cannot live without bread, and pork, and beef! But, you ought to know, that He—the Great Spirit—and Master of Life—has provided food for us, in these broad lakes, and upon these mountains.

> **Minavavana**, Chippewa leader, late 1700s. Attributed.

Hungry men have no respect for law, authority or human life.

> **Marcus Garvey**, Jamaican Black nationalist leader. *Philosophy and Opinions*, 1923

We have the temerity to declare that all have a right to bread, that there is bread enough for all, and that with this watchword of "bread for all" the revolution will triumph.

> **Peter Kropotkin**, Russian political theorist, writer. *Conquest of Bread,* 1892

Humanity is born free but everywhere is in supermarket chains buying 14.7 cm long carrots stripped of dirt, geography, effort, labour, stripped of content, context, joy and flavour buying 14.7 cm long carrots stripped of carrothood.
> **Steve Hancock**. *In Between Poems*, 2000

Population is a political issue, not an ecological issue. At this moment we produce twice as much food as needed to give every person on Earth a physiologically adequate diet. The real problem is poverty. Excess population is a symptom of poverty, not the other way around.
> **Barry Commoner**, biologist. *Mother Earth News,* March-April 1990

We are mining the soil of its fertility, and are draining oil and gas fields of their wealth to get the energy to do that... We can't afford to let our food system just "run out" some day.
> **Robert Rodale**, agriculturist, writer. *Organic Gardening*, September 1980

A farmer's duty, is protecting the earth, maintaining it's fertility, and maintaining the fertility of seed. That is part of being a farmer. A farmer is not a low-paid tractor driver, that's a modern definition of what a farmer is. The real definition of a farmer is a person who relates to the land and relates to the seed and keeps it for future generations, keeps renewing it, fertility.
> **Vandana Shiva**, Indian scientist, activist. Interview, *In Motion Magazine*, 8/14/1998

While much of the world starves, a major preoccupation in America is how to lose weight.
> **Colman McCarthy**, peace activist, educator. Interview, *Satya* magazine, November 2001

Chapter 46

"Chanting Down Babylon"
Spirituality, Religion, Liberation Theology

Well they tell me of a pie up in the sky
Waiting for me when I die...
But between the day you born and when you die,
They never seem to hear you when you cry...

> **Ekwueme Michael Thelwell**, writer, educator. *The Harder They
> Come,* 1980

You are the God of the poor, the God who is human and simple; The God
who sweats in the streets, the God with the weather-beaten face. That is why
I can talk to you the way I talk with my people: because you are God, the
laborer, Christ, the working man.

> **Carlos Mejía Godoy**, Nicaraguan singer. "The Mass to the God
> of the Poor, By the Poor," 1975

I'm fighting for the Black people on welfare, the Black people who have no
future, Black people who are wineheads and dope addicts. I am a politician
for Allah.

> **Muhammad Ali**, champion boxer, activist. Attributed.

God who has created the shining sun above, who stirs up the seas and
unleashes thunder, this God—you hear? While hiding in a cloud is watching
us and sees the misdeeds of the whites. Our God, who is so good, orders
us to take vengeance. He takes us by the arm and guides us. He will give
us assistance. Throw away the white God's image who is thirsting for the
water in our eyes. Listen to the call of freedom in our hearts.

> **"Zamba" Boukman Dutty**, Haitian revolutionary leader. From
> prayer, circa 1790

Don't let anybody make you think that God chose America as His divine
messianic force to be—a sort of policeman of the whole world. God has a
way of standing before the nations with judgment, and it seems that I can
hear God saying to America: 'You are too arrogant! If you don't change
your ways, I will rise up and break the backbone of your power!'

> **Martin Luther King Jr.**, civil rights leader. Speech, 1967

Many activists mistrust religion and spirituality, often for good reasons. But
each of us is in this work because something is sacred to us—sacred in the

sense that it means more than our comfort or convenience, that it determines all of our other values, that we are willing to risk ourselves in its service.

> **Starhawk**, activist, writer. Essay, "Only Poetry Can Address Grief," 2001

I say God is that place between belief and
what you name it
I believe holy is what you do when there is
nothing between your actions
and the truth

> **Staceyann Chin**, poet. From poem "Cross-fire," 2002

No one can say that Christianity has failed. It has never been tried.

> **Adam Clayton Powell, Jr.**, Congressman, writer. *Marching Blacks*, 1945

Christian ideology has contributed no little to the oppression of women.

> **Simone de Beauvoir**, French writer, philosopher. *The Second Sex*, 1949

The perception that Jesus is white has given whites the preening arrogance with which they have enslaved, oppressed and subjugated blacks and other non-whites not merely with impunity but with, as they choose to see it, blessings from above.

> **Miles Willis**, writer. Essay, "The Passion of the Whites," circa 2002

We do not want churches because they will teach us to quarrel about God.

> **Chief Joseph**, Nez Perce leader, 1840-1904

Unless a religion springs from within the people themselves, it is a weapon of the system.

> **Rigoberta Menchú Tum**, Guatemala Mayan human rights activist. *I, Rigoberta Menchu*, 1983

The church is a crutch. It is a white man's religion. They brought it here to conquer us and civilize us.

> **Lorraine Canoe**, educator. *New York Times*, 1/3/1995

When the white man came we had the land and they had the Bibles; now they have the land and we have the Bibles.

> **Proverb**, origin uncertain. Widely used in reference to European colonization since the 1800s.

The Church in the colonies is the white people's Church, the foreigner's Church. She does not call the native to God's ways but to the way of the white man, of the master, of the oppressor. And as we know, in this matter many are called but few chosen.

> **Franz Fanon**, Martiniquen psychiatrist, writer. *The Wretched of the Earth*, 1963

The attempted transformation of the Indian by the white man and the chaos that has resulted are but the fruits of the white man's disobedience of a fundamental and spiritual law.

> **Luther Standing Bear**, Lakota leader, writer, 1868-1939

When I found out I thought God was white, and a man, I lost interest.

> **Alice Walker**, writer, poet. *The Color Purple*, 1982

You can pray until you faint, but if you don't get up and try to do something, God is not going to put it in your lap. And it's no need of running, and no need of saying, 'honey, I'm not gonna get in the mess,' because if you're born in America with a Black face, you're born in the mess.

> **Fannie Lou Hamer**, civil rights leader, 1917-1977. Speech, in *The Roots of Resistance*, from the Freedom Archives, 2002

Long-haired preachers come out every night,
Try to tell you what's wrong and what's right;
But when asked how 'bout something to eat
They will answer with voices so sweet:
You will eat, bye and bye,
In that glorious land above the sky;
Work and pray, live on hay,
You'll get pie in the sky when you die

> **Joe Hill**, singer, labor movement martyr. From song "The Preacher and the Slave," 1911

We are not those who wait, naively, for justice to come from above, when it only comes from below. The liberty which can only be achieved with everyone.

> **Zapatista National Liberation** Army representative. Speech upon arriving with Zapatista marchers in Mexico City, March 2001

The most heinous and the most cruel crimes of which history has record have been committed under the cover of religion or equally noble motive.
Mahatma Gandhi, Indian activist, political leader. *Young India,* 1927

We're caught between Bin Laden who's a violent Islamic religious fanatic and Bush who's a violent Christian religious fanatic.
Ras Baraka, poet, Deputy Mayor of Newark, NJ. In *Another World is Possible,* 2001

Let us strangle the last king with the guts of the last priest.
Denis Diderot, French philosopher, 1750. Attributed.

Every day people are straying away from the church and going back to God.
Lenny Bruce, comedian. 1925-1966. Attributed.

The greatest threat to our country is religion and materialism. Religion has become an opiate, a sedative to calm a guilty conscience. We bask in religion to make ourselves feel good while at the same time we destroy two-thirds of the world.
Christoph Arnold, writer. *Blu Magazine,* 2000

You've got to have something to eat and a little love in your life before you can hold still for any damn body's sermon on how to behave.
Billie Holiday, singer. *Lady Sings the Blues,* 1956

Religion is the sigh of the oppressed creature, the sentiment of a heartless world, and the soul of soulless conditions. It is the opium of the people.
Karl Marx, German political theorist. "Critique of Hegel's Philosophy of Right," 1844

Spiritual reality is based upon responsibility. Religious realities are not spiritual. The religious reality that exists in these technologic industrial perceptions are not about responsibility, they're about authoritarianism and guilt and sin and blame, domination and submission.
John Trudell, poet, activist, former chairman of the American Indian Movement. Interview, 1999

God will unite us so that we understand one another. The world belongs to God, and God has given us land for us to live together. Everyone has a right to live on their land, and this is why we are all here. Some people create bombs to destroy the world, and others work to unify the world. May God bless His creation.

Lesikar Ole Ngila, Tanzanian Maasai activist. *Baobabconnections.org*, 2004

Some people think it's the only power. They're like the ones who take the uranium out of the ground where God put it and build an atomic bomb to kill human beings. Then they go to their church and call out, "God bless us! Help us rule your world!" Impossible! God's not helping them. They can't rule this world. This world is God's, and only God rules the world.

Mathew King, Lakota spiritual elder. *Noble Red Man*, 1994

Those of you that think that God, the Creator of heaven and earth, does not care about those little children in Afghanistan and their mothers and fathers ravaged by three decades of war as much as he cares about us here in America, then I question your God and wonder who it is that you are praying to at night.

Ewuare Osayande, educator, activist, poet. Speech, 1/21/2002

If a state makes welcome the Jewish French but not the Jewish Dissidents, could dissidence make one less Jewish?
or just less desirable?
We must remember our history about un desirables

Mary La Rosa, poet. From poem "Poem to the Israeli Government: 'I Have No More Secrets to Tell,'" 2004

Workers need poetry more than bread. They need that their life should be a poem. They need some light from eternity. Religion alone can be the source of such poetry.

Simone Weil, French philosopher, writer. *Gravity and Grace*, 1947

The religion that we have, the religion of Islam, the religion that makes us Muslims, the religion that The Honorable Elijah Muhammad is teaching us here in America today, is designed to undo in our minds what the white man has done to us. It's designed to undo the type of brainwashing that we have had to undergo for four hundred years at the hands of the white man in order to bring us down to the level that we're at today.

Malcolm X, Black nationalist leader, Speech, December 1962

In the conflict of poverty, all we had was nothing. But because of the divine spirit that we was raised with, it teaches us to bind nothing, and get something; zero with zero and get one.

Peter Tosh, Jamaican reggae artist. In "The Red X Tapes," 1992

What you believe and what you do are the same thing. In Indian way, if you see your people suffering, helping them becomes absolutely necessary. It's not a social act of charity or welfare assistance, it's a spiritual act, a holy deed.

Leonard Peltier, writer, U.S. political prisoner. *Prison Writings,* 1999

[Jesus] organized a working class movement...for no other purpose than to destroy class rule and set up the common people as the sole and rightful inheritors of the earth.

Eugene V. Debs, activist, labor organizer, socialist. "Jesus, the Supreme Leader," 1910

Lord, receive a thousand thanks that you, too, are a rebel. That day and night you wage your constant struggle against injustice. That you fight all inhumanity towards our fellow man.

Carlos Mejía Godoy, Nicaraguan singer. "The Mass to the God of the Poor, By the Poor," 1975

If a society desires to separate religion from the government of course it has to be done. This issue is not against Islam. The main point is the following: the Muslims all over the world in any country where they live should not be deceived by the claim that Islam is incompatible with democracy and we must choose between accepting democracy or the tradition our ancestors wanted. We can have both.

Shirin Ebadi, Iranian human rights activist. Speech, 5/14/2004

Creator got things fixed. If you don't do the right thing, you can't go forward and you can't go backward.

Sun Ra, jazz composer. In *In Defense of Mumia,* 1996

Chapter 47

"Overthrowing Our Inhibitions"

Love, Hate, Emotion

Love is contraband in Hell,
cause love is an acid
that eats away bars.

> **Assata Shakur**, former Black Panther, in exile in Cuba. From
> poem "Love," 1987

Love is the ability to tap into the largesse of the human spirit made evident
by struggle. Thus, struggle becomes a sacred act like prayer... Each day that
we're alive we're given the opportunity to stand in our own truth...this is
our struggle...this is what teaches us how to love.

> **Sybil Roberts**, playwright, educator. From play, "A Love Song
> for Mumia," 2000

In order to be a true revolutionary, you must understand love. Love, sacrifice,
and death.

> **Sonia Sanchez**, educator, poet, writer. In *Black Women Writers at
> Work*, 1983

Let me say, at the risk of sounding ridiculous, that the true revolutionary is
motivated by great feelings of love.

> **Ernesto "Che" Guevara**, Argentinean-Cuban revolutionary and
> military leader. "Socialism and Man in Cuba," 1965

The only antidote to fear is love. You're either in fear or in love. There's not
really any place in between.

> **Nina Utne**, publisher of *Utne Reader*, on coping with the 9/11
> World Trade Center attacks. In *Another World is Possible*, 2001

We give love
Knowing the scent
Bees follow
Is greater
Than the sum of war

> **Ann Filemyr**, educator, poet, activist. From poem, "Love's Great
> Equation," *Skin on Skin*, 2000

Sooner or later, all the peoples of the world will have to discover a way to
live together in peace, and thereby transform this pending cosmic elegy,

into a creative psalm of brotherhood. If this is to be achieved, man must evolve for all human conflict, a method which rejects revenge, aggression and retaliation. The foundation of such a method is Love.

> **Martin Luther King Jr.**, civil rights leader. Acceptance address for the Nobel Peace Prize, 1963

Love poses a threat to our political system, for it is difficult to convince a man who has a lot to live for in his personal relationships to be willing to fight and die for an abstraction such as the state.

> **CrimethInc. Worker's Collective.** *Days of War, Nights of Love*, 2000

I mean to resist the hatred of these times any way that I can.

> **June Jordan**, poet, educator. Attributed.

Love cannot conquer all if it is not conscious.

> **Ewuare Osayande**, educator, activist, poet. *So The Spoken Word Won't Be Broken*, 1999

It takes courage to love, it takes bravery to love, and love is not simply a feeling but an action. Love is the ability to stand up and speak the truth even when you know you will be standing alone.

> **Ewuare Osayande**, educator, activist, poet. Speech, Newtown, PA 1/21/2002

Let us the living love the living,
since gratefully dead things will be later.

> **César Vallejo**, Peruvian poet. Attributed.

The greatest resistance to war is love, and love is not resistance. Love is love.

> **Saul Williams**, hip hop MC, activist. Interview, *Satya* magazine, May 2003

I wanna love you militantly
make revolutionary love

> **Sharon Smith-Knight**, poet. From poem "Revolutionary Love," circa 1998

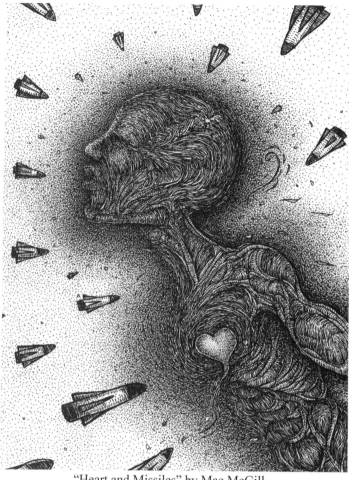

"Heart and Missiles" by Mac McGill

Life is subversive
Love is the agitator
    Ernesto Cardenal, Nicaraguan poet, liberation theologian.
    Attributed.

Love is not a doctrine. Peace is not an international agreement. Love and
Peace are beings who live as possibilities in us.
    Mary Caroline Richards. *Centering*, 1964

Hey baby I picketed in front of the jail today.
(Hmmm, keep it going don't stop)
I set fire to a nike store.

(Ooh, you know how covert actions turn me on)
I exposed government corruption at the highest level
(Oh god, that's what i'm talking about)
Girl, i dismantled this whole racist oppressive totalitarian capitalist regime,
(Oh yeah)
and replaced it with a nurturing respectful egalitarian and open society!
(oh yes, oh yes, right there RIGHT THERE it's sooooooo gooooood!)

> **Turiya Autry and Walidah Imarisha**, activists, poets. From poem "Political Man," 2000

In prison I realized that hate was beginning to destroy me. So I had to give up that hate and find a way to forgive these people. I learned that you cannot forgive anyone else until you first forgive yourself for being the very same thing that you end up hating. Because bitterness only consumes the vessel that contains it... See, hate put me in prison, no doubt about it, and love busted me out.

> **Rubin "Hurricane" Carter**, activist, former champion boxer framed for murder. *Blu Magazine*, 2000

We must remember that the enemy does not live half-way around the globe, but in our own hearts, and that only with love of our fellow man will the hatreds of the world be ended once and for all.

> **Wright Salisbury**, Father-in-law of Ted Hennessey, killed in 9/11 World Trade Center attacks. Essay, "Working for Bridges of Understanding," 2003

If you force people into an economical situation that is not productive, and if you demographically situate these people in a living condition that is subservient to the masses of society, you produce hate.

> **"Forty-Two Decades,"** interlude on "State of Emergency" music compilation, 1994

By taking a look at your anger it can be transformed into the kind of energy that you need—understanding and compassion. It is with negative energy that you can make the positive energy. A flower, although beautiful, will become compost someday, but if you know how to transform the compost back into the flower, then you don't have to worry.

> **Thich Nhat Hanh**, Vietnamese Buddhist monk, educator. In conversation with bell hooks, *Shambala Sun*, January 2000

Hateful things sometimes befall the hateful but the hateful are not rendered loveable thereby.

> **Gwendolyn Brooks**, writer, poet. From poem "In the Mecca," 1967

Hatred as an element of the struggle; a relentless hatred of the enemy, impelling us over and beyond the natural limitations that man is heir to and transforming him into an effective, violent, selective and cold killing machine. Our soldiers must be thus; a people without hatred cannot vanquish a brutal enemy.

> **Ernesto "Che" Guevara**, Argentinean-Cuban revolutionary and military leader. From "Message to the Tricontinental," April 1967

Love is fragile and gentle and seeks a like response. They used to sing "I Love Everybody" as they ducked bricks and bottles: Now they sing:
Too much love,
Too much love,
Nothing kills a nigger like
Too much love.

> **Julius Lester**, writer, activist, musician, circa 1965. In *A People's History of the United States,* 1980

I won't permit you to call it hate. Let's say I'm going to create an awareness of what has been done to them. This awareness will produce an abundance of energy, both negative and positive, that can then be channeled constructively.

> **Malcolm X**, Black nationalist leader, in response to question regarding whether he planned to use hate as a force to motivate people. *Village Voice*, February 1965

There's always someone to hate. The list of those who have earned our hatred—and spurned our hatred—is endless. Shall we draw up lists of each other's crimes? Must we hate each other for all time?

> **Leonard Peltier**, writer, U.S. political prisoner. *Prison Writings,* 1999

Oh, I must keep my heart inviolate
Against the potent poison of your hate.

> **Claude McKay**, poet, activist, writer. From poem "The White House," circa 1919

How with this rage shall beauty hold a plea,
Whose action is no stronger than a flower?

> **Stephen Spender**, English poet, writer. *The Year of the Young Rebels*, 1968

When we embrace victimization, we surrender our rage. My rage intensifies because I am not a victim. It burns in my psyche with an intensity that creates clarity. It is a constructive healing rage.

> **bell hooks**, writer, educator, activist. *Killing Rage: Ending Racism*, 1995

I'm African born in the u.s. and I understand the healing power of anger. White people don't want us to be angry, they would also like to take that right from us too. Anyone that has been raped or brutalized has the right to speak our minds.

> **Post on the Dead Prez internet message board**, 2004

Grab the broom of anger and drive off the beast of fear.

> **Zora Neale Hurston**, writer. *Dust Tracks on a Road*, 1942

I have suckled the wolf's lip of anger and I have used it for illumination, laughter, protection, fire in places where there was no light, no food, no sisters, no quarter.

> **Audre Lorde**, educator, activist, poet. Essay, "The Uses of Anger," 1981

An emotion we will all soon feel when we go to war...is comradeship. I want to warn you not to confuse this with friendship, with love. The ecstatic glow that makes us in war feel as one people, as one entity, is real. But this is part of war's intoxication.

> **Chris Hedges**, writer. *Harvard Gazette*, 4/3/2003

The reason why even revolutionaries...cannot change their social circumstances is because they do not recognize or just deny the existence of powerful unconscious, self-enslaving emotional habits, thought patterns and defense-mechanisms WITHIN THEM that overwhelms the best and most righteous of intentions and endeavors to change society.

> **Ashanti Alston**, former Black Panther member, anarchist activist. Essay, "Childhood & The Psychological Dimension of Revolution," 1983

Let us not grieve about anything, but forgive everyone, just as we must be forgiven everything, and go into the future radiant with joy.
> **Eberhard Arnold**, educator, writer. *Blu Magazine*, 1999

If you already know that you control your mind therefore controlling your life, then you know as a people we control our world.
> **Iriel Sayeed**, activist, poet. Essay, "Food: The Famine and the Feast," 2003

Hope is believing in spite of the evidence, and then watching the evidence change.
> **Reverand Jim Wallis**, writer, editor. Attributed.

The 20th century was born under the sign of revolution, and it dies marked by despair. Stop the world, I want to get off: in these times of stupor and collapse, the ranks of the regretful are swelling—regretful of political passion and regretful of all passion. There are many who apologize for having believed that it was possible to conquer heaven; there are many who fervently seek to kick over their own traces and climb down from hope, as if hope were a worn-out horse.
> **Eduardo Galeano**, Uruguayan historian, educator. Preface, *One Hundred Red Hot Years*, 2003

Do not mistake kindness for weakness or restraint for inability to act. Let us seek the high ground in all things.
> **David Hill**, Leonard Peltier Defense Committee. "Statement of Position: Seeking the High Ground," 2004

We are as human beings still capable of being gentle, still capable of kindness, of generosity. Given the cruelty of history, there is virtually no reason in the world any of us should have those qualities. Yet they persist.
> **Martín Espada**, poet. *Christian Science Monitor*, 1991

Chapter 48

"The Power is Final"

Truth and Falsehood

All great truths begin as blasphemies.
> **George Bernard Shaw**, Irish playwright, writer. Attributed.

A lie can travel around the world while the truth is just putting on its shoes.
> **Mark Twain**, writer. Attributed.

Justice is a master virtue: no light matter, no civil rights issue, just truth and falsehood, not nicely calculated less or more. Truth comes and falsehood is perished, and falsehood by its nature is bound to perish.
> **Jamil Al-Amin**, formerly H. "Rap" Brown, activist, U.S. political prisoner. *Blu Magazine*, 2001

All truth passes through three stages. First, it is ridiculed. Second, it is violently opposed. Third, it is accepted as being self-evident.
> **Arthur Schopenhauer**, German philosopher, 1788-1860

Apparently, 'conspiracy stuff' is now shorthand for unspeakable truth.
> **Gore Vidal**, writer. *The Observer*, 10/27/2002

Universal truth is not measured in mass appeal.
> **Immortal Technique**, hip hop MC. From song "Point of No Return," Viper Records, 2003

He who tells the truth is not well liked.
> **Proverb**, Mali and Senegal

Sometimes the truth hurts when it is spoken aloud, but it also heals.
> **Aishah Shahidah Simmons**, filmmaker. Interview, 2003

Truth came to market and could not be sold; we buy lies with ready cash.
> **Proverb**, Nigeria, Benin and Togo

They say there are three sides to a story: Your side of the story; my side of the story; and the side of the truth. And most of the time, you know, everybody is trying to pull the side of the truth to their side, and the truth is standing right there by itself.
> **Olga Tungi**, Jamaican musician. In "The Red X Tapes," 1992

Know the truth, and it shall make you free. Know the real truth, and it shall piss you off.

> **Kon Spyrysist**, writing alias of a computer programmer. *Blu Magazine*, 2000

As for speaking the truth, we don't have any other choice.

> **Mogauwane Mahloele**, South African musician, in exile in the U.S., 2004

The power of truth is final.

> **John Africa**, founder, MOVE Organization, circa 1975

To tell the truth is to become beautiful, to begin to love yourself, value yourself. And that's political, in its most profound way.

> **June Jordan**, poet, educator. Interview, *Essence*, September 2000

So often the truth is told with hate, and lies are told with love.

> **Rita Mae Brown**, writer. *Bingo*, 1988

I see everything that is deadly upon creation arranged to assassinate those who speak the truth.

> **Peter Tosh**, Jamaican reggae artist. In "The Red X Tapes," 1992

When the conspiracy of lies surrounding me demands of me to silence the one word of truth given to me, that word becomes the one word I wish to utter above all others.

> **Andre Brink**, South African educator. Attributed.

Chapter 49

"The Other Side"

Life and Death

Life pardoned me. History pardoned me. Violence passed me by. Death decided not to take me. I should have been at La Moneda Palace with Allende.

> **Ariel Dorfman**, Argentinean-born writer, former member of Salvador Allende's staff, on the 9/11/1973 CIA-assisted coup which initiated Chile's reign of terror under Augusto Pinochet.

They had to kill him to prolong the life of apartheid.

> **Nelson Mandela**, South African human rights and political leader, speaking of Stephen Biko. *BBC*, September 2002

I am as content to die for God's eternal truth on the scaffold as in any other way.

> **John Brown**, anti-slavery guerrilla leader. From letter to his children on the eve of his execution for his group's attack on Harper's Ferry, 12/2/1859

Since it seems that any heart which beats for freedom has the right only to a small lump of lead, I demand my share. If you let me live, I shall never stop crying for vengeance, and I shall avenge my brothers by denouncing the murderers in the Commission for Pardons.

> **Louise Michel**, French anarchist rebel leader in the 1871 Paris Commune. From statement to military court during her trial, 1871

It seems to me that one ought to rejoice in the fact of death—ought to decide, indeed, to earn one's death by confronting with passion the conundrum of life. One is responsible to life: It is the small beacon in that terrifying darkness from which we come and to which we shall return. One must negotiate this passage a nobly as possible, for the sake of those who are coming after us.

> **James Baldwin**, writer, educator. *The Fire Next Time*, 1963

When one falls, another must take his place, and the rage of each death renews the reason for the fight.

> **Ernesto "Che" Guevara**, Argentinean-Cuban revolutionary, military leader. Attributed.

A bullet cannot terminate the infinite.

> **Haydée Santamaría**, Cuban revolutionary fighter, political leader. From farewell letter to Ernesto "Che" Guevara after his death, 1968

Mother Earth, witness how my enemies shed my blood.

> **Tupac Amaru**, Incan resistance leader against Spanish colonialism. Last words before execution by the Spanish, 1572. Attributed.

We know that the road to freedom has always been stalked by death.

> **Angela Davis**, activist, educator, writer. "Tribute to George Jackson," 1971

I will
not kill for you. Especially
I will not die
for you. I will not mourn
the dead with murder nor
suicide.

> **Suheir Hammad**, poet. From poem "What I Will," circa 2002

Wherever death may surprise us, let it be welcome, provided that this, our battle cry, may have reached some receptive ear and another hand may be extended to wield our weapons and other men be ready to intone the funeral dirge with the staccato singing of the machine-guns and new battle cries of war and victory.

> **Ernesto "Che" Guevara**, Argentinean-Cuban revolutionary and military leader. "Message to the Tricontinental," April 1967

It is better to die on your feet than live on your knees!

> **Emiliano Zapata**, Mexican revolutionary and military leader. circa 1913. Attributed.

A coward dies a thousand deaths, a brave man dies but once.

> **Medgar Evers**, civil rights activist. Attributed.

There is a moment when all things can be beautiful, heroic. That moment when life defies death and defeat, because one holds on to it, because it's so important not to lose it. At such a moment, one risks everything to preserve what really counts. Life and death can be beautiful, and noble, when you fight for your life, but also when you give it up without compromise. All I have wanted to show our young Cubans is that life is more beautiful when you live that way.

Haydée Santamaría, Cuban revolutionary fighter, political leader. In *Haydée Santamaría*, 2003

If a messenger from the sky came down and guaranteed that my death would strengthen our struggle, it would be worth it. But experience teaches us the contrary. It's not with big funerals and motions of support that we're going to save the Amazon. I want to live.

Chico Mendes, Brazilian rubber tapper, union leader, environmentalist. Interview, *O Jornal do Brasil*, 12/9/1988

"Ernesto Che Guevara" by Ricardo Levins Morales

It must become a right of every person to die of old age. And if we secure this right for ourselves, we can, coincidentally, assure it for the planet.

Alice Walker, writer, poet. *Living By The Word*, 1988

Math
does not change from nation to nation. Its self
is not threatened with visa status nor border crossing. One
life always equals one life, though one never brings back
another. No matter the men in power—the math stands.

> **Suheir Hammad**, poet. From poem "September 4, 2002," 2002

He is not dead, because to die for one's homeland is to live forever.

> **Haydée Santamaría**, Cuban revolutionary fighter, political leader.
> Reply to a prison guard who informed her that they had killed her
> fiancé. Related by Fidel Castro in speech, "History Will Absolve
> Me," 1953

Chapter 50

"Politics By Other Means"

War and Militarism

We are peddling freedom to the world and daring them to oppose it and bribing them kindly to accept it and dropping death on those who refuse it.
> **W.E.B. Du Bois**, scholar, educator. Speech, Madison Square Garden, New York City, 1952

War is the continuation of politics by other...means.
> **Mao Tse-Tung**, Chinese revolutionary, political theorist. "On Protracted War," 1938

War...is a social tool by which governments have always mobilized larger social forces for their political ends.
> **Mumia Abu-Jamal**, journalist, U.S. political prisoner. Essay, "Why Being Anti-War Means Being Anti-Imperialist," 2003

When machines and computers, profit motives and property rights, are considered more important than people, the giant triplets of racism, extreme materialism, and militarism are incapable of being conquered.
> **Dr. Martin Luther King Jr.**, civil rights leader. Speech, New York, NY 4/4/1967

There isn't a trick in the racketeering bag that the military gang is blind to. It has its "finger men" to point out enemies, its "muscle men" to destroy enemies, its "brain men" to plan war preparations, and a "Big Boss" Super-Nationalistic-Capitalism. It may seem odd for me, a military man to adopt such a comparison. Truthfulness compels me to… I spent most of my time being a high class muscle-man for Big Business, for Wall Street and for the Bankers. In short, I was a racketeer, a gangster for capitalism.
> **Smedley Butler**, U.S. Marine Corps General, 1933

Imperialists blackmail humanity by threatening it with war.
> **Ernesto "Che" Guevara**, Argentinean-Cuban revolutionary and military leader. From "Message to the Tricontinental," April 1967

Is not Life miserable enough, comes not Death soon enough, without resort to the hideous enginery of War?
> **Horace Greeley**, writer, writing in protest of the war against Mexico. *New York Tribune*, 5/12/1846

"Oil Soldier" by Nicholas Lampert

American officials retain their unshakable belief that they have a god-given right to do whatever they want, for as long as they want, to whomever they want, wherever they want.

William Blum, writer. *Rogue State,* 2000

What if the enemy isn't in a distant land
What if the enemy lies behind
The voice of command
The sound of war is a child's cry
Behind tinted windows,
They just drive by
All I know is that those
Who are going to be killed
Aren't those who preside
On Capitol Hill

Ani DiFranco, singer. From song "Roll With It," 1991

"International community" is also the pseudonym that shelters the great powers in their military campaigns of extermination, also called "pacifying missions." The "pacified" are the dead. The third war against Iraq is already in the works. As in the two previous ones, the bombers will be called "allied forces" while the bombed will be "fanatic mobs serving the Butcher of Baghdad." And the attackers will leave behind a trail of civilian corpses which will be called "collateral damages."

Eduardo Galeano, Uruguayan historian, educator. Essay, "The Machine," 5/1/2002

"Sonia Sanchez and Lamont Steptoe, Poets Against War," collage by Theodore Harris

We'd thought they were little brown men and we were the great big white men. They were of a lessor species. The Germans were well known as tremendous fighters and builders, whereas the Japanese would be a pushover. We used nuclear weapons on these little brown men. We talked about using them in

Vietnam. We talked about using our military force to get our oil in the Middle East from a sort of dark-skinned people. I never hear about us using the military to get our oil from Canada. We still think we're a great super-race.
> **Gene Larocque**, former U.S. Navy Admiral who was present during the Japanese bombing of Pearl Harbor in 1941. Interview, 1985

I don't believe that the big men, the politicians and the capitalists alone, are guilty of the war. Oh no, the little man is just as guilty, otherwise the peoples of the world would have risen in revolt long ago!
> **Anne Frank**, German Jewish girl who kept a diary of her time in hiding from the Nazi Gestapo. *Anne Frank*, 1952

War is the health of the state.
> **Randolph Bourne**, writer. "The State," 1918

Militarism...is one of the chief bulwarks of capitalism, and the day that militarism is undermined, capitalism will fail.
> **Helen Keller**, educator, socialist activist. *The Story of My Life*, 1902

TWO MORE U.S. SOLDIERS PAY THE ULTIMATE PRICE FOR THE CONTINUED PROFITABILITY OF BP/CHEVRON/TEXACO/SHELL/UNOCAL/SUN
what an honor it must be to die for an oil company.
> **Terry Lodge**, attorney, activist. From "Lodge's War Digest" e-mail list serve, July 2003

I was walking to chow hall with my unit, and we were yelling, 'Train to kill, kill we will,' over and over again. I kind of snuck a peek around me and saw all my colleagues getting red in the face and hoarse yelling—and at that point a light went off in my head and I said, 'You know, I made the wrong career decision.'
> **Jeremy Hinzman**, paratrooper in the U.S. Army, recalling how he came to be a consciencious objector and sought refuge from military service in Canada. CBS, 12/8/2004

Real Soldiers Are
Dying In Their
Hummers

So You Can Play
Soldier in Yours

10 Miles Per Gallon
2 Soldiers Per Day
Hand-made signs on a U.S. highway, 2004

What a country calls its vital economic interests are not the things which enable its citizens to live, but the things which enable it to make war.
Simone Weil, French philosopher. Attributed.

Mass demonstration against U.S. war on Afghanistan, Iraq and military aid to Israel, Washington, DC, 2002. Photo by Hans Bennet

It is forbidden to kill; therefore all murderers are punished unless they kill in large numbers and to the sound of trumpets.
Voltaire, French writer, philosopher, 1694-1778

Murder is murder, and somebody must answer. Somebody must explain the streams of blood that flowed in the Indian country in the summer of 1838. Somebody must explain the 4000 silent graves that mark the trial of the Cherokees to their exile... Let the Historian of a future day tell the sad story with its sighs, its tears and dying groans. Let the great Judge of all the earth weigh our actions and reward us according to our work.

> **John G. Burnett**, a soldier who served in a federal militia which forced the Cherokee nation West on the "Trial of Tears." "The Cherokee Removal Through the Eyes of a Private Soldier," December 1890

This system train you to think when you kill, so long as patriotism exist in you, killing is neutralized in the same way love is supposed to neutralize hatred, but the American killer called a patriot for killing Russians is called a murderer in Russia.

> **John Africa**, founder, MOVE Organization, circa 1980

There's a consensus out that it's okay to kill when your government decides who to kill. If you kill inside the country you get in trouble. If you kill outside the country, right time, right season, latest enemy, you get a medal.

> **Joan Báez**, singer, activist. *Daybreak,* 1968

When you kill politicians you are called a murderer, when you kill *for* politicians you are called a patriot.

> **John Africa**, founder, MOVE Organization, circa 1980

After which war did you get free education? After which war did you get free healthcare? After which war did you get social security? U.S. wars do not help working people here. When the wars come, they turn working class people into killers.

> **Elias Rashmawi**, activist, educator. Speech, New York, NY 5/17/2003

America's "volunteer" army in fact depends on a poverty draft of poor whites, blacks, Latinos, and Asians looking for a way to earn a living and get an education.

> **Arundhati Roy**, Indian writer, activist. Speech, 5/13/2003

We're coming, Father Abraham, three hundred thousand more
We leave our homes and firesides with bleeding hearts and sore
Since poverty has been our crime, we bow to thy decree;

We are the poor and have no wealth to purchase liberty.
> **From "Song of the Conscripts,"** written about the draft during the U.S. Civil War and circulated in Northern cities, summer 1863

A lot of our family is being snatched away by military recruiters. They are being misled and tricked into joining the military and supporting war. They lure recruits from one culture of death to another. We have to stop what's happening in our communities. We have to stop the body snatchers.
> **Mario Hardy Ramirez**, activist, on military recruitment in economically poor communities of color. Speech, 1/31/2003

Political thugs in shark suits persuade us to pull triggers in army boots...
> **Nas**, hip hop MC. From song "Doo Rags," 2002

I hate it when they say, "He gave his life for his country." Nobody gives their life for anything. We steal the lives of these kids. We take it away from them. They don't die for the honor and glory of their country. We kill them.
> **Gene Larocque**, former U.S. Navy Admiral. Interview, 1985

I went to war because there were no jobs on the reservation.
> **Wilson Keedah, Sr.**, a former member of the Navajo "code talkers" of World War II. In *Warriors,* 1990

If there is a war, you will furnish the corpses and the taxes, and others will get the glory. Speculators will make money out of it—that is, out of you.
> **Bolton Hall**, American Longshoremen's Union, writing in opposition to the Spanish-American war. "A Peace Appeal to Labor," 1897

I ain't got no quarrel with the Vietcong... No Vietcong ever called me nigger.
> **Muhammad Ali**, champion boxer, activist, refusing to join the U.S. military, 1966. Attributed.

Join the Army, see the world, meet interesting people—and then kill them.
> **Bumper sticker**

If it's natural to kill, why do men have to go into training to learn how?
> **Joan Báez**, singer, activist. *Daybreak,* 1968

The recruiting of our classmates and friends is wrong. The military has been on a massive recruitment campaign, rallying the youth with half-truths and outright lies to blindly sign them up to fight endless wars that do not represent the interests of the people of this world.

From flyer by anti-war group Not In Our Name, 2003

whoop! whoop!
that's the military,
they tryin' to come and get me
to fight wars overseas
for some fake democracy!

Asian and Pacific Islanders Coalition Against War. From e-mail, July 2003

I am not a baby-making factory, my children are not war machine fodder, and I do not plan to bury them in Arlington Cemetery. My loyalties lie first with my God, then my children and neighbors, and my constitution third. I feel no ill-will to the people of the world. I also feel no loyalty to rich men in fancy suits with silver tongues. They have never owned responsibility, accepted accountability, nor have they been soaked with the blood of the dead. They leave all that to our children.

Kay Lee, activist. "To The Women Who Care And The Men Who Support Them," May 2004

YOUNG MEN: The lowest aim in your life is to become a soldier. The good soldier never tries to distinguish right from wrong. He never thinks; never reasons; he only obeys. If he is ordered to fire on his fellow citizens, on his friends, on his neighbors, on his relatives, he obeys without hesitation. If he is ordered to fire down a crowded street when the poor are clamoring for bread, he obeys and sees the gray hairs of age stained with red and the life tide gushing from the breasts of women, feeling neither remorse nor sympathy. If he is ordered off as a firing squad to execute a hero or benefactor, he fires without hesitation, though he knows the bullet will pierce the noblest heart that ever beat in a human breast.

Jack London, writer. Attributed.

CATHOLIC Irish, Frenchmen and German of the invading army!
The American nation makes a most unjust war to the Mexicans, and has taken all of you as an instrument of their iniquity. You must not fight against a religious people, nor should you be seen in the ranks of those who proclaim slavery of mankind as a constitutive principle. The religious man, he who possesses greatness of mind, must always fight for liberty and liberty is

not on the side of those who establish differences in mankind, making an unhappy and innocent people, earn the bread of slavery.

> **Juan Soto**. From leaflet printed by a group of Irish soldiers in the U.S. military who switched sides during the war on Mexico and took up arms against the U.S. and were known as San Patricio's (St. Patrick's) Battalion. June 1847

Military recruiters tour the country selling a dangerous product with glamorous ads, just like tobacco companies or drug pushers.

> **From website of the Central Committee for Conscientious Objectors**, 2002

One weekend a month, my ass.

> **Sign placed in the windshield of a U.S. Army truck by an American soldier in Iraq**, 2003. *New York Times*, 7/22/2003

Why should they ask me to put on a uniform and go ten thousand miles from home and drop bombs and bullets on brown people in Vietnam while so-called Negro people in Louisville are treated like dogs and denied simple human rights? No, I'm not going ten thousand miles from home to help murder and burn another poor nation simply to continue the domination of white slave masters of the darker people the world over... The real enemy of my people is right here. I will not disgrace my religion, my people or myself by becoming a tool to enslave those who are fighting for their own justice, freedom and equality.

> **Muhammad Ali**, champion boxer, activist, speaking to reporters, on his refusal to be drafted to the U.S. military to fight in Vietnam, Louisville, KY, 1966

One keeps healthy in wartime not by a series of religious and political consolations that something good is coming out of it all, but by a vigorous assertion of values in which war has no part.

> **Randolph Bourne**, writer. Essay, "A War Diary," concerning World War I, 1917

War is very profitable for politicians and other parasites.

> **Tee-shirt**, 2003

I've killed more people than the Unabomber because I've paid more taxes than he has.

> **Oprah Winfrey**, talk show host. Attributed. In *Days of War, Nights of Love*, 2000

Soldiers are natural political scientists, because politics can be a matter of life or death to them.

> **Stan Goff**, writer, former U.S. Army sergeant, quoting a friend in the military. *Truthout*, 7/16/2003

Militarism's a Package Deal:
Racism, Sexism, Homophobia
Don't Buy It!

> **Sign at protest against war on Iraq**, New York, NY 2/15/2003

100,000 people demonstrate in a series of mass actions against the U.S. invasion of Iraq, San Francisco, CA 2002. Photo by Bill Hackwell

Think. Speak out. And if you resist, there are hundreds of thousands who will support you, many of whom have already taken to the streets to oppose this war.

> **Jeff Patterson**, first active-duty U.S. military resistor to the Gulf War. *Awol Magazine*, 2002

We go AWOL against this militaristic society; we go AWOL from imperialist society. We are absent without leave from the business of killing and oppressing.

> **Editors**, *Awol Magazine*, 2002

The essential act of war is destruction, not necessarily of human lives, but of the products of human labor. War is a way of shattering to pieces, or pouring into the stratosphere, or sinking in the depths of sea, materials which might otherwise be used to make the masses too comfortable, and hence, in the long run, too intelligent. Even when weapons of war are not actually destroyed, their manufacture is still a convenient way of expending labor power without producing anything that can be consumed.

> **George Orwell**, English writer. *1984,* 1949

The irony of war is that it uses man's best to do man's worst.

> **Mark Twain**, writer. Attributed.

Militarism is the most energy-intensive, entropic activity of humans, since it converts stored energy and materials directly into waste and destruction without any useful intervening fulfillment of basic human needs.

> **Hazel Henderson**, environmental activist. *The Politics of the Solar Age*, 1981

Never counted in the "costs" of war are the dead birds, the charred animals, the murdered fish, incinerated insects, poisoned water sources, destroyed vegetation. Rarely mentioned is the arrogance of the human race towards other living things with which it shares this planet. All these are forgotten in the fight for markets and ideologies. This arrogance will probably be the ultimate undoing of the human species.

> **Arundhati Roy**, Indian writer, activist. Essay, "The Loneliness of Noam Chomsky," 8/24/2003

The sole purpose of war is to kill and destroy. There are no winners.

> **Douglas Rokke**, Vietnam veteran, former director of the U.S. Army's depleted uranium project. *Buffalo News*, 7/22/2003

Once you master people by force you depend on force for control. In your isolation you begin to make mistakes. Fear engenders cruelty; cruelty, fear, insanity, and then paralysis.

> **Chris Hedges**, writer. Speech at graduation ceremony at Rockford College, during which he was booed off stage for his opposition to the U.S. war on Iraq, Spring 2003

I tell people not to buy into the hype about US military invincibility. Person for person, and dollar for dollar, the US military is the most inefficient in the world. And the most fragile. They are fragile because of their overwhelming dependence on high technology, and fragile because the troops come out of a pampered consumer culture where real physical hardship is anecdotal.

> **Stan Goff**, writer, former U.S. Army sergeant. Interview, *Truthout*, 7/16/2003

When human society advances to the point where classes and states are eliminated, there will be no more wars, counter-revolutionary or revolutionary, unjust or just; that will be the era of perpetual peace for mankind.

> **Mao Tse-Tung**, Chinese revolutionary, political theorist. "Problems of Strategy in China's Revolutionary War," 1936

In proportion as the antagonism between classes within the nation vanishes, the hostility of one nation to another will come to an end.

> **Karl Marx and Friedrich Engels**, German political theorists. *Communist Manifesto,* 1848

We cry for Baghdad. Tonight, we shall be awake waiting for the bombs to fall, but we will also remember that God is stronger than oppression. Wars come and go, but Baghdad will remain.

> **Abdel-Jabar al-Tamimi**, Iraqi civil servant, Baghdad, one day before U.S. bombing. *Reuters*, 3/19/2003

The circle of violence is a death spiral; no one escapes. We are spinning at a speed that we may not be able to hold. As we revel in our military prowess—the sophistication of our military hardware and technology, for this is what most of the press coverage consisted of in Iraq—we lose sight of the fact that just because we have the capacity to wage war does not give us the right to wage war. This capacity has doomed empires in the past.

> **Chris Hedges**, writer. Speech at graduation ceremony at Rockford College, during which he was booed off the stage for his opposition to the U.S. war on Iraq, spring 2003

All wars are useless to the dead.

> **Adrienne Rich**, writer, poet. From poem "Implosions," 1969

I think we can be reasonably confident that if the American population had the slightest idea of what is being done in their name, they would be utterly appalled.

> **Noam Chomsky**, political analyst, linguist. In *Another World is Possible*, 2001

Very few people chose war. They chose selfishness and the result was war. Each of us, individually and nationally, must choose: total love or total war.

> **David Dellinger**, activist, one the "Chicago Eight" protestors arrested and charged for "conspiracy" during the Democratic Convention in Chicago, IL, 1968

War is not the answer
For only love can conquer hate

> **Marvin Gaye**, singer, composer. From song, "What's Going On," 1971

As long as we allow millions to be slaughtered in our name, and others to be manipulated into and forced to surrender themselves to what they think of—and justify—as a just war, we will never feel sufficiently human, sufficiently worthwhile, to become responsible for ourselves, our leaders, our country, our children, or our fate, we will die as our fathers and mothers have died, in their delusions.

> **Jafar Saidi**, U.S. political prisoner. From message to supporters, 3/30/2003

So finally I say,
that for a brighter future
a little bombing is a small price to pay.

> **David Roberts**, English poet. From satirical poem "A Message from Tony Blair to the People of Iraq," 2003

Heaven help the roses if the bombs begin to fall
Heaven help us all

> **Stevie Wonder**, singer. From song, "Heaven Help Us All," 1970

Let us not justify war. Because if the war should happen no one will come out of it proud.

> **Shirin Ebadi**, Iranian human rights activist. Speech, 5/14/2004

and after we win each war we wait in fear once more
the more we win the less time there is for living

> **Robert Adamson**, poet. From poem "My Collaboration with George Bush," 2003

The most beautiful victory will be the war that we avoid.
Greeting card, March 2004

War is unhealthy for children and other living things.
Author unknown

On the Ground by Brandon Bauer

War has crossed out the day and replaced it with horror, and now horrors are unfolding instead of days.
Zlata Filipovic, Bosnian girl who kept a journal of her experiences during the war in her country. *Zlata's Diary*, 1994

There has never been a war yet which, if the facts had been put calmly before the ordinary folk, could not have been prevented. The common man is the greatest protection against war.
Aneurin Bevan, English Minister of Health, 1945

So, who do you believe: the Iraqis digging shards of U.S. made rockets out of the rubble who say the bomb was a U.S.-made rocket? Or do you believe the sergeant from the freakin' 346th TACTICAL PSYCHOLOGICAL OPERATIONS COMPANY who says there's no evidence the explosion was caused by a U.S. attack?
Terry Lodge, attorney, activist. From Essay "PSYCHED OP— Just wondering?" 2003

War waged for empire or wealth in an age when those arrayed against us can also get apocalyptic weapons means we dance with our own destruction. We thrill in our own annihilation. In war, we suffer as much destruction as we wreak. When we unleash war's awful power, we become its pawn, its tool.

Chris Hedges, writer. The *Harvard Gazette*, 4/3/2003

Let it not be said that people in the United States did nothing when their government declared a war without limit and instituted stark new measures of repression.

The signers of this statement call on the people of the U.S. to resist the policies and overall political direction that have emerged since September 11, 2001, and which pose grave dangers to the people of the world.

We believe that peoples and nations have the right to determine their own destiny, free from military coercion by great powers.

Not in Our Name Coalition. From "A Statement of Conscience: Not in Our Name," signed by thousands of people during 2001-2002

But in wartime people lose their senses. There are flags and yellow ribbons and posters and every media outlet is beating the war drum and even sensible people can hear nothing else. In the US, God forbid you should suggest the war is unjust or that dropping cluster bombs from 30,000 ft on a city is a cowardly act.

Woody Harrelson, actor, activist. *The Guardian,* 11/17/2002

If I look up the street two blocks, I see three houses with flags on them. I've talked to some people who have flags, and they say they're doing it to show sympathy for the victims (of Sept. 11). But I know what that symbol really means: Let's rally the troops and go bomb someone. People need to connect the problems they're going through here with the problems that are going on in the Middle East because the people they're demonizing are part of the same economic exploitation.

Boots, of hip hop group The Coup. Interview, *San Francisco Chronicle*, 11/18/2001

This business of burning human beings with napalm, of filling our nation's homes with orphans and widows, of injecting poisonous drugs of hate into veins of people normally humane, of sending men home from dark and bloody battlefields physically handicapped and psychologically deranged, cannot be reconciled with wisdom, justice and love. A nation that continues year after year to spend more money on military defense than on programs of social uplift is approaching spiritual death.

> **Martin Luther King Jr.**, civil rights leader. Speech, New York, NY 4/4/1967

We are helpless people. It is all out of our hands. Why cannot the world find a solution? The whole world is watching us die and is doing nothing to help us.

> **Iraqi woman**, after U.S. missile killed civilians during 2003 war on Iraq. *Reuters*, 3/29/2003

Being a 'civilian' is a relative thing in a country occupied by Americans. You're only a civilian if you're on their side. If you translate for them, or serve them food in the Green Zone, or wipe their floors—you're an innocent civilian. Just about everyone else is an insurgent, unless they can get a job as a 'civilian.'

> **Riverbend**, alias of an Iraqi writer in Baghdad. Essay, "Rule of Iraq Assassins Must End," November 2004

If you assume that every military age male is an enemy, there can be no better sign that you are in the wrong country, and that, in fact, your war is on the people, not on their oppressors, not a war of liberation.

> **Rahul Mahajan**, writer, activist. *Guerrilla News Network*, November 2004

There is no flag large enough to cover the shame of killing innocent people.

> **Howard Zinn**, historian, educator. Attributed quotation on a tee shirt, March 2004

When will this cease?
The warheads will all rust in peace

> **Megadeth**, heavy metal band. From song "Rust In Peace," 1990

Chapter 51

"Arms Are For Hugging"

Weapons

You can have my gun when you pry it from the fingers of my cold, dead child.

> **Hand-made sign on a highway**, a spoof on the slogan of the
> National Rifle Association, 2004

The countries that sell the world the most weapons are the same ones in charge of world peace. Fortunately for them, the threat of world peace is receding.

> **Eduardo Galeano**, Uruguayan historian, educator. *Upside Down*,
> 1998

We don't believe in death-dealing guns, we believe in life. But we knew the cops wouldn't be so quick to attack us if they had to face the same stuff they dished out so casually on unarmed defenseless folk.

> **MOVE Organization**, on their armed vigil against police attack,
> Philadelphia, PA 1977

Enough of the illusion that the problems of the world can be solved by nuclear weapons. Bombs may kill the hungry, the sick, and the ignorant, but they cannot kill hunger, disease, and ignorance. Nor can they kill the righteous rebellion of the peoples. And in the holocaust, the rich—who have the most to lose in this world—will also die.

> **Fidel Castro**, Cuban revolutionary, political leader. Speech,
> United Nations, 1979

We have to prove that greatness is not to be measured in stock piles of atom bombs.

> **Kwame Nkrumah**, Ghanaian political leader. *Neo-Colonialism*,
> 1965

If having a 'weapon of mass destruction' is a violation of international law, then the USA must be a global criminal, for no nation possesses so much nuclear weaponry.

> **Mumia Abu-Jamal**, journalist, U.S. political prisoner. Essay,
> "More Bombs Over Baghdad," 2/24/2001

Arms are for hugging

> **Bumper sticker**

Nuke Bird by Richard Mock

Gun control is being able to hit what you aim at.
Bumper sticker.

We pray that justice will melt these bullets.
Broadcast Live. From song "50 Million and One," 2004

The contention that a standing army and navy is the best security of peace is about as logical as the claim that the most peaceful citizen is he who goes about heavily armed.
Emma Goldman, activist, writer, anarchist. Anarchism, 1910

There are 40,000,000 men under arms in the world today, and our statesmen and diplomats have the temerity to say that war is not in the making.
Smedley Butler, U.S. Marine Corps General. *War Is a Racket*, 1935

Melt down the bombs and the guns to build the ovens that will cook the food for the world's hungry. Melt down the bombs and the guns to make the tools that the world's oppressed will use to achieve the liberation and self-determination they desperately desire now.

> **Ewuare Osayande**, educator, activist, poet. Speech, 1/21/2002

I tell you, all men are created equal
But behind the trigger it's a different sequel

> **Buju Banton**, Jamaican reggae artist. From song "Murderer," 1995

Chapter 52

"Homeland Insecurity"

Terrorism

i do not know how bad a life has to break in order to kill.
i have never been so hungry that i willed hunger
> **Suheir Hammad**, poet. From poem "First Writing Since," 2001

The underlying logic of terrorist attacks, as well as "retaliatory" wars against governments that "support terrorism," is the same: both punish citizens for the actions of their governments.
> **Arundhati Roy**, Indian writer, activist. *The Hindu* newspaper, 8/24/2003

The designation terrorist is produced by the one-way gaze of power. Only one point of view, one vision, one story, is necessary and permissible, since what defines the gaze of power is its absolute, unquestionable authority.
> **John Edgar Wideman**, writer. Essay, "Whose War: The Color of Terror," 2002

A terrorist is someone who has a bomb but doesn't have an air force.
> **William Blum**, writer. *Rogue State,* 2000

The Americans said it was a war against terrorism. Who is doing the terrorism now? Didn't their radars tell them this is a press office and these are civilian houses? My message to you is that hatred grows more hatred.
> **Dima Ayoub**, wife of Al Jazeera news reporter Tariq Ayoub, killed when a U.S. tank fired at a hotel housing journalists in Baghdad. *Associated Press*, 2003

Air bombardment is state terrorism, the terrorism of the rich. It has burned up and blasted apart more innocents in the past six decades than have all the anti-state terrorists who ever lived... In the United States we would not consider for the presidency a man who had once thrown a bomb into a crowded restaurant, but we are happy to elect a man who once dropped bombs from airplanes that destroyed not only restaurants but the buildings that contained them and the neighborhoods that surrounded them.
> **C. Douglas Lummis**, political scientist. *The Nation*, September 1994

When I was in the Black Panther Party, they called us terrorists. How dare they call us terrorists when we were being terrorized? Terror was a constant part of my life. I was living under apartheid in North Carolina. We lived under police terror.

>**Assata Shakur**, former Black Panther, in exile in Cuba. Interview, "From Exile With Love," 2001

The notion that *they* hate *our* freedoms: a belief one can only have if one really thinks one lives in a free country in the first place.

>**Tim Wise**, activist, educator. Essay, "Reagan, Race and Remembrance," June 2004

The important thing to remember is that when it happens to others it's called collateral damage, when they do it to us it's terrorism.

>**Manus Chakravarty**. In *Another World is Possible,* 2001

I want to defend my home. If a stranger invades America and the people resist, does that mean they are terrorists? Everyone [in Fallujah] has been labeled a terrorist.

>**Ahmed Manajid**, member of Iraqi Olympic soccer team, competing in Athens, Greece. *Edgeofsports.com*, 2004

For all their posturing, the terrorists and the Bush regime might as well be working as a team. They both hold people responsible for the actions of their governments. They both believe in the doctrine of collective guilt and collective punishment. Their actions benefit each other greatly.

>**Arundhati Roy**, Indian writer, activist. Speech, 5/13/2003

All thinking people oppose terrorism both domestic & international... But one should not be used to cover the other.

>**Amiri Baraka**, poet, educator. From prelude to poem "Somebody Blew Up America," 2001

An act of torture is an act of terrorism. I must press for justice, or others will die as my husband did, either thrown from a helicopter or dismembered and scattered across a sugar cane field, all paid for by U.S. tax dollars and protected with U.S. secrecy. Here it must end.

>**Jennifer K. Harbury**, human rights activist whose husband, Efraín Bámaca Velásquez, a Guatemalan rebel fighter, was killed by forces working in association with the C.I.A. *Covert Action Quarterly*, Fall 2002

Terrorism is in the eye of the beholder.

>**Nidal Sakr**, human rights activist.

To label an enemy a terrorist confers the same invisibility a colonist's gaze confers upon the native. Dismissing the possibility that the native can look back at you just as you are looking at him is a first step toward blinding him and ultimately rendering him or her invisible.

> **John Edgar Wideman**, writer. Essay, "Whose War: The Color of Terror," 2002

Nations deny causality by ascribing blame to other terrorists, rogue nations, and so on. Singling out an enemy, we short-circuit the introspection necessary to see our own karmic responsibility for the terrible acts that have befallen us. Until we own causes we bear responsibility for, in this case in the Middle East, last week's violence will make no more sense than an earthquake or cyclone, except that in its human origin it turns us toward rage and revenge.

> **The Buddhist Peace Fellowship**, referring to the 9/11/2001 World Trade Center attacks. In *Another World is Possible,* 2001

Columnists decry Islam as a religion of violence, Muslims as wife-beaters, etc, etc. They judge the actions of the few and apply it to the many. Tonight then, by their own testament, I will apply the actions of the few to the intentions of the many... Next time someone asks you the most idiotic of questions—"why do they hate us"—ask them to see the pictures in question.

> **Firas Al-Atraqchi**, Canadian writer. "Racism at Heart of POW Abuse," on photos of abuse of Iraqi prisoners by U.S. soldiers. *YellowTimes*, 5/1/2004

As long as the gap between the haves and the have-not keeps getting bigger, there will be conflict, and the more people feel they are not heard, the more likely they will turn to violence. It is not surprising.

> **Robert LeBlanc**, killed in World Trade Center attacks, 9/11/2001. Quoted by his widow in essay "The Everyday, Small, Good Things in Life," 9/13/2003

By John Jonik

We wonder how come the world doesn't love us? Take it to the neighborhood level. Suppose the wealthiest person on the block routinely walks up to people and smashes them in the face or cracks their skulls with a crowbar. It keeps happening. But one day someone swings back. Are you surprised?

> **Colman McCarthy**, peace activist, educator. Interview, *Satya* magazine, November 2001

Today, people feel powerless. And so when America is hit they celebrate. They don't ask what such an act will achieve, what its consequences will be and who will benefit. Their response, like the event itself, is purely symbolic… Palestine suffers every day. The West does nothing. Our governments are dead. Our politicians are corrupt. Our people are ignored. Is it surprising that some are responsive to the Islamists?

> **Tariq Ali**, English historian, writer. *The Clash of Fundamentalisms*, 2003

So what were we to do when we in America were attacked on September 11, that infamous day? I say we should have done then what we never did before: stop speaking to the people we labeled our enemies and start listening to them. Stop giving preconditions to our peaceful coexistence on this small planet, and start honouring and respecting every human's need to live free and autonomously, to truly respect the sovereignty of every state. To stop making up rules by which others must live and then separate rules for ourselves.

> **Michael Berg**, father of Nick Berg, a U.S. contractor in Iraq beheaded on video by insurgents. *The Guardian*, May 2004

They know where the fruits of the planet, the oil and the spices, are going. And when your actions cause grief in some new corner of the world, they know about it. And when you kill people who are poor and desperate, no matter what explanation you give for what you've done, their anger against you grows. You can't kill all these millions of people, but almost any one of them, in some way, some place, or some degree, can cause damage to you.

> **Wallace Shawn**, writer. Essay, "The Foreign Policy Therapist," 12/3/2001

One of the problems is that we bring these guys in. They learn the techniques of what we call counter-terrorism, which is terrorism. These guys then went back to Afghanistan. The idea was that they were going to fight the Russians. We forgot that sometimes Frankensteins turn around and devour their creators?

> **Greg Palast**, writer. Interview, *BuszzFlash.com*, 8/29/2003

Injustice is the most eloquent recruiter for terrorism.

> **John Maxwell**. In *Another World is Possible*, 2001

But now everyone is cashing in on the 'war against terror.' When Macedonian cops gun down seven Arabs, they announce that they are participating in the global 'war on terror.' When Russians massacre Chechens, they are now prosecuting the 'war on terror'... Must we all be hijacked into America's dangerous self-absorption with the crimes of 11 September?

> **Robert Fisk**, English writer. The *Independent*, UK, 3/30/2002

My son had his head blown off. Why are they hitting the people? Why are they killing the children? Why are they doing this to us? Why are they attacking civilians? Didn't Bush say on TV that he won't attack civilians? But these people who died are all civilians. Is this [house] a target?

> **Arouba Khodeir**, Iraqi woman, after U.S. bomb killed civilians during 2003 war on Iraq. *Reuters*, 3/29/03

On September 11th, 2001, my husband Sean became something very alien to the America experience. He became a 'civilian casualty.' And because of that, I found that I had become something different, too—a member of a world-wide community numbering in the millions, whose lives have been torn apart by the effects of man's inhumanity to man.

> **Beverly Eckert**, widow of Sean Eckert, killed in the 9/11/2001 World Trade Center attacks. Speech, 8/8/2003

Those towers represented human triumph over nature. Larger than life, built to be unburnable, they were the Titanic of our day. For them to burn and fall so quickly means that the whole superstructure we depend upon to mitigate nature and assure our comfort and safety could fall.

> **Starhawk**, activist, writer, referring to 9/11/01 World Trade Center attacks. Essay, "Only Poetry Can Address Grief," 2001

We ask why, why, why? Why all this blood? They came to free us? This is freedom?

> **Ahmed Sufian**, physician at a Baghdad, Iraq hospital, after a U.S. missile killed civilians in a market during the 2003 war on Iraq. *Washington Post*, 3/31/2003

I will not side
with you nor dance to bombs
because everyone else is
dancing. Everyone can be
wrong.

> **Suheir Hammad**, poet. From poem "What I Will," circa 2002

the eagle flies talons sharpened
hungers for retaliation
a Muslim sister speaks
eyes locked on the TV screen
they will blame the Muslims
someone will feed the eagle

> **Marilyn Buck**, U.S. political prisoner, convicted of participating in prison escape of Assata Shakur. From poem, referring to the 9/11/2001 World Trade Center attacks, circa 2001

I am told to believe nothing I read
Then everything I read

I am given my own face to be wary of
I am told to fear colors as alerts
> **Suheir Hammad**, poet. From poem, "Beyond Words," 2004

To see Cuba called a terrorist country is an insult to reality. If people come to Cuba, they'll see a reality unlike what they're told in America.
> **Assata Shakur**, former Black Panther, in exile in Cuba. Interview, "From Exile With Love," 2001

If you choose to do nothing to help change things for the better, to find nonviolent means to end conflict, to break down the walls that alienate and divide, to feed and clothe all the children of the world, to provide health care for the poor and suffering, to make a difference in an unjust world, it could be your child who suffers or dies at the hands of someone whom we have oppressed, threatened, or harmed in some way.
> **John Titus**, father of Alicia Dexter, killed in 9/11/01 World Trade Center attacks. Essay, "Reflections of a Grieving Father," 8/1/2003

Chapter 53

"You May Say I'm a Dreamer"

Peace

Right now it's like we are unable to imagine world peace. Why? Because our imaginations have been stolen from us. We can imagine World War III because we've seen it in every movie, every TV show, etc. We cannot imagine world peace because we've never seen it before.

> **Saul Williams**, hip hop MC, activist. Interview, *Satya* magazine, May 2003

If the white man wants to live in peace with the Indian he can live in peace. There need be no trouble. Treat all men alike. Give them all the same law. Give them all an even chance to live and grow. All men were made by the same Great Spirit Chief. They are all brothers.

> **Chief Joseph**, Nez Perce leader. Statement, Washington, DC. *North American Review*, 1879

I am saying no to war; I have chosen peace. I went to Iraq and was an instrument of violence and now I have decided to become an instrument of peace.

> **Camilo Mejia**, former U.S. Army sergeant, on why he refused to return to duty in Iraq in 2004. *Associated Press*, 3/16/2004

Peace as the absence of War?
When over a thousand people have been killed unjustly, without trial, by the government's police state, isn't that already war?
When hundreds of thousands of people are imprisoned, robbed of their freedom and stripped of all human dignity, isn't that war?

> **Eberhard Arnold**, educator, writer. Essay, *Blu Magazine*, 1999

We Americans claim to be a peace-loving people. We hate bloodshed; we are opposed to violence. Yet we go into spasms of joy over the possibility of projecting dynamite bombs from flying machines upon helpless citizens… Our hearts swell with pride at the thought that America is becoming the most powerful nation on earth, and that it will eventually plant her iron foot on the necks of all other nations.

> **Emma Goldman**, activist, writer, anarchist. "Patriotism: A Menace to Liberty," 1908

If it were up to the people, there would be peace. It's the governments that

create war.
>   **Iraqi man**, speaking to actor/activist Woody Harrelson in the late
>   1980s. *The Guardian,* 11/17/2002

Youth demonstrate against U.S. war with Iraq, Philadelphia, PA, 2002.
Photo by Hans Bennet

I always think that the peace movement does not mean that you have to do something special. I think the peace movement starts with a little thing, for example, you try to be kind to the people around you. I think that is the peace movement. It begins with such a little thing, so I really want you to keep it in mind and always be kind to other people.
>   **Kwak Bok Soon**, Japanese Hiroshima atomic bomb survivor.

To achieve peace, we who abhor fighting must gain power.
>   **Adrienne Maree Brown**, activist. *How to Get Stupid White Men Out of Office*, 2004

There is no way to peace—peace is the way
>   **A.J. Muste**, activist, 1885-1967. Attributed.

Peace is not this utopian idea of dashing through a field of dandelions, you know, it's hard work. Sometimes the peacemakers lose their lives in the process.
>   **Aqeela Sherrills**, youth gang peace organizer. Interview, *Satya* magazine, November 2002

Peace is definitely not patriotic. The U.S.A. was founded on violence. If you don't kill someone on the 4th of July, you're not patriotic.
>   **Anonymous**, making a joke, Philadelphia, PA, July 2003

You can't separate peace from freedom because no one can be at peace unless he has his freedom.

> **Malcolm X**, Black nationalist leader. Speech, "Prospects for Freedom in 1965," January 1965

White folks don't want peace; they want quiet. The price you pay for peace is justice. Until there is justice, there will be no peace or quiet.

> **Jesse Jackson**, civil rights activist, reverend. Interview, *Playboy*, November 1969

See we all want peace
but the problem is crackers want a bigger piece

> **Dead Prez**, hip hop group. From song "Police State," 2000

The suppression of war is not the equivalent of peace.

> **Vida Dutton Scudder**, educator, activist. *The Privilege of Age*, 1939

We are willing to work for peace at any price, except at the price of liberty.

> **Lucy Ella Gonzales Parsons**, political activist. Speech, "The Principles of Anarchy," circa 1900

You can bomb the world to pieces, but you can't bomb it into peace.

> **Spearhead**, music group. From song "Bomb the World," 2003

I feel conflicted by the need to DO something for peace and also the need to BE peace...to do what I know how to do...to finish this row. I know that unless I am able to recognize the everyday, small, good things of life I have no chance of making anything better. Impoverished, I will have nothing to give.

> **Andrea LeBlanc**, widow of Robert LeBlanc, killed in 9/11/2001 World Trade Center attacks. Essay, "The Everyday, Small, Good Things in Life," 9/13/2003

You may say I'm a dreamer, but I'm not the only one.

> **John Lennon**, singer. From song "Imagine," 1971

Chapter 54

Bonus Quotations

The world is big. Some people are unable to comprehend that simple fact. They want the world on their own terms, its peoples just like them and their friends... Diversity is not an abnormality, but the very reality of our planet. The human world manifests the same reality and will not seek our permission to celebrate itself in the magnificence of its endless varieties. Civility is a sensible attribute in this kind of world we have; narrowness of heart and mind is not.

    Chinua Achebe, Nigerian writer, educator. Attributed.

There is an idealistic slogan within the social movements, which goes like this: 'We can change the world without taking power.' This slogan doesn't threaten anyone; it's a moral slogan.

    Tariq Ali, English historian, writer. Interview, *Venezuelanalysis. com*, 7/22/2004

'Race' disables us because it proposes as a basis for common action the illusion that black (and white and yellow) people are fundamentally allied by nature and, thus, without effort; it leaves us unprepared, therefore, to handle the 'intraracial' conflicts that arise from the very different situations of black (and white and yellow) people in different parts of the economy and the world.

    Kwame A. Appiah, Ghanaian educator. *In My Father's House*, 1992

Totalitarianism is never content to rule by external means, namely, through the state and a machinery of violence; thanks to its peculiar ideology and the role assigned to it in this apparatus of coercion, totalitarianism has discovered a means of dominating and terrorizing human beings from within.

    Hannah Arendt, German educator, political analyst. *The Origins of Totalitarianism*, 1951

So long as we are undaunted and determined to be a free people, the fire of freedom shall not be extinguished from our hearths, we shall march forward towards our national emancipation.

    Nnamdi Azikiwe, Nigerian writer, political leader. Attributed.

The state is the sum of the denials of the individual liberties of all its members.

    Mikhail Bakunin, Russian anarchist writer. Attributed.

To be black and conscious in America is to be in a constant state of rage.
    James Baldwin, writer, educator. Attributed.

To be born in a free society and not be born free is to be born into a lie.
    James Baldwin, writer, educator. Attributed.

In order to survive as a human, moving, moral weight in the world, America and all the Western nations will be forced to reexamine themselves and release themselves from many things that are now taken to be sacred, and to discard nearly all the assumptions that have been used to justify their lives and their anguish and their crimes so long.
    James Baldwin, writer, educator. *The Fire Next Time*, 1963

The destruction of the racist complex presupposes not only the revolt of its victims, but the transformation of the racists themselves and, consequently, the internal decomposition of the community created by racism.
    Etienne Balibar, French political theorist. Attributed.

Revolution begins with the self, in the self... We'd better take the time to fashion revolutionary selves, revolutionary lives, revolutionary relationships. Mouths don't win the war.
    Toni Cade Bambara, writer, activist. *The Black Woman*, 1970

I learned a long time ago that self-dignity and racial pride could be consciously approached through art.
    John T. Biggers, artist. Attributed.

We are aware that the white man is sitting at our table. We know he has no right to be there; we want to remove him…strip the table of all trappings put on by him, decorate it in true African style, settle down and then ask him to join us on our own terms if he wishes.
    Stephen Biko, South African anti-apartheid leader, killed by police in 1977. Attributed.

We must accept that the limits of tyrants are prescribed by the endurance of those whom they oppress. Our situation is not a mistake on the part of the whites but a deliberate act, and no amount of moral lecturing will persuade the white man to correct the situation.
    Stephen Biko, South African anti-apartheid leader, killed by police in 1977. Attributed.

We see a completely non-racial society. We don't believe, for instance, in the so-called guarantees for minority rights because guaranteeing minority rights implies the recognition of portions of the community on a race basis. We believe that in our country there shall be no minority; there shall be no majority; just the people. And those people will have the same status before the law and they will have the same political rights before the law.
> **Stephen Biko**, South African anti-apartheid leader, killed by police in 1977. Interview, circa 1975

We might remember that we were not taught Christianity that we might be saved. We were taught Christianity that we might be better slaves.
> **Reverend Young Blood**, activist, reverend, referring to antebellum America. Speech, New Orleans, LA, March 2005

The time has come for white people in this country to realize that their destiny is inextricably bound with ours... They will never be free as long as they have to lie awake at night worrying whether a black government will one day do to them as they are doing to us.
> **Allan Boesak**, South African religious leader. Speech, August 1983

Even so tyrants...the more is given them, the more they are obeyed, so much the more do they fortify themselves, become stronger and more able to annihilate and destroy. If nothing be given them, if they be not obeyed, without fighting, without striking a blow, they remain naked, disarmed and are nothing—like as the root of a tree, receiving no moisture or nourishment, becomes dry and dead.
> **Etienne de la Boétie**, French writer, judge, 1577

Cursed is the soldier who uses his arms against his own people.
> **Simón Bolívar**, Venezuelan revolutionary leader, military general, 1783-1830. Attributed.

It is a fallacy of radical youth to demand all or nothing, and to view every partial activity as compromise. Either engage in something that will bring revolution and transformation all at one blow, or do nothing, it seems to say.
> **Randolph S. Bourne**, writer. *Youth and Life*, 1913

To live means to finesse the processes to which one is subjugated.
> **Bertolt Brecht**, German playwright, poet. "Notes on Philosophy," 1941

On what does the survival of oppression depend? On us! On whom must we depend on for its demolition? On ourselves!

Bertolt Brecht, German playwright, poet. Attributed.

Those who take the most from the table, teach contentment. Those for whom the taxes are destined, demand sacrifice. Those who eat their fill, speak to the hungry, of wonderful times to come. Those who lead the country into the abyss, call ruling difficult, for ordinary folk.

Bertolt Brecht, German playwright, poet. Attributed.

It is not enough to demand insight and informative images of reality from the theater. Our theater must stimulate a desire for understanding, a delight in changing reality. Our audience must experience not only the ways to free Prometheus, but be schooled in the very desire to free him. Theater must teach all the pleasures and joys of discovery, all the feelings of triumph associated with liberation.

Bertolt Brecht, German playwright, poet. "Essays on the Art of Theater," 1954

The law was made for one thing alone, for the exploitation of those who don't understand it, or are prevented by naked misery from obeying it.

Bertolt Brecht, German playwright, poet. *The Threepenny Opera*, 1928

Unhappy the land that is in need of heroes.

Bertolt Brecht, German playwright, poet. *Life of Galileo,* 1939

If only more of today's military personnel would realize that they are being used by the owning elites as a publicly subsidized capitalist goon squad.

Smedley Butler, U.S. Marine Corps General, 1933

A people's struggle is effectively theirs if the reason for that struggle is based on the aspirations, the dreams, the desire for justice and progress of the people themselves and not on the aspirations, dreams or ambitions of half a dozen persons who are in contradiction with the actual interests of their people.

Amilcar Cabral, Guinean anti-colonial leader, assassinated in 1973. Attributed.

Always bear in mind that the people are not fighting for ideas. They are fighting to win material benefits, to live better and in peace, to see their lives go forward.

> **Amilcar Cabral**, Guinean anti-colonial leader, assassinated in 1973. *Revolution in Guinea*, 1969

Who are we? We are Puerto Ricans. In order to resolve Puerto Rico's political status, we must first understand who we are and our island's history. In order to destroy our nation, they will have to take our lives.

> **Pedro Albizu Campos**, Puerto Rican revolutionary leader, after the Ponce Massacre, Puerto Rico, 1937

What would become of the world if the condemned started to confide their heartaches to the executioners?

> **Albert Camus**, French-Algerian philosopher, writer, 1962

Methods of thought which claim to give the lead to our world in the name of revolution have become, in reality, ideologies of consent and not of rebellion.

> **Albert Camus**, French-Algerian philosopher, writer. "Rebellion and Revolution," 1953

It is probable that the most inhuman monsters, the Himmlers and the Mengeles, convince themselves that they were engaged in noble and courageous acts.

> **Noam Chomsky**, political analyst, linguist. *Necessary Illusions*, 1989

U.S. international and security policy...has as its primary goal the preservation of what we might call "the Fifth Freedom," understood crudely but with a fair degree of accuracy as the freedom to rob, to exploit and to dominate, to undertake any course of action to ensure that existing privilege is protected and advanced.

> **Noam Chomsky**, political analyst, linguist. *The Culture of Terrorism*, 1988

What we're saying today is that you're either part of the solution or you're part of the problem.

> **Eldridge Cleaver**, writer, former black power activist. Speech, 1968, San Francisco, CA

Information is the raw material for new ideas; if you get misinformation,

you get some pretty fucked-up ideas.
>**Eldridge Cleaver**, writer, former black power activist. Attributed.

All the gods are dead except the god of war.
>**Eldridge Cleaver**, writer, former black power activist. *Soul on Ice*, 1968

Now each day is fair and balmy,
Everywhere you look: the army.
>**Ustad Daman**, Punjabi poet, circa 1959

To understand how a society functions, you must understand the relationship between the men and the women.
>**Angela Davis**, activist, educator, writer. Attributed.

The joke goes: An anthropologist comes up to an Indian, and asks him what did the Indians call America before the whites came, and the Indian replies, "Ours!"
>**Vine Deloria**, educator, writer. Attributed.

The land's going to break its chains
Poverty's heyday's over
The hills, the valleys and plains
Are going to blossom through work
Down with the liars and traitors
The tyrants and usurers
The peasants will be masters
>**Pierre DuPont**, songwriter. "The Peasant's Song," 1850

We carry a new world here, in our hearts. That world is growing in this minute.
>**Buenaventura Durruti**, Spanish anarchist, assassinated in 1936. Attributed.

To celebrate the holidays we decided on a bonfire. Unfortunately for U.S. Forest Industries it was in their corporate headquarters office.
>**Earth Liberation Front**. Communiqué issued after arsonists destroyed the offices of a Medford, OR logging company which they said was devastating forest sites in Colorado, 1990s

I am an invisible man.... I am a man of substance, of flesh and bone, fiber and liquids—and I might even be said to possess a mind. I am invisible, understand, simply because people refuse to see me.

Ralph Ellison, writer. *The Invisible Man*, 1952

Whoso would be a man must be a nonconformist. He who would gather immortal palms must not be hindered by the name of goodness, but must explore if it be goodness. Nothing is at last sacred but the integrity of your own mind.

Ralph Waldo Emerson, philosopher, writer. "Self Reliance," 1841

Rebellion Is the Circle of a Lover's Hands

Martín Espada, poet. Title of book, 1990

Speak, your lips are free.
Speak, it is your own tongue.

Faiz Ahmed Faiz, Pakistani writer, poet, 1914-1978. From Poem, "Speak"

The suspense that lasts between killers and weapons
as they gamble: who will die and whose turn is next?

Faiz Ahmed Faiz, Pakistani writer, poet, 1914-1978. From poem, "So Bring the Order for My Execution"

Wishing for the roses of your lips
we offered ourselves to a gallows' twig

Faiz Ahmed Faiz, Pakistani writer, poet, 1914-1978. From poem inspired by the letters of Ethel and Julius Rosenberg, "We, Who Were Slain In Unlit Pathways," 1954

The law in its majestic equality forbids both the rich and the poor to beg for money, sleep under bridges, and steal bread.

Anatole France, French writer. *The Red Lily*, 1894

There is no such thing as a neutral educational process. Education either functions as an instrument which is used to facilitate the integration of the younger generation into the logic of the present system and bring about conformity to it, or it becomes the practice of freedom—the means by which men and women deal critically and creatively with reality and discover how to participate in the transformation of their world.

Paulo Freire, Brazilian educator. *Pedagogy of the Oppressed*, 1968

The principle of 'an eye for an eye' will some day make the whole world blind.

Mahatma Gandhi, Indian activist, political leader. Attributed.

Tell a man whose house is on fire to give a moderate alarm; tell him to moderately rescue his wife from the hands of the ravisher; tell the mother to gradually extricate her babe from the fire into which it has fallen; but urge me not to use moderation in a case like the present.

William Lloyd Garrison, slavery abolitionist. Editorial, *The Liberator*, 1/1/1831

As it happens, there are no columns in standard double-entry book-keeping to keep track of satisfaction and demoralization. There is no credit entry for feelings of self-worth and confidence, no debit column for feelings of uselessness and worthlessness. There are no monthly, quarterly or even annual statements of pride and no closing statement of bankruptcy when the worker finally comes to feel that after all he couldn't do anything else, and doesn't deserve anything better.

Barbara Garson, writer. Attributed.

The more stupid a white man is, the more stupid he thinks black men are.

André Gide, French writer, comment after visiting the Congo, 1930s. In *New African*, January 2003

While charity and religion are supposed to minister to the poor, both institutions derive their main revenue from the poor by the perpetuation of the evils both pretend to fight.

Emma Goldman, activist, writer, anarchist. *The Social Significance of the Modern Drama*, 1914

Until relief from oppression is granted, the only appropriate name for America is: "you hypocrite!"

Dick Gregory, activist, nutritionist, comedian. Attributed.

No one who has not been an integral part of a slaveholding community, can have any idea of its abominations...even were slavery no curse to its victims, the exercise of arbitrary power works such fearful ruin upon the hearts of slaveholders, that I should feel impelled to labor and pray for its overthrow with my last energies and latest breath.

Angelina Grimké, women's rights activist, slavery abolitionist. April 1839

I have not placed reading before praying because I regard it more important, but because, in order to pray aright, we must understand what we are praying for.

Angelina Grimké, women's rights activist, slavery abolitionist. "Appeal to the Christian Women of the South," September 1836

We have been given the responsibility of leading a country during very difficult times and all that ages you, naturally it takes its toll... But our work would not be complete if we did not know when to step down at the right time. One of your other duties is to create the people to replace us.

Ernesto "Che" Guevara, Argentinean-Cuban revolutionary and military leader. Attributed.

The people's heroes cannot be separated from the people, cannot be elevated onto a pedestal, into something alien to the lives of the people.

Ernesto "Che" Guevara, Argentinean-Cuban revolutionary and military leader. Attributed.

Revolutions, accelerated radical social changes, are made of circumstances; not always, almost never, or perhaps never can science predict their mature form in all its detail. They are made of passions, of man's fight for social vindication, and are never perfect. Neither was ours.

Ernesto "Che" Guevara, Argentinean-Cuban revolutionary and military leader. Attributed.

I'd tell the white powers that I ain't trying to take nothing from them. I'm trying to make Mississippi a better place for all of us. And I'd say, "What you don't understand is that as long as you stand with your feet on my neck, you got to stand in a ditch, too. But if you move, I'm coming out. I want to get us both out of the ditch.

Fannie Lou Hamer, civil rights leader. Attributed.

My aims as an artist, are at de-colonizing the mind, to decapitate capitalism in a collage, and rescue the heads of our comrades from it's wounded guillotine, under a government of philistines.

Theodore A. Harris, collage artist, poet. "Hunted Everywhere," 2004

We are rarely able to interact only with folks like ourselves, who think as we do. No matter how much some of us deny this reality and long for the safety and familiarity of sameness, inclusive ways of knowing and living offer us the only true way to emancipate ourselves from the divisions that limit our minds and imaginations.

>   **bell hooks**, writer, educator, activist. *Chronicle of Higher Education*, July 1994

The function of art is to do more than tell it like it is—it's to imagine what is possible.

>   **bell hooks**, writer, educator, activist. *Outlaw Culture*, 1994

The moment we choose to love we begin to move against domination, against oppression. The moment we choose to love we begin to move towards freedom, to act in ways that liberate ourselves and others. That action is the testimony of love as the practice of freedom.

>   **bell hooks**, writer, educator, activist. *Outlaw Culture*, 1994

The political core of any movement for freedom in the society has to have the political imperative to protect free speech.

>   **bell hooks**, writer, educator, activist. *Outlaw Culture*, 1994

Even the most subjected person has moments of rage and resentment so intense that they respond, they act against. There is an inner uprising that leads to rebellion, however short-lived. It may be only momentary but it takes place. That space within oneself where resistance is possible remains.

>   **bell hooks**, writer, educator, activist. *Yearning*, 1990

The classroom, with all its limitations, remains a location of possibility. In that field of possibility we have the opportunity to labor for freedom, to demand of ourselves and our comrades, an openness of mind and heart that allows us to face reality even as we collectively imagine ways to move beyond boundaries, to transgress. This is education as the practice of freedom.

>   **bell hooks**, writer, educator, activist. *Teaching to Transgress*, 1994

Great is truth, but still greater, from a practical point of view, is silence about truth. By simply not mentioning certain subjects...totalitarian propagandists have influenced opinion much more effectively than they could have by the most eloquent denunciations.

Aldous Huxley, English writer. 1949 forward to *Brave New World*, 1931

Drill and uniforms impose an architecture on the crowd. An army's beautiful. But that's not all; it panders to lower instincts than the aesthetic. The spectacle of human beings reduced to automatism satisfies the lust for power. Looking at mechanized slaves, one fancies oneself a master.

Aldous Huxley, English writer. *Point Counter Point*, 1928

The people who make wars, the people who reduce their fellows to slavery, the people who kill and torture and tell lies in the name of their sacred causes, the really evil people in a word—these are never the publicans and the sinners. No, they're the virtuous, respectable men, who have the finest feelings, the best brains, the noblest ideals.

Aldous Huxley, English writer. *After Many a Summer Dies the Swan*, 1939

Workers! The people have rights, which they can only secure by force. Such lessons are laid down in history… Nobody can feel the misery of the worker except the worker himself. Nobody can know the pain of hunger except the one who is famished. Why should we blame the persons who are eating the fruit of our labor…when we ourselves are encouraging them to rob us?

Iraqi communist activists, from appeal posted in the streets of Nasiriya, Iraq, December 1932

In America, you can segregate the people, but the problems will travel. From slavery to equal rights, from state suppression of dissent to crime, drugs and unemployment, I can't think of a supposedly Black issue that hasn't wasted the original Black target group and then spread like measles to outlying white experience.

June Jordan, poet, educator. *Moving Towards Home*, 1982

If you tie a horse to a stake, do you expect he will grow fat? If you pen an Indian up on a small spot of earth, and compel him to stay there, he will not be contented, nor will he grow and prosper. I have asked some of the great white chiefs where they get their authority to say to the Indian that he shall stay in one place, while he sees white men going where they please. They can not tell me.

Chief Joseph, Nez Perce leader. *North American Review*, April 1879

[There are] those "professional friends of the African" who are prepared to maintain their friendship for eternity as a sacred duty, provided only that the African will continue to play the part of an ignorant savage so that they can monopolize the office of interpreting his mind and speaking for him. To such people, an African who writes a study of [African people] is encroaching on their preserves. He is a rabbit turned poacher.

> **Jomo Kenyatta**, Kenyan political leader, making reference to his anthropological study of his Kikuyu culture. *Facing Mt. Kenya*, 1965

We are not fighting for the right to be like you. We respect ourselves too much for that. When we advocate freedom, we mean freedom for us to be black, or brown, and you to be white, and yet live together in a free and equal society. Our fight is not for racial sameness but for racial equality.

> **John Oliver Killens,** writer. Attributed.

I do not lead rebels but I lead Africans who want their self-government and land. I lead them because God never created any nation to be ruled by another nation forever.

> **Dedan Kimathi**, Kenyan Mau-Mau guerrilla leader, 1950s

The ultimate weakness of violence is that it is a descending spiral, begetting the very thing it seeks to destroy. Instead of diminishing evil, it multiplies it. Through violence you may murder the liar, but you cannot murder the lie, nor establish the truth. Through violence you may murder the hater, but you do not murder hate. In fact, violence merely increases hate. So it goes. Returning violence for violence multiplies violence, adding deeper darkness to a night already devoid of stars. Darkness cannot drive out darkness; only light can do that. Hate cannot drive out hate: only love can do that.

> **Martin Luther King, Jr.**, civil rights leader. *Where Do We Go from Here: Chaos or Community?*, 1967

Never forget that everything Hitler did in Germany was legal.

> **Martin Luther King, Jr.**, civil rights leader. Attributed.

I believe that unarmed truth and unconditional love will have the final word in reality. This is why right, temporarily defeated, is stronger than evil triumphant.

> **Martin Luther King, Jr.**, civil rights leader. Speech accepting the Nobel Peace Prize, December 1964

I just want to do God's will. And he's allowed me to go to the mountain. And I've looked over, and I've seen the promised land! I may not get there with you, but I want you to know tonight that we as a people will get to the promised land.
> **Martin Luther King Jr.**, civil rights leader. Speech in Memphis the night before his assassination, 4/3/1968

The means by which we live have outdistanced the ends for which we live. Our scientific power has outrun our spiritual power. We have guided missiles and misguided men.
> **Martin Luther King, Jr.**, civil rights leader. *Strength to Love,* 1963

We who engage in nonviolent direct action are not the creators of tension. We merely bring to the surface the hidden tension that is already alive.
> **Martin Luther King, Jr.**, civil rights leader. *Why We Can't Wait,* 1963

Law and order exist for the purpose of establishing justice, and...when they fail to do this purpose they become dangerously structured dams that block the flow of social progress.
> **Martin Luther King, Jr.**, civil rights leader. *Why We Can't Wait,* 1963

I have a dream that my four little children will one day live in a nation where they will not be judged by the color of their skin but by the content of their character.
> **Martin Luther King, Jr.**, civil rights leader. Speech, Washington, D.C., June 1963

Let's take Patrice Lumumba, for example. Former Prime Minister of the Congo, his party elected by popular vote. He was a socialist who believed in democracy. Then he was murdered, and the CIA replaced him with Mobutu, a capitalist who believes in dictatorship. In the Punch and Judy program of American history, that's a happy ending.
> **Barbara Kingsolver**, writer. *The Poisonwood Bible,* 1998

The law is an adroit mixture of customs that are beneficial to society, and could be followed even if no law existed, and others that are of advantage to a ruling minority, but harmful to the masses of men, and can be enforced on them only by terror.

> **Peter Kropotkin**, Russian political theorist, writer. *Words of a Rebel,* 1885

America is just the country that shows how all the written guarantees in the world for freedom are no protection against tyranny and oppression of the worst kind.

> **Peter Kropotkin**, Russian political theorist, writer. Speech, 1891

The struggle of man against power is the struggle of memory against forgetting.

> **Milan Kundera**, Czech writer. Attributed.

You already know enough. So do I. It is not knowledge we lack. What is missing is the courage to understand what we know and to draw conclusions.

> **Sven Lindqvist,** Swedish writer, educator. *Exterminate All the Brutes,* 1997

We have long suffered and today we want to breath the air of freedom. The Creator has given us this share of the earth that goes by the name of the African Continent; it belongs to us and we are its only master. It is right to make this continent a continent of justice, law and peace.

> **Patrice Lumumba**, Congolese political leader. Attributed.

Freedom is always and exclusively freedom for the one who thinks differently.

> **Rosa Luxemburg**, German revolutionary. *The Russian Revolution,* 1922

We have a special responsibility to the ecosystem of this planet. In making sure that other species survive we will be ensuring the survival of our own.

> **Wangari Maathai,** Kenyan environmental/political activist, educator. Attributed.

When we plant trees in Kenya, we know that we will eventually have our hands on politics, on economics, on culture, on all aspects that either destroy or create a sustainable environment.

> **Wangari Maathai,** Kenyan environmental/political activist, educator. *Africa News,* June 1992

The public functionaries are not, as is commonly believed, the guardians of order. Order, which is harmony, doesn't need guardians, precisely because it is order. That which needs guardians is disorder and a disorder which is scandalous, shameful, and humiliating to those of us who weren't born to be slaves, a disorder which reigns over the political and social life of humanity.

> **Ricardo Flores Magón**, Mexican writer, organizer, rebel leader. *Regeneración*, 1911

A tragic paradox: freedom, the very symbol of life, is won through the taking of life.

> **Ricardo Flores Magón**, Mexican writer, organizer, rebel leader. *Regeneración,* 1911

That which we at present call laziness is, rather, the disgust which men feel over breaking their backs for beggars' salaries and being, moreover, looked down upon and depreciated by the class which exploits them—while those who do nothing useful live like princes and are deferred to and respected by all.

> **Ricardo Flores Magón**, Mexican writer, organizer, rebel leader. *Regeneración*, 1911

There is a paradox at the core of penology, and from it derives the thousand ills and afflictions of the prison system. It is that not only the worst of the young are sent to prison but the best—that is the proudest, the bravest, the most daring, the most enterprising, and the most undefeated of the poor. There starts the horror.

> **Norman Mailer**, writer. In Introduction to *In the Belly of the Beast*, 1981

I look at an ant and I see myself: a native South African, endowed by nature with a strength much greater than my size so I might cope with the weight of a racism that crushes my spirit.

> **Miriam Makeba,** South African singer. *Makeba, My Story*, 1988

Freedom is not defined only in terms of color. If it is wrong for whites to oppress blacks, then it is even more immoral and shameful for black African leaders to oppress their own people.

> **Makaziwe Mandela**, South African educator, February 1992

After climbing a great hill, one only finds that there are many more hills to climb. I have taken a moment here to rest, to steal a view of the glorious vista that surrounds me, to look back on the distance I have come. But I can rest only for a moment, for with freedom comes responsibilities, and I dare not linger, for my long walk is not yet ended.

> **Nelson Mandela**, South African human rights and political leader. *Long Walk to Freedom*, 1994

I can't say I'm Che's secretary, because I'm a fighter. I fought beside him in the Las Villas campaign and took part in all the engagements there...when it became practically impossible for me to continue living in Santa Clara, due to my revolutionary activities, I decided to join the ranks of those fighting the dictatorship by taking up arms.

> **Aleida March**, Cuban political leader, widow of Ernesto "Che" Guevara. Attributed.

Only for the powerful is history an upward line, where their today is always the pinnacle. For those below, history is a question which can only be answered by looking backwards and forwards, thus creating new questions.

> **Subcomandante Marcos**, Mexican Zapatista revolutionary, writer. Attributed.

Men make their own history, but they do not make it just as they please; they do not make it under circumstances chosen by themselves, but under circumstances directly found, given and transmitted from the past. The tradition of all the dead generations weighs like a nightmare on the brain of the living.

> **Karl Marx**, German political theorist. *The Eighteenth Brumaire of Louis Bonaparte,* 1852

Work, as long as it is oppressed in a black skin, will never become free in a white skin.

> **Karl Marx**, German political theorist. *Das Kapital*, 1867

The writer may very well serve a movement of history as its mouthpiece, but he cannot of course create it.

> **Karl Marx**, German political theorist. "Moralizing Criticism and Critical Morality," 1847

The bourgeoisie of the whole world, which looks complacently upon the wholesale massacre after the battle, is convulsed by horror at the desecration of brick and mortar.

Karl Marx, German political theorist. Speech on "The Civil War in France,"1871

European colonial rule in Africa was more effective in destroying indigenous African *structures* than in destroying African *culture*. The tension between new imported structures and old resilient cultures is part of the post-colonial war of cultures in the African continent.

Ali A. Mazrui, Kenyan educator. *The Africans*, 1986

A people denied history is a people deprived of dignity.

Ali A. Mazrui, Kenyan educator. Attributed.

I muse upon my country's ills—the tempest bursting from the waste of time on the world's fairest hope linked with man's foulest crime.

Herman Melville, writer. "Misgivings," 1860

Subjugated people tend to feel that if they are not religious, they are nothing.

Albert Memmi, Tunisian writer, educator. *Air France Magazine*, June 1999

What I think the political correctness debate is really about is the power to be able to define. The definers want the power to name. And the defined are now taking that power away from them.

Toni Morrison, writer, educator. *New York Times Magazine*, 9/11/1999

The liberation of women is not an act of charity. It is not the result of a humanitarian or compassionate position. It is a fundamental necessity for the Revolution, a guarantee of its continuity, and a condition for its success.

Samora Moises Michel, Mozambican political leader. Attributed.

I wonder if it will prove to have been easier to fight the oppression of apartheid than it will ever be to set women free in our societies... Male domination does not "burn down."

Lauretta Ngcobo, South African writer. In *African Women's Writing*

We have the right to govern and even misgovern ourselves.
Kwame Nkrumah, Ghanaian political leader. Attributed.

Without discipline, true freedom cannot survive.
Kwame Nkrumah, Ghanaian political leader. Attributed.

The future beckons at us to dare the monsters that menace us. We are no fools for entering the social struggle even though we perish, for wise men still believe that it is better to be maimed or killed in their affray than to live like a slave.
Mowugo Okoye, Nigerian writer. Attributed.

A world in which it is wrong to murder an individual civilian and right to drop a thousand tons of high explosive on a residential area does sometimes make me wonder whether this earth of ours is not a loony bin made use of by some other planet.
George Orwell, English writer. Attributed.

Who controls the past controls the future: who controls the present controls the past.
George Orwell, English writer. *1984*, 1949

In every one of those little stucco boxes there's some poor bastard who's never free except when he's fast asleep and dreaming that he's got the boss down the bottom of a well and is bunging lumps of coal at him.
George Orwell, English writer. *Coming Up for Air*, 1939

All animals are equal. But some animals are more equal than others.
George Orwell, English writer. *Animal Farm*, 1946

Stories need communities to be heard, but communities themselves are also built through story tellings. Stories gather people around them…Rape stories, coming out stories and recovery stories feed upon and into community— shifting the spheres of what is public and private, secret and known about.
Ken Palmer, writer. *Telling Sexual Stories*, 1995

The worst forms of tyranny, or certainly the most successful ones, are not those we rail against but those that so insinuate themselves into the imagery of our consciousness, and the fabric of our lives, as not to be perceived as tyranny.
Michael Parenti, historian, writer. Attributed.

I've always believed that the biggest excuse for doing nothing is the what-I-do-is-a-drop-in-the-ocean problem. We have to learn to think in puddles, not ponds.

> **Ina Perlman**, South African activist. Interview, 1994

Yes, art is dangerous. Where it is chaste, it is not art.

> **Pablo Picasso**, Spanish painter. In *Pablo Picasso*, 1957

If I were to be murdered I would not want my murderer executed. I would not want my death avenged. Especially by government—which can't be trusted to control its own bureaucrats or collect taxes equitably or fill a pothole, much less decide which of its citizens to kill.

> **Helen Prejean**, Catholic nun, activist. *Dead Man Walking*, 1993

Only equals can be friends.

> **Proverb, Ethiopia**

Where there is doubt, there is freedom.

> **Proverb, Latin**

A man without religion is like a horse without a bridal.

> **Proverb, Latin**

A senile fairytale, the freedom of women in our countries

> **Nizar Qabbani**, Syrian poet, activist, 1923-1998. From poem, "A Letter from a Stupid Woman"

And of me say the fools:
With my poetry I violated the sky's commands.

> **Nizar Qabbani**, Syrian poet, activist, 1923-1998. From poem, "Clarification to My Poetry-Readers"

This is the revolution of notebooks
And ink

> **Nizar Qabbani**, Syrian poet, activist, 1923-1998. From poem, "The Wrathful"

To all the women who've been made fun of, called ugly
and dirty and fat; you are so beautiful....
Yo' mama's so ugly!...
She was able to
avoid the slave master's gaze

As he constantly went through his phases
of seeking prey—
At night time or even in broad day,
he waited
on the plantation
For the right one to free his own hands from masturbation
So that he could release the poisonous ejaculation
To ensure the enslavement of the future generations
of a young female slave child
And while he was busy detesting Yo' Mama
for being so 'damn ugly'—
She was busy building the underground railroad...

> **QueenGodIs**, artist, lyricist, active-ist. From song/poem "Yo' Mama!" 1999

The existence of the white race depends on the willingness of those assigned to it to place their racial interests above class, gender, or any other interests they hold. The defection of enough of its members to make it unreliable as a predictor of behavior will lead to its collapse.... Treason to whiteness is loyalty to humanity.

> **Race Traitor Journal**. "What We Believe," 1992

I have never blamed the American people for misunderstanding Cuba's revolution, because there is a lie about Cuba which is repeated so often that it becomes the truth.

> **Representative** from the Ministry of Foreign Affairs, Cuba. Statement to visiting American activists, Havana, Cuba 7/17/2004

The faces and the tactics of the leaders may change every four years, or two, or one, but the people go on forever. The people-beaten down today, yet rising tomorrow... The people are the real guardians of our hopes and dreams.

> **Paul Robeson**, activist, scholar, athlete, 1952

Advocates of capitalism are very apt to appeal to the sacred principles of liberty, which are embodied in one maxim: The fortunate must not be restrained in the exercise of tyranny over the unfortunate.

> **Bertrand Russell**, English philosopher, mathematician. "Freedom in Society," 1928

Work is of two kinds: first, altering the position of matter at or near the earth's surface relatively to other such matters; second, telling other people to do so.

Bertrand Russell, English philosopher, mathematician. Attributed.

Every man is encompassed by a cloud of comforting convictions, which move with him like flies on a summer day.

Bertrand Russell, English philosopher, mathematician. Attributed.

No gods, no masters!

Margaret Sanger, women's rights activist. Attributed.

Seize the time!

Bobby Seale, co-founder, Black Panther Party. Speech, circa 1967

Colonialism has nothing to do with the color of the colonizer and the colonized. Any group of people that uses the advantages of power—military or material—to oppress, exploit, and inferiorize another group of people can be justifiably described as a colonizing group.

Ropo Sekoni, Nigerian educator. *The Isokan News*, Spring 1995

The history of mankind is the history of repeated injuries and usurpations on the part of man toward woman, having in direct object the establishment of an absolute tyranny over her.

Seneca Falls Declaration, at a conference for women's suffrage and women's rights, Seneca Falls, NY, 1848

We can say "Peace on Earth," we can sing about it, preach about it, or pray about it, but if we have not internalized the mythology to make it happen inside of us, then it will not be.

Betty Shabazz, activist, widow of Malcolm X. Attributed.

The fact that a believer is happier than a skeptic is no more to the point than the fact that a drunken man is happier than a sober one.

George Bernard Shaw, Irish playwright, writer, speaking on religion. Attributed.

[George W. Bush], You tell me the truth. You tell me that my son died for oil. You tell me that my son died to make your friends rich. You tell me that my son died to spread the cancer of Pax Americana, imperialism in the Middle East. You tell me that, you don't tell me my son died for freedom and democracy. Cuz, we're not freer. You're taking away our freedoms. The Iraqi people aren't freer, they're much worse off than before you meddled in their country.

> **Cindy Sheehan**, anti-war activist whose son, U.S. Army Specialist Casey Austin Sheehen was killed in Iraq in 2004. Speech to Veterans for Peace Conference, Irving, TX 8/5/05

When I was growing up, it was Communists. Now it's Terrorists. So you always have to have somebody to fight and be afraid of, so the war machine can build more bombs, guns, and bullets and everything. But I do see hope. I see hope in this country. 58% of the American public are with us. We're preaching to the choir, but the choir's not singing. If all the 58% started singing, this war would end... The opposite of good is not evil, it's apathy. And we have to get this country off their butts, and we have to get the choir singing.

> **Cindy Sheehan**, anti-war activist whose son, U.S. Army Specialist Casey Austin Sheehen was killed in Iraq in 2004. Speech to Veterans for Peace Conference, Irving, TX 8/5/05

It's up to us, the people, to break immoral laws, and resist. As soon as the leaders of a country lie to you, they have no authority over you. These maniacs have no authority over us. And they might be able to put our bodies in prison, but they can't put our spirits in prison.

> **Cindy Sheehan**, anti-war activist whose son, U.S. Army Specialist Casey Austin Sheehen was killed in Iraq in 2004. Speech to Veterans for Peace Conference, Irving, TX 8/5/05

We are not waging a war on terror in this country. We're waging a war *of* terror. The biggest terrorist in the world is George W. Bush. How many more people are we going to let him kill before we stop him?

> **Cindy Sheehan**, anti-war activist whose son, U.S. Army Specialist Casey Austin Sheehen was killed in Iraq in 2004. Speech, San Francisco State University, CA 4/27/05

Liberty isn't a thing you are given as a present. You can be a free man under a dictatorship. It is sufficient if you struggle against it.

Ignazio Silone, Italian writer, socialist. "The God That Failed," 1949

The Truth shall set you free? Maybe. But first the Truth must be set free.
Wole Soyinka, Nigerian playwright, educator. *The Burden of Memory, The Muse of Forgiveness*, 1999

It may surprise some of our American citizens to learn that in this country of "free speech" there is no easier thing in the world than to sentence persons to death for expressing their views.
August Spies, labor organizer and one of eight anarchists tried and executed for their alleged involvement in the Haymarket bombing. Statement, 1886

Legal right is synonymous with power; whoever or whatsoever has the power, has the right.
Charles T. Sprading, writer. *Freedom and its Fundamentals*, 1923

Once I made you rich enough
Rich enough to forget my name
Bruce Springsteen, singer. From song "The Ghost of Tom Joad," 1995

To no form of religion is woman indebted for one impulse of freedom, as all alike have taught her inferiority and subjection.
Elizabeth Cady Stanton, women's rights activist, slavery abolitionist. Attributed.

booted and forested
we fell from the sky like stones
our mission
to preserve a democracy of bone
children
we were puppets
on the fingers of old men
whose wealth brought stealth
how could we know
we were torching the robes
of our lives

eating the strawberries of nightmares
lost in a land
that hated our footprints
and cut our throats
with the wind

> **Lamont B. Steptoe**, poet, publisher, reflecting on time served as a U.S. soldier in Vietnam. Poem "Booted and Forested," 2000

The State calls its own violence, law; but that of the individual, crime.

> **Max Stirner**, German philosopher. *The Ego and His Own*, 1845

Dissent...is a right essential to any concept of the dignity and freedom of the individual; it is essential to the search for truth in a world wherein no authority is infallible.

> **Norman Thomas**, socialist activist. Attributed.

It is not desirable to cultivate a respect for the law, so much as for the right. The only obligation which I have a right to assume is to do at any time what I think right.

> **Henry David Thoreau**, writer, philosopher. *Civil Disobedience*, 1849

There will never be a free and enlightened State until the State comes to recognize the individual as a higher and independent power, from which all its own power and authority are derived, and treats him accordingly.

> **Henry David Thoreau**, writer, philosopher. *Civil Disobedience*, 1849

They who are continually shocked by slavery have some right to be shocked by the violent death of the slaveholder, but no others. Such will be more shocked by his life than by his death.

> **Henry David Thoreau**, writer, philosopher. "A Plea for Captain John Brown," 1859

Where there is a man who does not labor because another is compelled to work for him, there slavery is.

> **Leo Tolstoy**, Russian writer. "The Slavery of Our Times," 1900

We don't hate America. We want America to live up to its potential. We want this to be a better place than it is. And when you have, especially as you do right now, a gang of cutthroats and thieves running everything, then the only way this country's going to be a better place and live up to its potential is if we are out there, jumping up and down and shouting and screaming…that the Emperor has no damn clothes on.

> **Tom Tomorrow**, cartoonist. Interview, *Buzzflash.com*, October 2003

The cartoons are a way of—how can I put this?—allowing people to laugh at things rather than just get so angry that their heads explode. It's admittedly bleak humor right now.

> **Tom Tomorrow**, cartoonist. Interview, *Buzzflash.com*, October 2003

To take part in the African revolution, it is not enough to write a revolutionary song; you must fashion the revolution with the people. And if you fashion it with the people, the songs will come by themselves, and of themselves.

> **Sekou Toure**, Guinean political leader. Attributed.

We prefer the poverty in freedom to riches in slavery.

> **Sekou Toure**, Guinean political leader. Attributed.

America owes to my people some of the dividends… She can afford to pay, and she must pay. I shall make them understand that there is a debt to the Negro people which they never can repay. At least, then, they must make amends.

> **Sojourner Truth**, activist, slavery abolitionist, former slave. Attributed.

I looked at my hands, to see if I was de same person now I was free. Dere was such a glory ober eberything, de sun came like gold trou de trees, and ober de fields, and I felt like I was in heaven.

> **Harriet Tubman**, Underground Railroad conductor, recalling the feeling of reaching free soil after escaping slavery. In *Harriet, the Moses of Her People*, 1869

On the 12th of May, 1828, I heard a loud noise in the heavens, and the Spirit instantly appeared to me and said the Serpent was loosened, and Christ had laid down the yoke he had borne for the sins of men, and that I should take it on and fight against the Serpent, for the time was fast approaching when the first should be last and the last should be first… And on the appearance of the sign I should arise and prepare myself, and slay my enemies with their own weapons.

>   **Nat Turner**, anti-slavery guerrilla leader. *The Confessions of Nat Turner*, 1831

The animals of the world exist for their own reasons. They were not made for humans any more than black people were made for white, or women created for men.

>   **Alice Walker**, writer, poet. In foreword to *The Dreaded Comparison*, 1988.

If they really believe there is danger from the Negro it must be because they do not intend to give him justice.

>   **Booker T. Washington,** activist, educator, writer. Attributed.

In the midst of disrespect and degradation, I promote the practical wisdom of dialogue—that thin reed in the whirlwind of our times doomed to strong lip service and weak action that stakes a high moral ground in a cynical age.

>   **Cornel West**, theologian, writer, educator. "Walking the Tightrope: Some Personal Reflections on Blacks and Jews," 1997

We have frequently printed the word Democracy, yet I cannot too often repeat that it is a word the real gist of which still sleeps, quite unawakened… It is a great word, whose history, I suppose, remains unwritten, because that history has yet to be enacted.

>   **Walt Whitman**, poet. *Democratic Vistas*, 1871

For 500 years, first spain and then united states have colonized our country. Billions of dollars in profits leave our country for the united states every year. In every way we are slaves of the gringo. We want liberation and the Power in the hands of the People, not Puerto Rican exploiters.

>   **Young Lords Party**, U.S. based Puerto Rican rights and liberation organization. From 13-Point Program and Platform, adopted October 1969

Under capitalism, our women have been oppressed by both the society and our own men. The doctrine of machismo has been used by our men to take out their frustrations against their wives, sisters, mothers, and children.

Our men must support their women in their fight for economic and social equality, and must recognize that our women are equals in every way within the revolutionary ranks.

> **Young Lords Party**, U.S. based Puerto Rican rights and liberation organization. From 13-Point Program and Platform, adopted October 1969

We did not launch our revolt to conquer illusory political rights which provide not a crumb to eat, but to procure a piece of earth which provides nourishment and liberty, a happy home, and a bright and independent future.

> **Emiliano Zapata**, Mexican revolutionary, August 1914

A strong people do not need a government.

> **Emiliano Zapata**, Mexican revolutionary. Attributed.

Is not nationalism—that devotion to a flag, an anthem, a boundary so fierce it engenders mass murder—one of the great evils of our time, along with racism, along with religious hatred? These ways of thinking—cultivated, nurtured, indoctrinated from childhood on—have been useful to those in power, and deadly for those out of power.

> **Howard Zinn**, historian, educator. "The Scourge of Nationalism," May 2005

Index

Estes, Carol, 174
Evers, Medgar, 305
expression, 164–79

F

Faiz, Faiz Ahmed, 343
Fajarina, Mercy, 140
falsehood, 302–303
Faludi, Susan, 184
Fanon, Franz, 105, 109, 280, 291
Farrakhan, Louis, 217, 228
Fawkes, Guy, 127
Featherstone, Alan Watson, 61
Feinberg, Leslie, 272
feminism, 180–94
Filemyr, Ann, 55, 116, 295
Filipovic, Zlata, 321
Finger, Simon, 75
First, Ruth, 265
Fisk, Robert, 331
Fitzgerald, Albert, 212
Fitzgerald, Kevin, 170
Flanagan, Fionulla, 263
Flying Hawk, 286
Flynn, Elizabeth Gurley, 102, 215
food, 287–88
Ford, Glen, 34
Fortune, T. Thomas, 86
"Forty-Two Decades," 298
Foucault, Michel, 254
Four Guns, 147
Fox, Michael, 79
France, Anatole, 343
Frank, Anne, 311
Franti, Michael, 105, 110–11
freedom, 120–24
freedom of speech, 142–45
Freire, Paulo, 90, 343
Fromm, Erich, 63
Fuentes, Carlos, 271
Fuller, Margaret, 196–97
Funkadelic, 176
Futerman, Dion, 268

G

Galeano, Eduardo, 13, 66, 67, 150, 178, 198, 203, 204, 205, 228, 301, 309–10, 324
Gama, Antonia Díaz Soto y, 52–53
Gamble, Peter, 34
Gandhi, Mahatma, 25, 87, 92, 101, 104, 109, 111, 115, 221, 292, 344
Garrigue, Jean, 79
Garrison, William Lloyd, 272, 344
Garson, Barbara, 344
Garvey, Marcus, 23, 26, 40, 120, 273, 287
Gaye, Marvin, 320
gays, 195–201
Geizer, Nell, 66
generations, 278–82
Geoghegan, Thomas, 210, 214
Geronimo, 161–62
Gerould, Katharine Fullerton, 262
Ghetto Bastard, 171
Gibbs, Michele, 44, 154
Giddings, Paula, 185–86, 189
Gide, André, 344
Gilbert, David, 11, 30, 33, 105–106, 129, 267–68
Gillian, Ayanna, 152
Ginsberg, Allen, 138, 260, 261, 282
Giovanni, Nikki, 171
Godoy, Carlos Mejía, 289, 294
Goethe, Johann Wolfgang von, 47, 225
Goff, Stan, 27, 35, 138, 203, 227, 243, 247, 279, 317, 319
Goldman, Emma, 92, 127, 139, 153, 175, 219, 237, 251, 265–66, 325, 334, 344
Gomez, Cynthia, 34, 38, 40
Gómez, Ermilo Abreu, 150
Gómez-Peña, Guillermo, 117
González, Gloria, 130
Gonzales, Rodolfo "Corky," 26, 151, 167
Goodie Mob, 50
Goodman, Amy, 94
Goodman, Ellen, 286
Gordon, Thomas, 240
Gorky, Maxim, 280

ACKOWLEDGEMENTS

A great debt is owed to the many people who have supported this book. I am grateful to Greg Bates and everyone else at Common Courage Press, whose belief in this project made it possible. Quinn Eli supplied invaluable advice while the book was in its infant form. Taina del Valle Asili, Theodore Harris, Walidah Imarisha and Joel Latner provided additional editorial support for which I'm thankful. To all of the graphic artists who so generously contributed work, as Toni Cade Bambara said, you "make revolution irresistible!" To the poets and hip hop MCs who allowed the use of their work, Ho Chi Minh might have envisioned you when he said that "the poet should also be able to lead an attack!" To all those too numerous to mention who contributed ideas and love, you are so greatly appreciated.

ABOUT THE EDITOR

Teishan Latner is a 28-year-old political activist and organizer living in Philadelphia, Pennsylvania. He has been involved in community and international social justice work for ten years. An occasional citizen journalist, his work has appeared in the *Antioch Record*, the *Antiochian*, *Awol Magazine, Blu Magazine, Impact Weekly/Dayton Weekly News, Onward,* and *Poor Magazine* online.